The Houseplant Book

KU-611-535

The Houseplant Book

A complete guide to creative indoor gardening

Cynthia Wickham

MARSHALL
CAVENDISH
EDITIONS

Published by Marshall Cavendish Editions
a division of
Marshall Cavendish Books Limited
58 Old Compton Street
London W1V 5PA

© Marshall Cavendish Limited 1977, 1978, 1979

Printed in Great Britain

ISBN 0 85685 147 7

Typeset in Monotype Plantin Light by
Unwin Brothers Ltd The Gresham Press
Old Woking, Surrey

Colour reproduction by
Photoprint Plates Ltd Rayleigh, Essex and
Colour Workshop Ltd Hertford, Hertfordshire

Printed in
Great Britain by Redwood Burn Ltd Trowbridge,
Wiltshire

Editors:
Heather Maisner
Jane Kenrick

Art Editor:
Mike Rose

Assistant editors:
Julia Blackburn
Vivianne Croot
Marjory Lampard

Design:
Bridget Heal
Pedro Prá-Lopez
Peter Saag
Sally Smallwood
Trevor Vertigan

Picture editor:
Antonia Gaunt

**Picture research
and styling:**
Ann Davies
Sue Hoyle

Editorial assistant:
Katy Franklin

Special consultant:
Michael Dawes
(JP Dip Hort Kew)

Production:
Mike Emery

Publisher:
Frances Lincoln

Art Director:
John Strange

Contents

History of house plants

The techniques and traditions of taking decorative and useful plants out of their natural habitat and growing them indoors in pots has a long history. As many as 5000 years ago the Chinese were constructing ornate palace gardens and filling them with carefully cultivated shrubs and flowers, each one standing in its own earthenware container. Much has happened in the way of innovations, advances, and occasional regressions since those distant times. Here we give just some of the highlights in the varied and fascinating history of plant cultivation.

One of the earliest surviving images of plants in pots comes from the palace of Queen Hatsheput of Egypt, who reigned from c. 1503–1482 BC. It is a carved stone bas-relief, showing a row of highly formalized trees each one standing in a small pot. The Queen wanted frankincense; this rare perfume comes from the gum of the *Boswellia* tree, which at that time was only to be found in the land of Punt in East Africa. An expedition was sent out to find trees and bring them back. The mission was successful and the trees apparently flourished in their new country, each in its own small container.

There is a tendency to presume that in early times plants were only cultivated for their medicinal or culinary value, but this was far from the case. In many ancient civilizations decorative plants were highly prized and even revered as status symbols. Paintings from early China show azaleas and lilies in ornate pots lending their fragile beauty to interior settings. The luxury of growing such plants was considered the prerogative of the rich alone. In India it was a criminal offence for a common man to grow an orchid. In Japan the same mystique surrounded roses and a palm called the Kan-non-chiku, the buddess, or princess, of light, which has maintained its elite status to this day.

The charm of house plants was well known to the Chinese, as is shown by the delightful twelfth-century interior (above).

A frieze of *Boswellia* adorns the tomb of Egyptian Queen Hatsheput (left).

The splendour of Babylon's hanging gardens depended on plants in porous troughs.

The unassuming form of *Rhapis excelsa*, the Kan-non-chiku palm, (left) belies the privileged position accorded to the plant in Japan. When first imported there from China 300 years ago it became a favourite with the Imperial family and soon became synonymous with power and position. Today it is owned by the rich and collected by enthusiasts who discern an especial beauty in the positioning of its leaves; it is grown in exquisitely designed, handmade porcelain pots decorated with gold.

The Babylonians were technically skilled gardeners and King Nebuchadrezzar's famous Hanging Gardens had trees growing in porous earthenware containers. The King had the gardens planted for his wife who in her exile yearned for the plants of her distant homeland.

Solomon, King of Israel, was reputed to be a brilliant gardener. He cultivated a great variety of herbs, experimented with water gardening and introduced many new plants propagated from cuttings. Apparently one of the chambers of his great temple was a garden room decorated with a profusion of potted plants.

Most early plant displays were extremely formalized. It is to ancient Greece that we must turn to find the origins of the more informal way of grouping together varied containers, each with an attractive plant. Every year Greece had a festival of Adonis, the god of plant fertility, and 'Adonis gardens' were planted to symbolize the seasonal death and rebirth of the young god. Quickly germinating seeds such as fennel, barley and lettuce were sown in pots, baskets and other small containers. For eight days they were carefully tended until the little seedlings were quite sturdy. Then they were grouped around the shrines of Adonis and left in the sun without water for the eight days of the festival, during which time they withered and died. This custom later developed into a children's game and led to the use of flower pots by people in general. Today a continuation of this early heritage can be seen in the tradition peculiar to Mediterranean countries of grouping together a large number of assorted pots so that they stand in a decorative cluster on stairways, window ledges and patios.

This adornment of the outer house with plants (above) is a remnant of the use of plants in ancient rites dedicated to Adonis (left).

In early Rome pot gardening was also a feature of many town houses, compensating for limited garden space. The most important contribution the Romans made was in the development of an artificial means of cultivating plants out of season. During Seneca's reign shiploads of roses were brought to Rome from Alexandria and Cartegena and, in order to make them bloom in winter, special hothouses were constructed. A transparent crystal called selenite was used to make the roof, while hot water pipes kept the building warm. Another sophistication was the development of a technique for 'forcing' plants. The method involved surrounding the plants with a ditch filled with warm water.

While missions were specially planned by kings and generals to fetch a certain plant from a distant land and induce it to survive in unfamiliar surroundings, varieties of plants also travelled from one part of the world to another by more haphazard means. Merchants, soldiers and other intrepid travellers would carry living plants with them on their journeys, either because they were useful for medicinal purposes or good to eat or simply because they served as a reminder of the homeland. Chance and circumstance led to all sorts of unlikely varieties taking root. In this way the beautiful Madonna lily was carried by Roman legionaries from camp to camp until it became known in every part of Europe.

In Europe throughout the dark and Middle Ages it was the monks who studied the techniques of plant cultivation and learnt the secrets of plant remedies and flavours. This was a useful art since food at that time was generally comprised of rather tasteless grain produce which needed livening up to make it palatable, while meat was of dubious freshness and needed its 'high' flavour concealed by the equally strong taste of herbs. Herbs were also used for strewing on the floor, releasing their perfume when crushed underfoot and permeating houses with freshness.

Medicine was based on herb lore. First, monastic gardens and, later, simple cottage gardens had as many as 400 different herbs growing in them, although barely one flowering plant was grown purely for its beauty. Herbs such as basil were grown indoors in pots, but again for solely practical reasons.

The Renaissance with its passion for rediscovering the splendours of classical antiquity revived the art of formalized container gardening. The Florentine humanist and architect Leon Battista Alberti designed a garden in the late fifteenth century in which myrtle, ivy, juniper, vines and lemon trees were displayed in terracotta tubs with brightly flowering plants growing around their base. The aristocracy began to cultivate a taste for rare and exotic plants and explorers brought back finds from all corners of the New World. Many varieties died in transit locked in dark, damp storerooms, or on arrival when they were not understood. Others were used in what seems now a totally unfamiliar fashion. The tomato, or Love Apple as it was called in the sixteenth century, was considered dangerous to eat and was kept as a purely decorative plant indoors and outside. The scarlet runner bean which arrived from South America in the seventeenth century was also treated as a purely ornamental plant for the first hundred years of its life in Europe.

A simple painting of borage from medieval herbal.

The Madonna lily, here drawn by Leonardo (left), was carried all over Europe by Roman soldiers.

The detail from *Grammar* by de la Hyre (above) reflects the Renaissance interest in the art of indoor gardening.

As more and more new plants poured into Europe, certain rare, beautiful varieties suddenly became the subject of crazes. No plant, not even the orchid, could compete with the tulip mania that hit Europe in the early seventeenth century. Wild tulip bulbs were brought back from the Levant, and hybridized to produce new colours and forms for indoor and outdoor display. The Netherlands became the centre of the tulip market, and during the Thirty Years War the real boom took place. Tulips were fought for and died for, fortunes were made and lost. They even became a form of currency and over 10 million paper tulips, promises to pay the bearer a certain bulb or number of bulbs, exchanged hands. In 1637 a law was passed to halt the racketeering. The market died down, although from then onwards Holland was firmly established as the tulip centre of the world.

These parrot tulips painted by Claude Aubriet c. 1690 reflect the tulip mania that swept seventeenth-century Europe.

While on the one hand pot plants had always been the luxurious possessions of the aristocratic elite, they were also moving into a position of more general use in the homes of the working people. Early settlers to America took many European plants with them which they grew in containers in the home and garden. These were African and French marigolds, *Calendula*, scarlet beans, sweet williams, wallflowers, hyacinths, ivy, lilies, tulips, passion flowers, and a large number of herbs and vegetables. In return they brought back from America to Europe the *Agave* and the *Opuntia*.

Plants brought colour and beauty into the often bleak and dreary homes of the Industrial Revolution. *Auricula*, hyacinths, tulips, carnations, pinks and pansies were grown on an enormous scale by Lancashire cotton workers, who were responsible for cultivating a large variety of resilient indoor plants, especially those impervious to city conditions.

Sailors working for the vast East India company brought home from all corners of the world camellias, azaleas, peonies and chrysanthemums. However, before the development of good and efficient means of transporting plants, only a very small proportion survived the journey. Until the beginning of the nineteenth century, the most professional collector would consider it a triumph if eight out of twenty azaleas were still alive by the time they reached their new destination. In 1819 the problems of transportation were improved when Dr Livingstone, surgeon to the East India Company in Canton, also a botanist, suggested that the Chinese method of growing plants in pots of fibrous loam should be adopted and that plants should be potted two months before their journey.

The most crucial step forward in the history of pot plants was made accidentally in 1834 by a Victorian gentleman called Nathaniel Ward. He discovered that plants could thrive in an enclosed glass case recycling their own moisture by the process of respiration. Wardian cases in the home enabled people to grow their own miniature jungles of tropical plants, and also led to new developments in the techniques and technicalities of glasshouse growing. The invention of the Wardian travelling case enabled delicate specimens to be transported from afar safely and in perfect condition.

Fuchsias, geraniums and *Auricula* cheered the hard, monotonous life of the nineteenth-century industrial worker (left).

The ingenious Wardian portable greenhouse (above) could ensure that imported plants reached their destination safely.

By the mid-nineteenth century the indoor plant craze had reached its zenith as this 1845 Italian salon shows (left).

Glass plant containers ranged from the modest heated rotunda housing cacti (left) to this room-high plant window.

With the sudden availability of a wide range of exotic plants and the possibility of growing them successfully in an enclosed case, a conservatory or simply in a decorative pot standing aloof and alone in a corner of the room, indoor plants became the rage in the smart societies of England, Europe and America. Whereas growing strange and exotic specimens had once been the exclusive hobby of the very rich, it now became possible for the less rich to join in. Ferns, orchids, *Dracaena*, *Cissus*, *Grevillea*, *Ixora* and crotons were in great demand. To answer this need numerous fearless plant hunters set out on dangerous explorations into unknown regions to find new specimens. The orchid was the biggest prize and, since these plants in their natural habitat grow perched high up in the branches of tall trees, whole forests fell to the ground in the scramble to find new types. Orchids were indeed very big business. When one English grower sold his stock to an American syndicate at the end of the century, he netted what in those days was the staggering sum of £24,000. At the same time less rare plants were pouring in from all parts of the world and nurserymen experimented with hybridization and propagation to produce specimens ideally suited for indoor growing. In England the Veitch family were important figures in this experimentation and developed the hybridized orchids, *Streptocarpus*, *Hippeastrum* and begonias that are still grown commercially today.

From the mid-nineteenth century onwards plants became an essential feature in many homes. Elaborate ferneries like miniature greenhouses were constructed. Palms gained popularity, and specially designed palm stands and palm tables became dominant features in every chic interior setting.

The *Ficus* (rubber plant) grew in popularity after the first world war and has remained popular ever since, while cacti and succulents came into their own in the twenties and thirties with the construction of large framed glass windows. Today interior architectural design has taken plants to heart and our plants now share our rooms with us. Never before have there been so many exotic plants flourishing in so many different interiors. This is as a result of the fascination which plants have always held, together with the intrepid expeditions of the plant hunters and the determined perseverance of the plant cultivators.

Palms were an essential part of the late-nineteenth-century parlour (above).

In the 1930's cacti came into their own encouraged by architectural developments.

Geography of house plants

It is a remarkable fact that plants gathered from such varied environments as Mexican deserts, Amazonian rain forests, Tibetan foothills, Indian jungles and windy Pacific islands can be found living happily under the roofs of houses in London, New York, Stockholm or Berlin.

Of course a plant from a damp woodland in Indonesia is not going to flourish when given the same conditions as a spiny flowering cactus from Bolivia or Peru, but every house interior has a wide range of plant areas. There is no reason to presume that a sunny window sill and regular inundations of water are the ideal way of life for all plants. Some peculiarly resilient ones have a habit of surviving in spite of all kinds of adverse conditions, but most of them need to be grown in an environment which is as close as possible to their natural habitat. Even today many cacti and succulents are drowned by careful over-watering, while palms and ferns go brown and wizened from being exposed to too much direct sunlight.

The appearance of a plant, the shape and size of its leaves and flowers, the nature of its root system, and any outstanding feature of its form are adapted to suit the conditions imposed by a given environment. Its seasonal rhythms, whether it is an evergreen or a plant that loses its leaves in the winter, depend on the type of climate it is accustomed to. Even when a plant has been taken right out of its natural habitat and is seen growing in the thoroughly tame setting of a plastic or terra-cotta pot in a modern house interior, it is still possible to tell something about the part of the world that it came from originally, whether it was a barren desert, a tropical humid jungle or a cool forest region.

Because indoor plants naturally tend to suffer from a lack of direct sunlight the majority of types we are accustomed to see in our houses come from the tropical regions of the world. Plants which come from the floor of jungles and forests have adapted themselves to surviving with a minimum amount of light. The large leaves of the rubber plant, the *Monstera* and other similar types have the maximum amount of leaf surface to receive all available sunlight. The stems of the *Chlorophytum* and many types of *Cissus* and *Tradescantia* are creeping to enable them to contort themselves towards leaf-filtered patches of light, and they adapt themselves similarly as they twine and trail around a doorway or window.

Tropical plants are almost all evergreens; they have a dormant season when growing ceases, but they never drop all their leaves, so you are never left with a naked ungainly plant for months on end.

In their natural habitat some tropical plants grow in a leafy compost mixture on the forest ground, while others called epiphytes, such as bromeliads and orchids, establish their root system among the leaves and mosses to be found in the angle of tree branches way up above the ground. The various compost mixtures available are ideal soil substitutes for such plants, all of which tend to have shallow root systems.

High temperatures are not essential for these plants, but a level of humidity does have to be maintained. In the home this can be done very simply by regular misting of the leaves. Alternatively you can set up a self-sufficient warm and humid tropical world in the enclosed atmosphere of a terrarium or bottle garden.

The transition from an arid desert wasteland to a sunny window ledge is comparatively easy. Cacti and succulents which have evolved in ever changing conditions of both rain and severe drought, burning heat in the day and sharp cold at night find normal indoor life an easy transition and demand very little attention. They will not grow to a height of 6 m (20 ft) as they do in Mexico or Arizona, but they will thrive in a miniature way in the desert of a small flower pot.

Plants which are naturally suited to dryish conditions are *Pittosporum* from the mountain forests of China and New Zealand, *Grevillea* from western Australia, and the *Aspidistra*,

from the cool Japanese mountain forests. There are a number of resilient plants that like a certain degree of dampness and as much light as possible. These are various *Ficus* (rubber plants), *Tradescantia* and *Philodendron*.

Palms and ferns come from damp, shady places such as the South American rain forests (*Adiantum*), Asia and Africa (*Asplenium*) and temperate woods all over the world (*Phyllitis*). Apart from changes in fashion, one of the reasons for the comparative disappearance of the fern from the indoor stage is due to the rise in room temperatures. Cold, dark winter gloom was one thing, central heating and picture windows are quite another, and many poor ferns have shrivelled and died

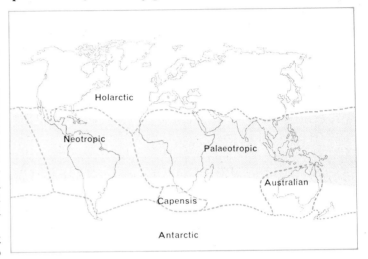

☐ boundary of floristic realms   tropical regions

Most houseplants come from the tropics and subtropics but the distribution of particular genera and species depends on geology as well as plant evolution and history. As the continents separated from each other plant life in them developed independently and the most recent group of plants to develop—the flowering plants —shows the widest differences between regions. Six major floristic realms are distinguished. The list below gives some of the genera found in the various regions.

Australian	Impatiens	Palaeotropic
Acacia	Jasminum	Adiantum
Adiantum	Primula	Aglaonema
Blechnum	Rhododendron	Begonia
Callistemon		Blechnum
Chorizema	Neotropical	Cissus
Cissus	Adiantum	Codiaeum
Grevillea	Aechmea	Coleus
Hoya	Agave	Conophytum
Passiflora	Anthurium	Cordyline
Platycerium	Begonia	Cyperus
	Blechnum	Dizygotheca
Capensis	Bougainvillea	Dracaena
Adiantum	Calceolaria	Ficus
Blechnum	Cephalocereus	Hedera
Chlorophytum	Cissus	Hoya
Lithops	Cyperus	Hydrangea
Pelargonium	Dieffenbachia	Impatiens
Rhoicissus	Fittonia	Ipomoea
	Fuchsia	Jasminum
Holarctic	Hydrangea	Kalanchoë
Adiantum	Impatiens	Lithops
Agave	Ipomoea	Nephrolepis
Blechnum	Monstera	Passiflora
Camellia	Neoregelia	Pelargonium
Campanula	Nephrolepis	Peperomia
Chrysanthemum	Passiflora	Pilea
Cyclamen	Peperomia	Platycerium
Cyperus	Philodendron	Primula
Fatsia	Pilea	Rhododendron
Hedera	Tradescantia	
Hyacinthus		Antarctic
Hydrangea		Primula

10

because we like to keep ourselves far too warm in winter. In other words we have changed our climate, which is ideal for some plants but not so good for others.

The best indoor plants now, as always, are those able to take differing conditions in their stride. *Dracaena* from the tropics and sub-tropics of Africa, Asia and Australia, *Philodendron* from the tropical rain forest of Mexico, Peru, Brazil and the West Indies, *Ficus* from India, Indonesia, Australia and West Africa, *Aspidistra* from China, *Chlorophytum* from tropical America and Africa, *Pandanus* from Indonesia, Africa and Madagascar and *Sansevieria* from Africa. Ivy is to be found growing in all parts of the world, and it is a most amenable

and adaptable plant, able to do well in most indoor conditions and in need of very little attention.

There are certain plants which really do need fostering and pampering if they are to survive, and others which are by nature tough and resilient and able to withstand the most thoughtless treatment. A lot depends on your understanding of their background and the realization that even one room in your house can have many different climatic conditions; a little careful thought can make use of all the 'regions' of a room. It is quite miraculous to think that plants coming from so many distant and different lands can be persuaded to live happily in the confines of one small home.

Columbia
Peru
Bolivia
The Andes
R. Amazon
Amazon Basin
Equator
Tropic of Capricorn
Plateau of Bolivia
Atacama Desert

Dry steppe and semi-desert

Andean tropical rain forest

Paramo

Andean tropical rain forest (above left) clings to the lower slopes of the Andes where rising warm air forms water vapour. The forests, which are continually shrouded in cloud, form an ideal site for epiphytes which take their water from the air and for flowering plants like the *Fuchsia* (above right). In their upper reaches, the trees diminish in size and ferns, which prefer a damp, cool climate, predominate (left).

In the north and western Andes above the tropical rain forest stretches an intermittent alpine belt known as the paramo. Vegetation is sparser and trees are no longer found, partly because rain is scarce, partly because the soil temperature remains too low. Most of the vegetation hugs the soil. The largest plants are the trunk-forming *Espletia* species (seen below) and bushy shrubs such as the one shown in flower (right).

Trade winds sweep inland from the Caribbean depositing rain on the slopes of the Andes and leaving this coastal region in Colombia free from rain during at least half the year. Thorn bush and cacti grow here, the former spreading their roots wide just below the surface of the soil to take advantage of the rain that does fall, the latter using specially developed reservoirs in their stems to store water. Cacti like the one above right are also among the few plants to survive on the Plateau of Bolivia 3,500 m (11,500 ft) high.

Plant psychology

A friend of mine used to hide her begonia in the attic whenever a certain neighbour came to visit, because she declared that the plant wilted when left in the same room as her neighbour. At that time people laughed at her and declared her to be eccentric; today her behaviour is not considered so odd, especially when you learn that she is also a very good gardener. She loves plants and they thrive under her care.

Plant psychology is still in its infancy, but more and more is being written and researched on the subject. All kinds of experiments are being devised to test the reaction, the behaviour, even the emotions of plants. Much information has been uncovered, which lends a new truth to old superstitions and beliefs. Some people said to have 'green fingers' succeed with their plants because they do not just look after them correctly, they also really seem to love them. They say that in ancient times you had to apologize to the Elder Mother before cutting down an Elder Tree. More than 2000 years later we realize that plants do appreciate this kind of consideration; there is even the recent story of a pine tree which was given chloroform in order to lessen the emotional shock of being transplanted.

Obviously to go so far as acquiring a plant at all, you must like the look of it and intend to keep it healthy. However, while some people see their plants as decorative additions to a room, others treat them as living creatures and do their best to keep them happy by being attentive to their needs. Observers have noticed that plants in the centre of a showroom lost among other beautiful objects do less well than those in an entrance hall where they are constantly being admired by passers-by. The more practical minded will simply dismiss this observation, declaring that plants receive more light when they are in an entrance hall. It is now believed that farmers who play music to cows have a happier herd and therefore more milk. Plants are also believed to react to music, and experiments show that they tend to grow towards the sounds of Bach and Handel and Indian sitar music, although for some reason they lean away from modern rock. In general it is now believed that plants grown to the constant strains of music do better than those grown in silence.

In the late eighteenth century people were beginning to become aware of the psychology of plants, although the real initiator was an American plant breeder called Luther Burbank. In the 1890's he was working at cross-fertilization of plants in order to produce new types. He had an unselfconscious sympathy and understanding of plants and, when he wanted a certain plant to develop in a way that was not natural to it, he would sit beside it and talk to it. He reassured it that he loved it dearly and had no wish to do any harm and in return he asked the plant to help him. He certainly produced some remarkably strong varieties, including potatoes and plums that we cultivate and eat today, although whether this was due to his words of reassurance or his natural skill as a gardener is open to question.

Another important figure in the history of plant psychology was the American agricultural chemist, George Washington Carver (1864–1943), among whose many other contributions to modern society was the discovery of peanut butter. As a young man he took care of sick plants and to do this he set them out in his own specially prepared soil mixture and sang to them. When people asked him for the secret to his miraculous cure, he replied that the plants themselves held the secrets inside them, and anyone who understood them would be able to achieve the same results as he did.

The Indian scientist Sir Jagadis Chadra Bose (1858-1937) experimented with plants in all kinds of inventive ways. It was he who anaesthetized the pine tree and also discovered that too much carbon dioxide caused it to suffocate while oxygen could revive it. His work led him to the conclusion that plants were extremely sensitive in unexpected ways and he therefore postulated that they had a definite form of nervous system.

In the last ten years some important new advances in plant psychology have been made. An American lie-detector expert, Cleve Backster, carried out a number of experiments monitoring plants with the electrodes of his lie-detecting machine. The results were quite startling. He found that when he was just thinking about burning a leaf the plant became agitated, even before the match had been lit. A plant that was confronted with someone intending to hurt it appeared to faint as soon as the would-be culprit appeared in the room. Backster was able to demonstrate that plants have memories and can recognize a person who has previously done them harm. He also proved that this awareness is not limited to their own experience alone but that they possess a 'cellular consciousness', which enabled them to react to what was happening to all forms of life.

With the countless new theories on plant psychology, people are beginning to look again at their plants. While only extremists are willing to declare that a plant has hopes, fears and aspirations, it is no longer considered absurd to wonder if a plant does indeed let out a silent cry of pain when a leaf or a flower is cut from it. A living plant is more than a beautiful piece of green sculpture. Whether you go along with scientific speculations or not, liking a plant is obviously a good reason for acquiring it, and helping it grow with a little praise and encouragement goes a long way towards ensuring that it is happy and healthy with you.

Empirical evidence points to the fact that the right kind of music can encourage and soothe plants just as it does human beings. With love and affection as well as the basic requirements, plants will flourish in your interior.

The scope of indoor plants

There is a plant for every situation and for every time of year. Plants can be kept as an absorbing and rewarding hobby, or as beautiful objects demanding the minimum of time and attention.

We all know about the easy plants, the humble begonias and geraniums, the *Fatsia* and *Chlorophytum*, but the scope of indoor plants ranges wide and the dramatic effects possible today are almost limitless.

With architectural help and a certain amount of building work, forest glades, rockeries and rush-lined pools can be part of an interior design scheme. Large sheets of glass linking the inside with the outside can give plants enough light for an indoor tree like *Ficus benjamina* or *Sparmannia* to reach the ceiling, and enable you to sit beneath its spreading boughs. A group of chairs and tables, like islands, can look out through an interior landscape of banana, *Ficus*, *Cyperus* and *Dracaena* with ivy garlanding the walls and large leaves reflected in shallow rectangular pools.

Tall plants in a plant window give the necessary dappled jungle light to little plants which flourish in the shade below. A dense thicket or small copse of green can be happily maintained, even some distance from a window, with the help of artificial light and automatic watering or water culture. A small room may be entirely devoted to growing orchids or to a collection of cacti and succulents, and the night-flowering cactus will produce a bloom worth waking every member of the family and every neighbour to see. Given the right warmth and humidity you can sit under your curving palm fronds or giant banana leaves sipping your sundowner with none of the insect life of the tropics to contend with. Or, if your taste is more in tune with northern romanticism, you could create a mysterious hermit's grotto, hung with ivy and shaded with ferns, filled with mossy statuary and the soporific tinkle of water from an interior fountain, where small fish swim in a leaf-ringed pool.

But to return to the geranium, even this need not be so humble after all. There is no reason why it should not be given its head and grow two or three metres up a wall, dotted with brilliant vermilion or cerise flowers. Similarly an ivy-leaved type may trail down from an eminence such as a gallery or landing, as it would in its native home on the bare rocky hillsides of South Africa. And stout, portly *Mammillaria*, usually bought very small for a miniature garden, need not necessarily remain so, as given the right conditions they can grow half a metre round, and raised on a stone or concrete plinth, they crouch like creatures from outer space or giant prickly sculptures.

Severe, metal-framed windows can be laced with the delicate tracery of triangular ivy-leaved garlands or the star-shaped leaves of *Passiflora*, while vigorous *Allamanda* will very soon cover a whole wall with its glossy leaves.

We have come a long way since a Chinese gardener first put a chrysanthemum in a pot or a Roman realized that basil not only kept the flies away but also greatly improved the look of his solarium, or even since the Duke of Devonshire's gardener carefully tended some storm-tossed exotic from the Amazon in his Grace's hot-house. Whatever your life style and whatever your surroundings, today there are the right plants for you and your interior.

Familiar house plants such as ferns, *Hedera*, *Chlorophytum*, *Philodendron* and *Howeia* respond to a warm, humid atmosphere by reaching the luxuriant dimensions associated with growth in the wild. Together with parakeets and tropical fish they create the impression of an exotic jungle within the confines of this city interior.

Visual glossary

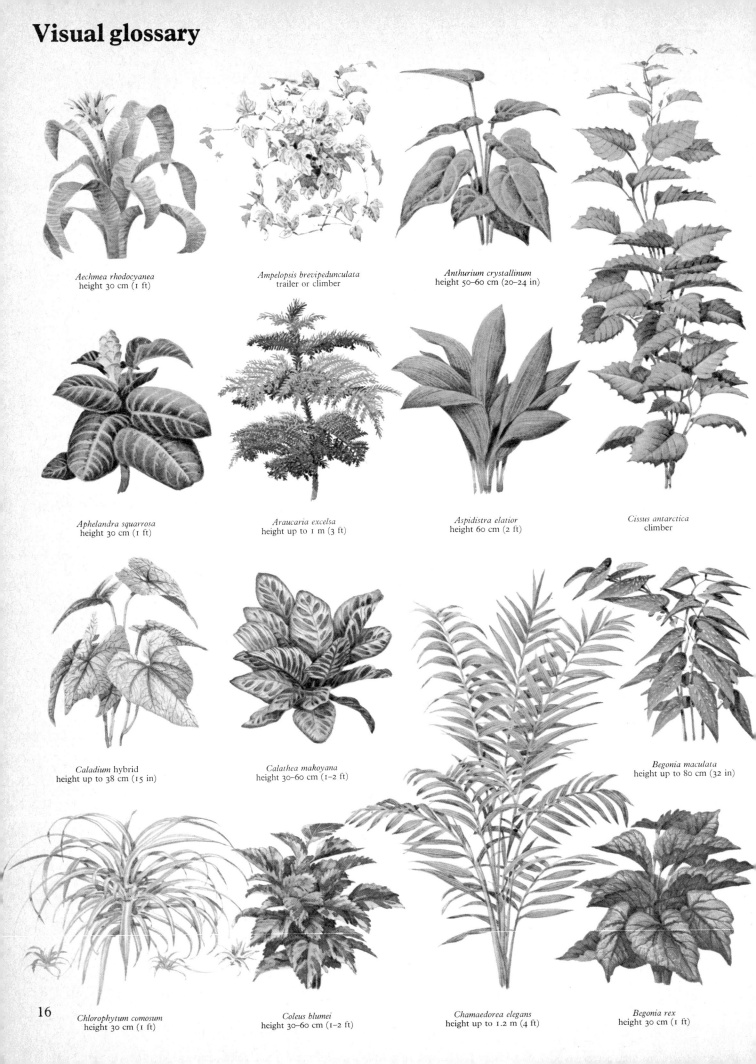

Aechmea rhodocyanea
height 30 cm (1 ft)

Ampelopsis brevipedunculata
trailer or climber

Anthurium crystallinum
height 50–60 cm (20–24 in)

Aphelandra squarrosa
height 30 cm (1 ft)

Araucaria excelsa
height up to 1 m (3 ft)

Aspidistra elatior
height 60 cm (2 ft)

Cissus antarctica
climber

Caladium hybrid
height up to 38 cm (15 in)

Calathea makoyana
height 30–60 cm (1–2 ft)

Begonia maculata
height up to 80 cm (32 in)

Chlorophytum comosum
height 30 cm (1 ft)

Coleus blumei
height 30–60 cm (1–2 ft)

Chamaedorea elegans
height up to 1.2 m (4 ft)

Begonia rex
height 30 cm (1 ft)

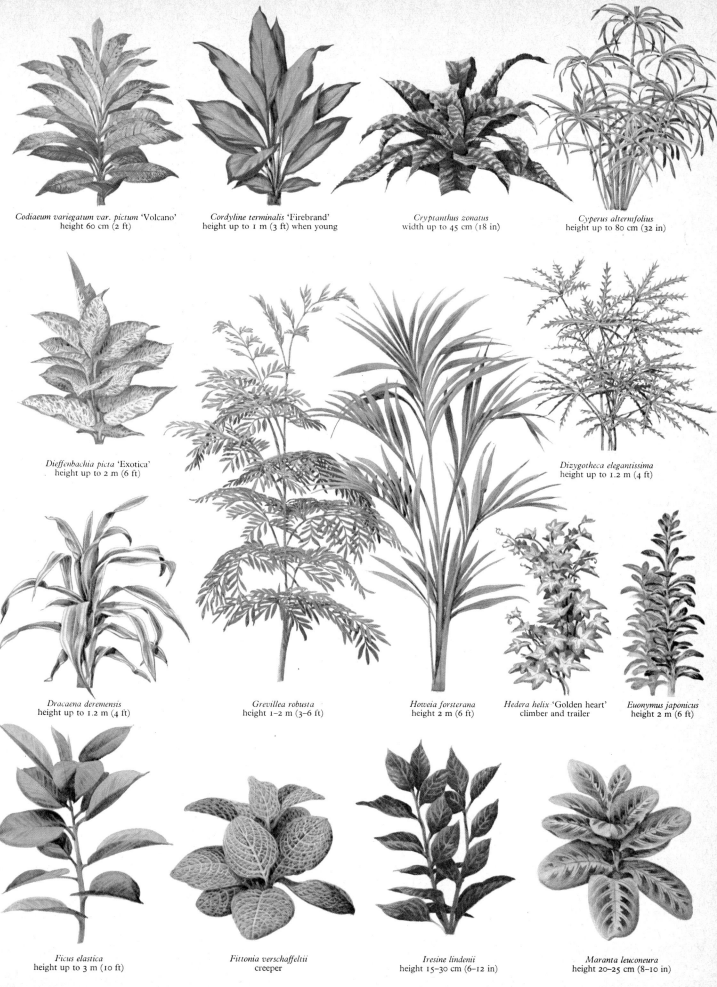

Codiaeum variegatum var. pictum 'Volcano'
height 60 cm (2 ft)

Cordyline terminalis 'Firebrand'
height up to 1 m (3 ft) when young

Cryptanthus zonatus
width up to 45 cm (18 in)

Cyperus alternifolius
height up to 80 cm (32 in)

Dieffenbachia picta 'Exotica'
height up to 2 m (6 ft)

Dizygotheca elegantissima
height up to 1.2 m (4 ft)

Dracaena deremensis
height up to 1.2 m (4 ft)

Grevillea robusta
height 1–2 m (3–6 ft)

Howeia forsterana
height 2 m (6 ft)

Hedera helix 'Golden heart'
climber and trailer

Euonymus japonicus
height 2 m (6 ft)

Ficus elastica
height up to 3 m (10 ft)

Fittonia verschaffeltii
creeper

Iresine lindenii
height 15–30 cm (6–12 in)

Maranta leuconeura
height 20–25 cm (8–10 in)

Microcoelum weddellianum
height up to 1.2 m (4 ft)

Neoregelia carolinae
width 30–38 cm (12–15 in)

Peperomia argyreia
height 20–25 cm (8–10 in)

Philodendron scandens
climber and trailer

Phoenix canariensis
height 4 m (13 ft)

Pilea cadierei
height up to 25 cm (10 in)

Pittosporum tobira
height up to 1.2 m (4 ft)

Rhaphidophora aurea
trailer

Monstera deliciosa
height 2.5 m (8 ft)

Rhoeo spathacea
height 20–35 cm (8–14 in)

Rhoicissus capensis
climber

Schefflera actinophylla
height 2 m (6 ft)

Sparmannia africana
height 1.2–2 m (4–6 ft)

Syngonium auritum
climber

Tradescantia fluminensis
height 20 cm (8 in)

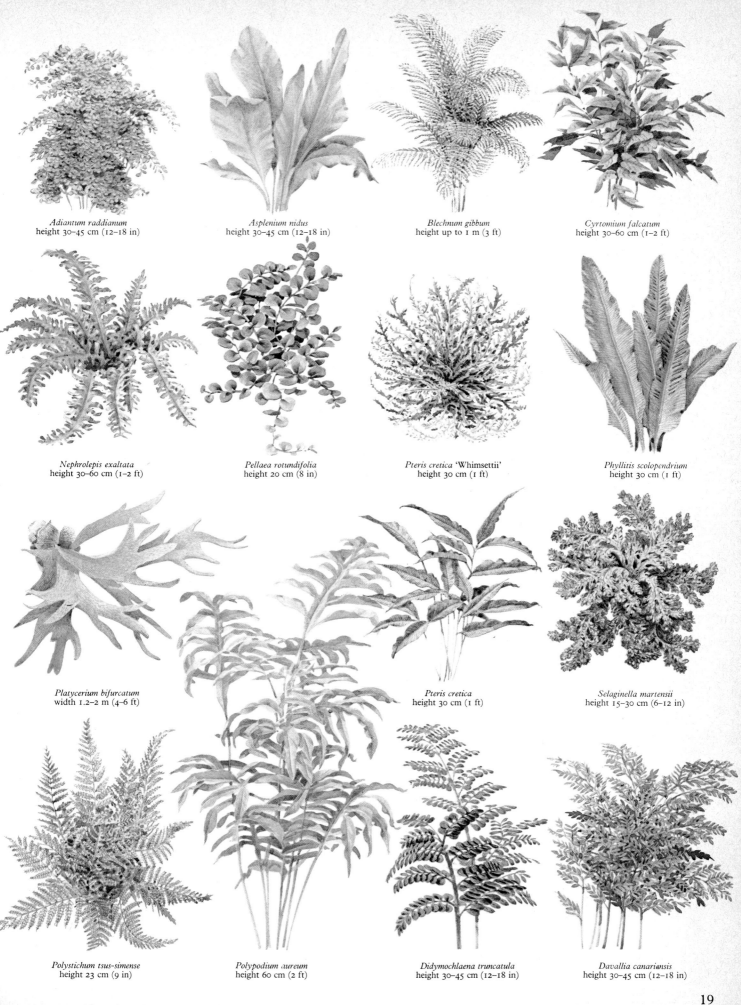

Adiantum raddianum
height 30–45 cm (12–18 in)

Asplenium nidus
height 30–45 cm (12–18 in)

Blechnum gibbum
height up to 1 m (3 ft)

Cyrtomium falcatum
height 30–60 cm (1–2 ft)

Nephrolepis exaltata
height 30–60 cm (1–2 ft)

Pellaea rotundifolia
height 20 cm (8 in)

Pteris cretica 'Whimsettii'
height 30 cm (1 ft)

Phyllitis scolopendrium
height 30 cm (1 ft)

Platycerium bifurcatum
width 1.2–2 m (4–6 ft)

Pteris cretica
height 30 cm (1 ft)

Selaginella martensii
height 15–30 cm (6–12 in)

Polystichum tsus-simense
height 23 cm (9 in)

Polypodium aureum
height 60 cm (2 ft)

Didymochlaena truncatula
height 30–45 cm (12–18 in)

Davallia canariensis
height 30–45 cm (12–18 in)

Anthurium scherzeranum
height 45 cm (18 in)

Begonia × tuberhybrida 'Harlequin'
height 30–45 cm (12–18 in)

Billbergia nutans
height 45 cm (18 in)

Bougainvillea glabra
height up to 1.2 m (4 ft)

Calceolaria × herbeohybrida
height up to 30 cm (1 ft)

Callistemon citrinus
height up to 1 m (3 ft)

Camellia japonica
height up to 2 m (6 ft)

Campanula isophylla
height up to 30 cm (1 ft)

Cineraria cruenta hybrid
height 45 cm (18 in)

Clivia miniata
height 45 cm (18 in)

Cyclamen persicum
height 30 cm (1 ft)

Drejerella (*Beloperone guttata*)
height up to 30 cm (1 ft)

Euphorbia pulcherrima
height 45 cm (18 in)

Canna × hybrida 'J. B. van der Schoot'
height 1–2 m (3–6 ft)

Fuchsia triphylla
height 60 cm (2 ft)

Gardenia jasminoides
height up to 2 m (6 ft)

20

Hibiscus rosa-sinensis
height 2 m (6 ft)

Hoya bella
height up to 30 cm (1 ft)

Hydrangea macrophylla
height up to 1 m (3 ft)

Jasminum mesnyi
height up to 2 m (6 ft)

Pelargonium × hortorum hybrid
height 30–60 cm (1–2 ft)

Primula obconica
height 15–30 cm (6–12 in)

Rechsteineria cardinalis
height 23–45 cm (9–18 in)

Rhododendron simsii
height 45–60 cm (18–24 in)

Passiflora caerulea
climber

Saintpaulia ionantha
height 20 cm (8 in)

Sinningia speciosa
height 30 cm (1 ft)

Spathiphyllum wallisii
height 30–40 cm (12–16 in)

Streptocarpus × hybridus
height 25 cm (10 in)

Thunbergia alata
climber

Vriesia splendens
height 45 cm (18 in)

Zantedeschia aethiopica
height 60 cm–1.2 m (2–4 ft)

21

Agave victoria-reginae
height up to 15 cm (6 in)

Astrophytum myriostigma
height 10 cm (4 in)

Cereus peruvianus
height up to 1 m (3 ft)

Cephalocereus senilis
height up to 23 cm (9 in)

Conophytum ficiforme
diameter 7.5 cm (3 in)

Crassula falcata
height 30–60 cm (1–2 ft)

Echinocactus grusonii
diameter up to 15 cm (6 in)

Echinocereus pectinatus
height 15 cm (6 in)

Faucaria tigrina
diameter 8–13 cm (3–5 in)

Ferocactus latispinus
height up to 13 cm (5 in)

Gasteria liliputana
height 5–8 cm (2–3 in)

Epiphyllum hybrid
height 30 cm–
1.5 m (1–5 ft)

*Gymnocalycium
mihanovichii* 'Friedrichii'
height 3.5 cm (1–2 in)

Haworthia fasciata
height 10 cm (4 in)

Kalanchoë blossfeldiana
height 25 cm (10 in)

Lithops fulleri
diameter 5–8 cm (2–3 in)

Mammillaria zeilmanniana
diameter 10–20 cm (4–8 in)

Opuntia rufida
height 30 cm (1 ft)

Parodia chrysacanthion
height 5–8 cm (2–3 in)

Rebutia minuscula
height 2·5–4 cm (1–1½ in)

Sansevieria trifasciata
height 30–45 cm (12–18 in)

Sedum sieboldii
trailer

Chionodoxa luciliae 'Gigantea'
height 15 cm (6 in)

Crocus vernus hybrids
height 15 cm (6 in)

Freesia × hybrida
height up to 45 cm (18 in)

Hyacinthus orientalis hybrids
height 30 cm (1 ft)

Narcissus (Daffodil, Trumpet type)
height 50 cm (20 in)

Narcissus (Tazetta type) 'Cragford'
height 50 cm (20 in)

Hippeastrum equestre
height 50–70 cm (20–28 in)

Iris reticulata
height 15 cm (6 in)

Nerine bowdenii
height 30–45 cm (12–18 in)

Ornithogalum nutans
height 23 cm (9 in)

Puschkinia scilloides
height 10 cm (4 in)

Scilla peruviana
height 25 cm (10 in)

Tulipa kaufmanniana
height 25 cm (10 in)

Sparaxis tricolor
height 30 cm (1 ft)

Lilium auratum
height 1.2–2 m (4–6 ft)

Valotta speciosa
height 60 cm (2 ft)

23

Design with house plants

Any interior, from a small cottage bedroom to a gleaming open plan apartment, is improved by well chosen and well placed plants. They give an added dimension to a room bringing it to life with their freshness and colour.

Your interest in plants may begin in one of many ways. You might have a large window or too much space in a light hall and decide that a plant or two will be just the thing. You may see a plant which is so beautiful that you just have to have it, and then walk around with it in your hands looking for the ideal place for it. A plant may be given to you as a present, or you may be trying to evoke a certain interior style or period feeling which can only be completed by the addition of palms, cacti or bonsai. Perhaps you just love plants and find it impossible to live without them.

There are plants which settle down happily into your life style, perhaps taking a background role, and there are others which demand a lot of time and care to keep them in the manner to which they have become accustomed. One small succulent may inspire you to buy another, and another, and, before you know it, you have a whole collection of them. After a while you may find that your plants are doing so well that they change from being mere accents in a room into dominating centre-pieces or focal points. In time as you buy more and more plants, they may seem to be taking over the whole environment, but this can never really be so. They are not Triffids, they do not invade a room and take possession; they grow and thrive only if you are attentive to their needs. As an apparently negligent style of dress often takes the most time and thought, so an apparent jungle has to be controlled to give the effect of profusion.

When designing your home with plants you must consider the space to be occupied and the size, form, texture and colour of the plant or plants which would suit it. Also whether you want your plants to enhance the beautiful features of your room, or disguise faulty paintwork and ugly pipes. Consider carefully whether a tall tree-like plant would give added height to the ceiling, or simply look trapped in the corner? Do you want one specimen, dramatically lit with spotlights, or many plants crowded together. Perhaps your room needs dividing with trailing plants which could act as a partial screen, or a graceful arch could be shown off to its best advantage, its form traced by delicate trailing ivies.

You must know not only what function your plant is to serve in a particular interior, but also what facilities you are going to provide it in return. You will get nowhere by placing an azalea on a sunny window sill because you like the way the light shines on it, for it will soon wilt and then die; nor can you set flowering geraniums in a sunless and airless corner without the light and fresh air they need. Designing with indoor plants goes a long way beyond purely aesthetic considerations, and it is only when you are able to understand your plants that you can use them to their best advantage.

Plants are the most important elements in this lofty, split-level room. Architectural features are minimal and unobtrusive, using white walls and simple materials like pinewood and glass. Free-floating chrome and glass shelves offer new and interesting views of potted plants and a large wall mirror doubles the already abundant image of foliage.

Plant planning

Most plant collections accumulate in a haphazard way: as a gift or bought at random and, although this contributes greatly to their charm, it can cause many problems if the wrong plants are kept together or plants are kept in unsuitable parts of the room. You may not consider that you have enough plants to merit a cogent plan, but if you are not careful, those you do have could quickly decline into a wilting assemblage of brown leaves.

There are several factors you should consider before beginning or adding to your collection. You need to assess carefully the demands made on your life: will you have the time and inclination to tend to your plants' needs? Do you lead a solitary existence or do you entertain on a large scale? What about the other members of the household—small children, pets, people with allergies—all of whom must share the environment. You must think about the size, architectural features and decor of the area in which you intend to house the plants, how light it is, what kind of heating it has, how damp it is, and how you would ultimately like it to look. Bearing all these things in mind you can select the number and kind of plants best suited to your circumstances.

If you are starting your collection, the best way to begin is cautiously, with one easy-to-care for flowering plant such as

a *Hydrangea*. You can choose the colour to fit the decor. If the plant fails, it can be whisked away unnoticed and, if it thrives, which it should if placed in a fairly cool, shaded position, it will become a small, decorative piece rather than a wholesale commitment to greenery. It adds colour to an otherwise quiet room bringing it alive in an unobtrusive way.

You may wish to enliven your room in a more dramatic way, in which case you could choose a full, mature palm such as a *Howeia*, and even reinforce its effectiveness by having two palms symmetrically positioned; or you may prefer one of the larger varieties of *Dracaena*. A similar grand effect can also be achieved by using a single even larger plant, such as a *Yucca*.

You may, however, decide that you would like a mass of greenery to decorate your interior, that you want almost to create the effect of the plants having taken over your living area. And this is where true plant planning comes into its own. With a spacious room, choice windows, several shelves, and ceiling beams capable of taking climbing plants, you can achieve an astounding effect with the right plants in the right place, creating an ever-changing contrast between flowers and foliage, large and small plants, sprawling trailers and the compact shapes of cacti. Be sure to instigate a systematic watering and feeding system. Indiscriminate rounds with a watering can and plant food will give some plants more than they need and leave others lacking.

A regiment of ferns, ranged along a long, low shelf, will not only look attractive but will appreciate their shady position. Fill corners with taller plants such as the rough-barked *Dracaena*, perhaps contrasting it with the small-leaved delicacy of *Ficus benjamina*. If you have large windows you can either fill them with sun-loving plants like *Impatiens* or build shelves for the spiny rotundity of cacti. An alternative is to screen the window with rubber plants (*Ficus elastica*), but make sure these don't grow so large as to obscure the whole window. Dull ceiling beams, on the other hand, can be disguised with climbers such as the indestructible *Rhoicissus*.

Plant planning can make the same room look like many different rooms, but when planning your urban display remember that every plant has a certain character which is based on the conditions imposed by its original habitat. Nothing can alter its basic needs, and so it is important when planning or adding to a collection of indoor plants, that you make sure that there will not be a major and insoluble personality clash between the human and vegetable world.

Plants and interior design

An old Chinese proverb declares that the 'superior man adapts the environment to suit himself'. On the larger scale of society in general this can present difficulties, but it can be done, and to great effect, in the private territory of your own home. Whatever sort of space you inhabit, whether it's a country cottage, a city apartment or an artist's garret, you need not necessarily allow it to impose a style of interior on you. Obviously, basic structural considerations have to be taken into account and, if they are to your liking, they can even be accentuated, but it is up to you to create a unique environment which both reinforces and reflects your own personality.

Different moods can easily be created in the most unpromising interiors with the right furniture and accessories, and the right plants. These can either intensify the established style of a room or evoke an entirely new and different style. You may have the right choice of paint, wallpaper, furniture and fabrics, but it is often the selection of plants that saves an otherwise perfect interior from looking unlived in. The oppressively clinical appearance of gleaming glass and chrome, for example, can be relieved by a large *Ficus benjamina*, a humanizing yet not distracting element among the sleek lines of the overall design. Similarly, a stylish recreation of the charm and dignity of the nineteenth century might be in danger of becoming a museum piece were it not brought alive by the traditional green presence of ferns, palms or an *Aspidistra*. These are plants which are indelibly associated with the nineteenth century, just as succulents and cacti are an instant evocation of the 1930s. You might want to evoke a culture rather than a period—for example, an interior that evinces the simplicity of the east, and this can be achieved by the addition of a bonsai delicately balanced in its special container, carefully positioned in relation to its setting.

On the other hand you may decide to let your architectural parameters dictate the terms of your interior. Perhaps you are fortunate enough to live in a nineteenth-century house with a built-in plant window or conservatory so beautiful that you willingly allow it to shape the rest of your design. Similarly, a country cottage, with thick-walled window embrasures and wooden beams demands the kind of plants that it has always enjoyed, a clutter of decorative pots filled with timeless country plants such as geraniums or sweet scented herbs. City dwellers in compact high rise apartments can grow plants very successfully on their sunny window sills high above ground level pollution. Urban apartments are usually all-too-efficiently heated, which means that vegetables thrive as well as exotic tropical plants.

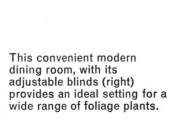

Hedera canariensis and a vase of ivy-leafed geraniums combine to enhance the rustic style of this interior (left).

This convenient modern dining room, with its adjustable blinds (right) provides an ideal setting for a wide range of foliage plants.

The striking shapes of a palm, cactus and *Dracaena* offset the classical lines of this modern apartment (left).

Tubs of *Cyperus alternifolius* with their elegant, erect stems contribute to the charm of this luxurious lounge (below).

The colonial style of this dining room with its flowered wallpaper and carpet is complemented by the delicacy of trailing *Hedera* leaves and *Nephrolepis* fronds (above).

Some of your architectural features may not be very pleasing, so your plants can be used to disguise them. A tiny attic, in which it seems impossible to achieve any design coherence, can be transformed by plants. In fact, many attics have the advantage of receiving plenty of sunlight. Basements on the other hand present their own problems: they may be damp and gloomy and blighted with a hideous outlook. You can change all this by filling your window with plants that prefer darkish shady conditions. As you won't be receiving much light anyway, you won't miss the little extra you will lose, and the plants will form an effective and beautiful screen hiding whatever you have outside, railings, dustbins or a brick wall.

You might have a studio in which you both live and work or you may live in a building that wasn't specifically designed to be a house—a converted warehouse, chapel, railway carriage or barn, for example. Often the architectural features in these larger living spaces are more exaggerated than in the ordinary house. Dramatic roof beams, large windows or pleasing yet non-functional industrial elements can all be emphasized or disguised with plants. Areas that are too large to live in, yet not worth obscuring with a structural wall can be pleasingly screened with plants, and these can easily be moved around as the need arises.

Whatever your interior, when designing with plants remember that you have made the habitat which suits your own way of life, but that your plants must enjoy the same consideration. Plants are living creatures and cannot for ever be shunted around from pillar to post in search of the best place for them to be seen. They must have a stable home in your home, with all the nourishment and comforts that they need. A pleasing harmony between their life and yours must be found.

An exuberant *Philodendron* with its deeply cut leaves provides a focal point for this sunny attic bedroom (above).

A capacious converted warehouse (right) makes an ideal plant home, affording many display areas.

A certain antique elegance is easily created (above) with the use of several potted palms and a *Chlorophytum*.

An eastern 'still life' with a *Cordyline terminalis*, *Patchypodium* and parasol brightens a dull corner (above).

An ugly basement outlook (below) can be screened with hard-wearing plants liking a medium light.

Plants, colour and texture

One of the most interesting approaches to the extensive use of plants in interior design is the juxtaposition of contrasting forms, shapes and colours, and the visual impact which can be made.

The leaves of plants are no more uniformly green than the sky is uniformly blue. They encompass countless permutations and variations of tone, shade and intensity, as well as variations in texture ranging from the velvety softness of African violet to the shiny gloss paint look of a healthy *Monstera*, and flowers covering the whole colour spectrum from the single smooth perfect white of the Calla lily to the massed bloom of deep purple *Heliotropium*.

Most plants have a natural affinity with organic materials, such as wood or stone, marble or indeed other plants. They can also contrast strikingly with the bright colours, unusual textures and hard edge forms of man-made products. The right decor is important; neither plant nor background should be camouflaged. The more simple the plant colour, the plain green leaves of the *Aspidistra* or a white-flowered hydrangea come to mind, the more suited it is for setting against a highly decorative background. A patterned wallpaper or curtain brings to life the rather subdued nature of an *Aspidistra* while some of the simple forms and colours of cacti and succulents are ideally complemented when they stand in front of a painting or wall hanging.

On the other hand any pattern will detract from the delicate tracery of foliage and leaf. Such splendid egocentrics as *Dizygotheca* and coconut palm are only seen at their best when they are given a backdrop which doesn't rival them. A complete contrast of colour is always effective and can create startling visual shocks. Try setting a pink begonia or azalea against a dark green wall or even against an orange background to introduce a planned discord. The large oval leaves of *Dieffenbachia* or dark polished leaves of *Ficus lyrata* are strong enough to stand their own when placed against vermilion or purple paint. Red *Cordyline* or *Begonia rex* have an equally jazzy effect when seen against green or blue. On a gentler note, the pale apple-green leaves of *Sparmannia* or ferns are well contrasted against dark wood panelling. The brilliant cerise and iridescent pinks of *Impatiens* and geraniums look particularly good when set against a blue-grey background.

Contrasting texture is well worth considering and responding to. Ferny, furry, or velvety leaves which seem to merge with a soft background suddenly come into their own when set against gloss paint or marble. The polished leaves of the many tropical foliage plants are emphasized by hessian (burlap), pinoleum velvet or the traditional split cane or woven grass blinds which come in a range of natural colours.

Some plants must be considered as objects which are complete in themselves and which need only an unobtrusive frame to hold them. One thinks of the intricate patterns and subtle colours of *Maranta* or *Calathea* as an example. Others are best seen as part of a larger composition, a tableau and then the overall use of colour combinations and the contrasts of texture must be considered as a whole.

The following charts listing some of the more common indoor plants have been drawn up as a general guide to choosing plants according to the colour and texture of their flowers or foliage.

A mass of greenery (right)— *Dieffenbachia*, *Nephrolepis* and chrysanthemums—gives colour to a white and silver decor.

White/grey/silver foliage and flowering plants

White flowering plants

Begonia semperflorens eg 'Coffee and Cream'
Campanula isophylla 'Alba'
Chrysanthemum many types
Cyclamen persicum eg 'White Swan'
Gardenia jasminoides
Hyacinthus orientalis eg 'L'innocence'
Narcissus many types
Stephanotis floribunda

Grey/silver foliage plants, cacti and succulents

Aglaonema crispum
Begonia rex many types
Caladium bicolor hybrids
Echeveria species
Fittonia argyroneura
Pilea many types

Vivid geraniums (above) increase the impact of a white window in a stark black wall.

Natural textures often serve to enhance one another. Pale, black-veined marble (above) finds an echo in creamy *Poinsettia* and the crisped ribbon fronds of a *Pteris*.

Cream/brown foliage and flowering plants

Cream flowering plants

Chrysanthemum many types
Cineraria cruenta hybrids
Narcissus many types

Cream and green foliage plants

Ananas comosus hybrids
Chlorophytum comosum
Dieffenbachia picta hybrids
Euphorbia pulcherrima hybrids
Peperomia magnoliifolia 'Variegata'

Brown/bronze foliage plants

Begonia rex many types
Coleus blumei hybrids
Dizygotheca elegantissima

A spiky cactus and a weathered terracotta pot (above right) match the rough textures of an unrendered brick wall.

The matt leaves of a succulent serve to enhance a simple, polished pine surface (right).

Red foliage and the brown glaze on a lamp base (below) create a warm corner setting.

The arching fronds of *Howeia* (above) rise gracefully against bands of cream bricks.

Natural pine (below) contrasts richly with chrysanthemums, crotons and *Dieffenbachia*.

33

Purple foliage and flowering plants

Flowering plants

Browallia species
Brunfelsia calycina
Cineraria cruenta hybrids
Crocus many types
Saintpaulia ionantha hybrids
Streptocarpus many types

Foliage plants

Gynura species
Iresine herbstii

The flowers of *Browallia speciosa* heighten the blues of this interior (far left).

A display of white blooms and grey and silver foliage echoes the restrained luxury of pastel upholstery (left).

The green fronds of *Adiantum raddianum* make a bright patch on plain blue tiles (above).

The striated leaves of an *Aechmea* subtly mirror the texture of raw silk (left).

A dramatic wallpaper demands an equally dramatic plant like this *Cordyline* (above).

Blue/green foliage and flowering plants

Flowering plants

Campanula species
Hyacinthus many types
Hydrangea macrophylla
hybrids
Ipomoea rubro-caerulea
Passiflora caerulea
Plumbago capensis

Foliage plants, cacti and succulents

Aechmea rhodocyanea
Cereus chalybaeus
Crassula falcata
Eucalyptus species
Sedum species

Solanum capsicastrum makes a lively splash (right) against a rough-textured wallpaper and the grain of natural wood.

A pleasing combination of the represented and the actual (above) sets leafy patterned wallpaper and antique wall tiles against the real thing— *Chlorophytum*, *Ficus pumila* and *Begonia rex*.

The display of ferns and palms (left) relieves the severity of strongly coloured, checker patterned furnishings.

Orange/yellow foliage and flowering plants

Flowering plants

Begonia (Hiemalis) eg
'Eveleen's Orange'
Begonia × *tuberhybrida* eg
'Guardsman'
Calceolaria × *herbeohybrida*
many types
Chrysanthemum many types
Citrus mitis (orange fruits)
Crocus many types
Hibiscus rosa-sinensis eg
'Miss Betty'
Narcissus many types
Primula many types
Thunbergia alata

Foliage plants

*Codiaeum variegatum var.
pictum* hybrids
Dieffenbachia picta hybrids

The distinctive shape and
colour of a *Philodendron*
make a dramatic contribution
to a yellow bedroom (right).

A sunny rusticity (below) is
achieved by teaming white
chrysanthemums and African
violets with yellow walls.

Orange and yellow chrysanthemums reinforce the tones
of bamboo hangings (bottom
left).

The elegance of a primrose
coloured polygonal room
(below right) is enhanced by
a *Chamaerops* and a
Cordyline.

Red/pink foliage and flowering plants

Flowering plants

Achimenes coccinea
Begonia many types
Chrysanthemum many types
Cyclamen many types
Fuchsia many types
Hyacinthus orientalis eg 'Rosalie'
Hydrangea macrophylla hybrids
Impatiens many types
Primula many types
Rhododendron simsii hybrids
Saintpaulia ionantha eg 'Grandiflora Pink'
Cineraria cruenta many types
Sinningia many types

Foliage plants

Begonia rex hybrids
Caladium bicolor hybrids
Coleus blumei hybrids
Cordyline terminalis eg 'Firebrand'
Iresene lindenii

Cyclamen pink and apple green unify a kitchen corner (below) where flowering plants offset the formal floral wallpaper.

Two magnificent fuchsias echo the red theme that runs through the decor of this spacious converted barn (above).

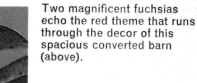

A simple and stunning effect is created by placing a glossy green *Monstera* against a vermilion background (left).

Clashing colours make a lively display happily tempered by green foliage (left).

Plants in groups

By grouping together many plants you create the effect of a garden which has been brought inside the house. Visually there is a world of difference between solitary plants, even when there are several of them standing in different corners of the room, and a group of plants standing shoulder to shoulder, filling one whole area with their greenery. You could have a row of little cacti and succulents standing demurely at one end of a table or an authentic Douanier Rousseau jungle corner, lacking only a wide-eyed tiger, composed of banana plants, arums arching their huge leaves and epiphytes on mossy branches.

The number of plants you use will depend on the amount of territory you want to keep for yourself and the amount you are prepared to give over to your plants. Perhaps you have a conservatory or plant window which was specially constructed to hold a jostling crowd of exotic tropical plants, or you may have decided that one third of the available floor space, table space or window ledge space is going to be given over to your plants.

There are several practical reasons for having plants in groups. Those needing the same conditions and the same environment really do seem to do much better when they are set close together. Maintenance is often easier as watering and spraying takes place in one spot, or large self-watering containers can be used. Having a group of plants together creates an ideal atmosphere, since the tiny workings of all the pores in each leaf contribute to the desired level of humidity. Low plants needing dappled shade are supplied with it naturally by taller plants, and in this way a proper jungle atmosphere is created.

A group of plants can be used to make a leafy dividing screen in a large open-plan room. Smaller scale groups fill in awkward shaped niches in the room, or perhaps occupy an empty fireplace during the summer months. Large plants like *Monstera*, *Ficus*, *Schefflera* and *Sparmannia* can form a grove in one corner, or the effect of a shrubbery. At the other end of the scale, pretty African violets make a decorative centre piece when they are set on a small table.

Groups can be chosen for their contrasting leaf shape, form and texture, or they can be composed of many plants of the same family. One cactus, one young avocado, one *Araucaria* tends to look bereft and naked when made to stand alone, yet comes into its own when flanked by many compatriots. Familiar and undramatic plants, like ferns or *Tradescantia* are suddenly given a new status when placed in groups, where the subtlety of each individual plant is seen in contrast to its neighbour.

A group of varied *Dracaena* is particularly effective. They grow high and tall on their slender stems, while younger shorter plants fill up the spaces with tufts of narrow leaves. *Begonia rex* are beautiful enough when they stand alone, but a group of them, displaying their enormous range of satiny, velvety texture and colour, can be breathtaking.

An interesting group effect is achieved by contrasting leaf shapes: the distinctive slits of *Monstera*, the violin shapes of *Ficus lyrata* and *Dieffenbachia's* characteristic speckles.

Contrast the shape of tall, elegant *Philodendron* with the squat outlines of *Neoregelia carolinae* (left).

Convivially grouped on a sill are *Ficus benjamina, F. radicans, Sparmannia, Fittonia* and *Chlorophytum*.

This brace of *Aechmea rhodocyanea* (above) makes a serene flower and foliage ornament for the table.

In a light, airy position (right), fuchsia, geraniums and *Plumbago capensis* make a well-matched flowering group.

Plants alone

A solitary plant does not need to be enormous in order to play a vital part in the overall design of a particular interior. Obviously a huge *Monstera* looming greenly in a corner of the room will have a definite impact on all who enter, but it might be caused primarily by the shock of seeing so large a creature apparently trying to hide behind a lamp-stand. A simple, delicately shaped and carefully placed *Cyperus* could well have a much more commanding and aesthetically pleasing presence standing alone.

Displaying groups of plants involves one set of considerations, displaying one or two specimens, carefully nurtured as objects to be appreciated for their own individual qualities is altogether another issue. A place must be found that not only answers the plant's needs, but also illuminates it, whether by daylight or artificial light, in such a way that it is enhanced and its best features are brought out. A bronzy black *Dizygotheca* looks particularly beautiful when seen silhouetted against the light. A maidenhair fern can look like an undifferentiated mass of greenery until it is placed so that the daylight strikes its feathery fronds from behind, and then it comes alive with a brilliant patina of luminous greens. But remember that ferns do not respond to an overgenerous amount of light.

Some plants are best seen at eye level; some, such as the representatives of the bromeliad family, should be seen from above, as only in this way can the form and colour of these strange flattened rosettes be fully appreciated. The large-scale charm of a *Monstera* or *Schefflera* is best seen from a distance, whereas the colours and designs on the leaves of *Maranta* and *Calathea* must be studied at close quarters.

All palms look effective standing alone. They have such a uniquely graceful and evocative shape, which would be lost if another plant were placed beside them. The date palm actually insists on isolation since its leaves are so sharp and spiky. The same antisocial trait is shared by the *Pandanus*, whose leaves have such sharp edges, that it needs to be given a generous space to stand in and a wide berth by passers-by.

It goes almost without saying that any plant singled out for the honour of standing alone must be in top form. This will be the case if it is carefully situated, so that it has the right amount of light, humidity and warmth, and carefully tended, so that its leaves are glossy and its general appearance speaks of regular attention.

A mass of *Adiantum raddianum* (above) comes alive when light strikes its fronds, but beware of direct sunlight.

Ficus benjamina (left), probably the best known house plant, can be very attractive standing alone.

The complete strangeness of the bromeliads can be fully realized by focusing on one member of the family, the *Nidularium*. The flower head of this plant never emerges from its nest, but lies snugly in the centre of the leaves, like a jewel.

The pale green, almost transparent leaves of *Sparmannia africana* stand in solitary magnificence (below).

The long, curved leaves of *Dracaena fragrans* (above) lend an exotic touch to an informal interior.

The timeless appeal of the palm in an elegant setting is exemplified by this interior (left) which uses a *Howeia forsterana* as a focal point.

A small, abundant *Howeia* cleverly positioned plays intriguing tricks with the scale of a room.

Plants as sculpture

Living with plants you gradually become conscious of their shape, colour and pattern, and their very different and distinctive forms. In fact, you begin to look at them as art objects in themselves. They are as pieces of moving sculpture, endlessly changing as a new leaf unfolds or a flower blossoms. A splendid specimen captivates your attention and makes you look at it again and again, rather as you return over and over again to an intriguing piece of sculpture. A plant can be more than a mere accessory chosen to match your decor. Like a painting or a bronze figure, it can become the focus of the whole room, when its unique shape, form and colour, in a word its personality, is given a chance to shine.

There are many ways to bring out the latent powerful characteristics of a plant and emphasize its sculptural qualities. Carefully chosen background colour and lighting contribute to a plant's importance in the overall design scheme. All plants have their own sculptural presence, whether they are tall like the four metre *Ficus rubiginosa*, small and solid like *Dieffenbachia*, slender like *Dracaena*, as leafy as a croton or as stark and intriguing as a cactus. With ingenuity and imagination you can elicit these qualities and use them to enhance the many different rooms and corners of your interior.

Placed on a window sill where each shape can be fully appreciated, a row of cacti demands the aesthetic response usually reserved for pieces of sculpture (left).

A pleasingly diverse but symmetrical composition (right) is achieved by juxtaposing the skeletal grace of a miniature palm with a pair of sturdy *Dracaena*.

A tall and splendid *Ficus* (below) serves as the centrepiece of a grandly designed split-level room.

Plants need not be large to make their presence felt: the distinctive leaves of bromeliads make an effective focal point for this tablescape (above).

The impact of a single plant can be even more striking when it is encountered in an unusual position, such as the corner of a landing (right).

Making the most of good features

A room may have obvious good features: elegant proportions, a large bay window overlooking a beautiful landscape or a spacious and gracefully designed interior. But there are also good features which are less obvious and far more personal. These are the subtle things that make you prefer one particular space rather than another, and it is these features that you want to emphasize when planning an interior, making it into your own personal space. Maybe you live in a large area sparsely furnished and with few decorations, or a cosy nest with low ceiling and even lower wooden beams. Perhaps your space is shared by a numerous family and the many visitors who happen to drop in, or it is your own private territory used as a study or a work room. Whatever your interior, it is for you to emphasize the features which you find the most attractive, and plants will always serve this function with great effectiveness.

As always with plant planning, you must choose a place which suits the plant just as well as it suits you. The best features of any room, which agree with people and plants alike, are plenty of space, light and fresh air, no uncomfortable draughts and a reasonably stable temperature.

A window is a focal point in many rooms, and carefully chosen and placed plants will draw attention to it. A large window with a good view can be framed with plants, thus drawing the eye towards the scenery outside, presenting the view as if it were a beautiful painting. A window which receives low sunlight late in the day can be used for a collection of all those delicately fronded ferns which look so beautiful as the light filters through them. The cosy quality of an interior is heightened by a group of gaily flowering plants all standing in a row along a window sill. Depending on which direction your window faces it can house a collection of cacti, *Tradescantia* or geraniums. The attractive but stark lines of a large picture window make an ideal setting for a *Ficus benjamina*, which diffuses the light through its delicate weeping branches. A small window in a passage, bathroom or bedroom can look nondescript when left empty, but suddenly comes into its own when it holds a begonia or two, a few ferns or the interesting, irregular shape of one or two cacti.

In an open plan interior plants serve to define areas, zoning for instance a study from a living room, but without in any way separating them off from each other and spoiling the

freedom of having one large spacious unit. A single tall plant or group of plants is ideal for drawing attention to an attractive alcove or niche which might otherwise pass unnoticed, and resilient growers such as *Cissus antarctica* or trailing ivy can line and soften an archway. An expanse of plain wall can be broken up by the strategic placing of tall plants such as *Ficus*. In a large space plants act as a restful focal point when they are placed in the centre of a room, so that they can be seen and admired from all sides. If the room has high ceilings what better way to show them off than with hanging baskets or a column of plants.

Staircases and landings should always be fully exploited for plant displays. A trailing cascade of *Chlorophytum* or ivy, lit by a skylight high above will emphasize the sweep of a stairway, and it is fascinating to see plants from unusual angles. A light cool landing is an ideal home for such plants as *Schefflera* or *Crassula arborescens*.

You can of course also use your plants to attract attention to one treasured piece of furniture, ornament or sculpture and it can happen that the two complement each other so perfectly that they become inseparable.

A delicate tumbling display of *Campanula isophylla* 'alba' reflects the innocent beauty of this tiny window niche.

Arching doorways decorated and emphasized with *Crassula*, ivy-leaved geraniums and *Chamaerops*.

Syngonium podophyllum with tubs of *Camellia* frame an attractive balcony with greenery (left).

Adiantum raddianum, the maidenhair fern, makes a superb blaze of green filling a fireplace (above).

A hammock, together with a screen of *Araucaria excelsa* and palms, makes a perfect divide in a spacious studio.

Disguising bad features

Rooms, like most other things, have a habit of not being perfect in every way. However, few of them are unredeemable given some careful thought and consideration. The appearance of any room, no matter what its shape or size, is greatly enhanced by the addition of healthy plants. They always make a space look well loved and lived in, and that goes a long way towards improving the overall effect of an interior.

Unfortunate features in a room range from faults in the original architectural design, such as an awkward door, a ceiling that is too high, a window that is too small or a room shaped small and square like a sugar cube, to the unsightly additions of radiators, switches, air vents and unaesthetic plumbing fixtures. There are also external factors such as a far from desirable view onto the outside world or no view at all beyond an expanse of brick wall, something which confronts many people living in basement apartments. The room may also be subject to too much direct sunlight or none at all. Remember that a number of the features in a room which you consider to be bad might turn out to be ideal for certain plants.

A *Monstera* would be a disastrous choice for concealing a bad view in front of a south-facing window, but it would be most content to be placed in a semi-shaded corner and used as a disguise for some of the mysteries of the plumber's art or an unsightly bump in the wall. Undesirable architectural features can also be hidden behind a screen of *Cissus antarctica*, *Fatsia*, *Philodendron* and the resilient *Aspidistra*. A long narrow hall with some light can be effectively foreshortened if an imposing, large scale plant such as a *Ficus benjamina* is placed at the end and, conversely, too short a space can be lengthened by the use of trailing plants made to grow along the length of a wall, or by setting a mirror directly behind a plant, producing a *trompe-l'oeil* of added depth. Any awkward corner or alcove can be given a function when it holds plants, as long as there is sufficient light. Deep sills in a north or north-east facing window may not let in very much light, but they form an ideal resting place for a luxuriant mass of cool-loving ferns.

The seasonal changes in the year are as strongly felt inside the house as they are outside. A radiator or a central heating vent can be covered by a prettily leaved bower only in the summer as in the winter the plants will need a cooler place. A summer fireplace which otherwise looks so bleak can be the temporary home of a plant group, composed perhaps of ferns and arums, with ivies and *Ceropegia* cascading down from the mantle, as long as the flue is blocked off to prevent draughts, and, of course, unblocked when fire-lighting time comes round again. Also in summer a large window can be shaded by climbing annuals, blue flowering *Ipomoea*, perhaps, or climbing runner beans. In winter you will not miss these temporary decorative plants too much since you will be glad of every beam of sun that finds its way into your room.

Tall plants with thin trunks like *Dracaena* will take the eye upwards thus heightening a low ceiling. Any one of the many strong charactered, 'personality' plants will transform a blank expanse of undecorated wall, especially if dramatic shadows are formed by a nearby window or by the use of artificial light.

Enliven a dull kitchen view by erecting a plant shelf across the window. Fill it with whatever plants you like, bearing in mind individual demands. This group (below) includes *Tradescantia*, *Asparagus* and *Zygocactus*.

Ugly corner pipes which spoil the effect made by an antique dresser (right) can be hidden by the tumbling, glossy leaves of a strategically placed *Philodendron scandens*; *Glechoma hederacea* 'Variegata' adds to the display.

Trailing ivy, × *Fatshedera*, cacti and *Platycerium* transform a narrow unusable area into a pleasant retreat (right).

A triangular cupboard topped with *Philodendron erubescens* fills an otherwise useless corner between door and wall.

Plants in the bathroom

Conditions in the average bathroom, which tend not to prevail elsewhere, are periods of steam and heat and general lack of light, with a background temperature varying from warm to chilly according to the bathroom concerned. Obviously those plants happiest in such conditions are the tough, natural inhabitants of shady, often damp and steamy places. The main plants to avoid are those best suited to hot sun such as cacti and those needing a cool undisturbed environment such as *Cyclamen* or African violets.

Generally speaking, and it must be generally, as all bathrooms are not alike, it is the arum from the dense green of the South American rain forests and the *Begonia rex* from the shady damp regions at the foothills of the Himalayas that seem to thrive best. The giant arum *Monstera deliciosa*, the Swiss cheese or Hurricane plant, so called because of the attractive slits in its leaves, is dramatic, and easy to keep happy in most places; and its relative, *Philodendron scandens* with heart-shaped leaves, also likes shady conditions and can be trained either as a climber or a trailer. Other decorative *Philodendron* can also be trained happily in bathrooms. The *Begonia rex* with their asymmetrical pointed leaves are available in a large variety of colours from silver or crimson to rich green and pink. These grow low and look especially good massed together in a group. A large mirror makes an excellent background to plants, giving more apparent space to a small room, and doubling the amount of light especially when positioned opposite a window.

Any of the least demanding and most easily kept plants are worth trying in a bathroom: rubber plants, *Cissus antarctica*, ivies and ×*Fatshedera* should do well, although you will have to keep the glossy leaves wiped and free from flying talcum

A charming bathroom (above) with *Ficus elastica*, *Fatsia*, *Pteris cretica*, ivy, *Asparagus sprengeri* and *Zebrina*.

In complete contrast the simple presence of a single *Cyperus diffusus* enlivens an austere washing area.

A single *Monstera* (left) placed in a Chinese container takes on an oriental beauty, complementing the decorated hand-basin.

A glorious clump (above) of *Nephrolepis exaltata* 'Crispa' makes a dramatic ornament for a tiled shower area.

The luxurious understatement of chrome and bronze is reflected in the glossy green leaves of *Spathiphyllum wallisii* and *Spathiphyllum floribundum* (above).

The period flavour of an old-fashioned marble bathroom table is reinforced by two splendid *Rhaphidophora* and a bowl of golden chrysanthemums (right).

powder. The *Aspidistra* always looks good as a single plant. You may have a high window, a skylight or a high shelf, which can be made into an ideal support for trailing plants, and from which ivies, *Philodendron, Chlorophytum, Tradescantia* and *Zebrina* could cascade decoratively.

Two handsome, good natured plants are *Grevillea robusta,* the silk oak, and *Begonia metallica* with its luminous leaves. Both should be happy in a bathroom, but need as much light as possible. They always strain towards the light source and will therefore need turning from time to time.

Ferns of the tougher sort should do well; one of the best looking ferns I know stands above the cistern of a dark bathroom and its fronds cascade down in the healthiest possible manner. A delicate and grotto-like effect can be created with some of the more robust ferns like *Asplenium, Blechnum* and *Pteris,* but these will not be happy if the temperature is too high. You can also try palms such as *Howeia forsterana*; these do not mind the shade, and give great elegance to any interior.

As with most rooms containing indoor plants a certain amount of moving about is necessary. Various plants which have become a little jaded elsewhere in the house may well be improved by a spell in the bathroom, though they may not be entirely happy to settle in as permanent residents. For temporary decoration at flowering time geraniums and begonias are excellent. As with all indoor plants a little experimentation may well produce astonishing results, since every room, shelf and window sill produces a different effect.

Rhapis humilis, which reaches a satisfactory but not overwhelming height, looks good in a spacious bathroom.

The idiosyncratic charm of two small *Nephrolepis exaltata* (below) is doubled by the use of a background mirror.

Use the bathroom as a home for food plants, such as seedling lettuces, tomatoes and citrus, planted here in yoghurt pots and egg boxes.

Unlike most ferns, *Asplenium nidus* (right), the classic bath room choice, can thrive even in the warmest conditions.

A large mirrored bathroom easily accommodates *Nephrolepis* and *Adiantum*, *Philodendron* and geraniums (below right).

Plants in the kitchen

A kitchen is a hectic place and probably needs the soothing presence of plants more than most places in the house. Herbs are, of course, the first plants you think of in connection with the kitchen. The fresher they are and the nearer the cooking the better. Small plants are usually best in kitchens, and herbs grow modestly in pots and on trays. You can also hang up your successful harvest to dry in decorative bunches. Food plants such as green peppers and tomatoes are both useful and pleasing to look at. Cucumber vines can be gracefully trained round a window and, outside, a green curtain of climbing beans from a window box affords both privacy and produce, while scented leaved geraniums not only look good but can be used to give subtle flavour to drinks and puddings.

However, you needn't feel confined to food plants. Decorative plants can be put to work as part of the design in what is, after all, the most popular room in the house, where at least one member of the household spends much of the day. Whether your kitchen style is rustic or sophisticated plants will enhance it. If there is a dining area, this could be semi-screened with *Cissus* or *Philodendron*. Palms lend an atmosphere of luxury to the most frugal of rooms; *Howeia* should do well and will look particularly good with bentwood chairs and marble-topped surfaces. Pine or hardwood kitchens are an ideal background for most plants, and greenery does a lot to soften the sometimes overwhelmingly clinical line of some modern kitchens. Kitchen utensils themselves, copper pots, china tureens, even teapots, make excellent *cache-pots* for flowering plants or ivy trailing down from a dresser shelf.

Washing up is a great deal more pleasant if there is a group of bright, pink *Tradescantia*, trailing *Zebrina* or vermilion geraniums sunning themselves on the sill. Other sun lovers are the prickly *Euphorbia splendens* and the vivid crimson and purple *Irisene herbstii*.

Many plants are capable of standing up to the rigorous hazards of life among the saucepans, providing there is room enough for them to breathe. These include *Fatsia japonica*, *Ficus benjamina*, *Dracaena*, *Impatiens*, *Chlorophytum* and asparagus ferns. Avocados grow easily from stones and an *Aspidistra* of course will grow anywhere. *Grevillea robusta* makes an excellent screen in front of a window which otherwise gives onto unsightly dustbins, but it may grow too tall for your requirements. However, do remember that you can always rearrange the plants when they outgrow their situation or need a change of light conditions.

It is worth remembering that the kitchen is not the easiest place in which to grow plants. A small kitchen is never good, and the fluctuating temperature present in any kitchen is not the most healthy for plants. There are also the dangers of cooking fumes, and occasional steamy periods, if washing goes on. On the other hand, there is little danger of the plants being neglected or forgotten by the kitchen's frequent inhabitants. As long as you keep in mind the essential requirements, light, air, water and as undisturbed an environment as possible, and take extra care in the positioning and choosing of plants, there is no reason why you should not have a successful kitchen garden both indoors and on your window sill.

Palms and ferns will only do well in a spacious kitchen. *Nephrolepis* and *Chamaedorea* are shown (left).

Window sills make safe homes for delicate plants, poinsettia, African violet and *Asplenium*, as well as *Chlorophytum*.

A wide, open kitchen (above) can easily contain the expansive leafiness of *Chlorophytum, Cyperus, Pteris* and × *Fatshedera*.

Only the toughest of plants such as *Hoya carnosa, Zygocactus, Crassula, Tradescantia* and *Callisia* can survive in a busy compact kitchen area (left).

A flowering begonia teamed with a delicate *Asparagus sprengeri* stand out of harm's way in a quiet corner (right).

Campanula, Syngonium and *Adiantum* intensify the rustic atmosphere of a country-style kitchen (right).

Plants in the bedroom

The bedroom is possibly the least observed room in the house. Even so, there is no reason why it should not be a reposeful haven of welcoming greenery, as long as you choose the plants wisely and remember to feed them regularly; a guilty midnight promise will not be enough.

Bedrooms have certain features that can be exploited to the advantage of your plants. They are generally cooler, more tranquil and less troubled by damaging fumes than other rooms, and so make a splendid home for a variety of the more temperate plants. Provided there is enough light, most plants that were happy in the cooler domestic environment of a house without central heating, will do well in a bedroom. *Araucaria*, for example, whose popularity has declined as it cannot take the heat in the average living room, makes a good bedroom plant. And ferns are among the first choice since they simply will not survive in the warm, dry conditions of most living rooms. *Adiantum*, *Asplenium*, *Blechnum* and the many varieties of *Pteris* will thrive in the bedroom particularly if they are regularly sprayed and fed.

Many flowering plants that need plenty of light but a cooler atmosphere than that in the normal living room will also do well in the bedroom. *Camellia*, *Oleander*, myrtle and scented leaved geraniums are certainties. Others are *Bougainvillea*, *Ceropegia*, cyclamen, hydrangea, *Impatiens*, *Kalanchoë*, *Pelargonium*, *Pittosporum*, *Plumbago* and *Begonia rex*. African violets are a possibility but need a shady position. Their relations the *Sinningia* (*Gloxinia*) also respond well to the bedroom atmosphere.

You need not stop at flowering plants. *Plectranthus* is reputed to cure rheumatism and, apart from its therapeutic powers, makes a pretty green shrub that roots easily in water. *Fatsia japonica* will be happy near a north-facing window as will *Ficus benjamina*. This grows into a small, weeping tree, so be careful where you site it. *Grevillea robusta* thrives in the bedroom growing into a feathery tree, but can reach 2 m (7 ft), so only those with high ceilings should try it. *Aspidistra*, the universal survivor, will also do well in the bedroom.

For the more ambitious, there are various climbers which can be trained to frame a mirror, doorway or arch. *Rhaphidophora* (also called *Scindapsus* or *Pothos*), *Philodendron scandens* and *Cissus rhombifolia* all do well in minimum light conditions and coolish winter temperatures.

The bedroom makes a safe winter storage place for many plants such as *Chamaerops*, × *Fatshedera*, *Schefflera* and *Tradescantia*. A light corner of the bedroom is the best place for a citrus tree to spend winter where its leathery evergreen leaves make it a decorative addition. Cacti and succulents can successfully spend their winter resting period in the bedroom. You can cover the window sill with many small plants, placed on trays for easy removal. The sill is a suitable autumn home for pruned and tidied geraniums, while in the summer all the cottage window plants such as begonias, *Chlorophytum*, *Echeveria* and *Billbergia nutans*, will bloom prettily there.

If you want a bright, flowering plant in your bedroom choose *Streptocarpus*, the Cape primrose (left). This obliging plant, with its coarse leaves and trumpet-shaped flowers comes in a wide variety of colours, and will bloom for months if kept in a warm but shaded spot.

The elegant *Howeia* (right), at home in any spacious area, lends its sophisticated grace to a plain, austere bedroom.

Ideal for a traditional bedroom *Sparmannia* (left) grows quickly if well watered, and produces white flowers.

Pelargonium, African violets and *Primula* provide a colourful, scented screen for a summer fireplace.

This generously opulent *boudoir* (left) is decoratively draped and festooned with the greenery of the Kangaroo vine, the dark green *Rhoicissus rhomboidea* (grape ivy) and the small leaves of the trailing *Ficus pumila*.

The bedroom window sill makes a suitable home for *Campanula fragilis* (below). The small blue flowers of this trailing perennial often grow so enthusiastically that they obscure the foliage altogether.

Plants in the conservatory

If you are fortunate enough to possess a conservatory, even a small one, it introduces a new dimension into your plant world. The conservatory truly belongs to the plants. Unlike a garden room, which is primarily for people, the conservatory is the plants' domain and you are the intruder.

Humidity, not heat is the keynote. A conservatory is not a hot house although the temperature in winter should not go much below 7°C (45°F). Heating can be either extended from the house, or greenhouse heating may be used. Thermostatic control is useful. A constant humidity can be maintained within the conservatory. Deep beds of peat keep plants moist at all times and, in the summer, the floors, which should be of tile or stone, can be damped down with water.

In these surroundings many house plants grow to twice the size they would normally attain in a room. *Hoya* do well in this atmosphere, and *Dieffenbachia*, which tend to lose their lower leaves in a normal living room, thrive here. *Caladium*, notoriously difficult in rooms, will do well and can be kept to overwinter in their pots in a warm dark corner before repotting in spring. Other plants which both look and grow better in conservatories are *Cordyline*, *Fittonia*, *Sonerila*, *Aglaonema* and many types of lily.

A cool glasshouse can hold ferns and ivies and is the best place for many orchids such as *Odontoglossum*, some varieties of *Paphiopedilum*, *Epidendrum*, *Dendrobium*, *Oncidium* and *Coelogyne*. Climbing plants such as *Thunbergia*, *Stephanotis* and passion flower can be trained up wires and posts, as can *Abutilon*, *Lapageria rosea* and *Philodendron*. Bromeliads may be grown on a 'tree', and arums and *Musa* make for a jungle atmosphere. Shade may be desirable in summer and slatted blinds of various kinds are available, but the judicious use of climbers will give the plants below the chequered shade they need. Under shade, ferns and tree ferns will revel in the moist atmosphere.

A glass entrance hall with cylindrical multi-height steps makes a good setting for *Asparagus*, *Cyperus*, *Cereus* and *Bouganvillea*.

A light, colourful area filled with *Nephrolepis*, *Philodendron bipinnatifidum*, *Nicotiana*, *Blechnum*, *Ficus*, *Asparagus sprengeri* and *Coleus* (right).

Specially-constructed shelves lead the eye through from a living room to a glass dining area set among *Howeia*, *Jasminum*, *Cyperus* and chrysanthemums (right).

In a conservatory of these dimensions you can relax among *Jasminum*, *Acacia*, *Eucalyptus*, *Polypodium aureum*, *Nerium oleander*, *Chamaerops* and *Adiantum*.

Plants in the hallway and on the stairs

Providing there is no draught and some light, a hall or staircase can be the ideal place for those plants that need cool, relatively undisturbed surroundings and plenty of space to expand in. A narrow dark hallway can be improved with the judicious use of mirrors, which will not only make it appear wider, but will also reflect extra light and make your choice of plants look doubly luxuriant.

Large plants that are particularly at home in a hall and tend to look best standing alone are *Ficus benjamina*, *Dracaena*, *Monstera deliciosa* and *Schefflera*. Really large tub shrubs, like *Aucuba japonica*, which grows to 2 m (6 ft) are readily accommodated in a hall, and miniature indoor trees such as *Sparmannia* and *Crassula arborescens* will grow handsomely. An ideal plant for a large hall or stairwell is *Phoenix*, the date palm. It is happy in a low temperature and needs plenty of space around it, as its leaves are sharp and spiky like those of *Pandanus*. *Grevillea robusta* will also thrive in a cool hall, as long as there is enough light in the form of a skylight or roof lantern for it to grow towards.

If your hall is of more modest dimensions, a small hall table can be used to display exotic *Begonia rex* or *Chlorophytum*, the spider plant, giving it enough room to spread its green fountains adequately. *Cyrtomium*, the holly fern, is also very good as a table plant.

Ferns once graced every well-appointed hall, and in a good light and cool conditions *Asplenium nidus*, the bird's nest fern, will do well. It will look especially good if placed on a fern stand or column. Serious fern lovers might create a fernery in a north- or east-facing glazed porch. South-facing porches, however, are best reserved for a colourful blaze of geraniums or even fruiting tomatoes.

If the stairway can take it, climbing plants can be used to great decorative advantage. A shelf under the skylight is the ideal anchor position for trailers like ivy (*Hedera*), *Ceropegia* and *Chlorophytum*. They look equally good trailing down a stairwell edge from a landing, perhaps meeting climbers such as × *Fatshedera lizei*, *Plectranthus* and the sweetheart vine, *Philodendron scandens* spiralling upwards. *Rhaphidophora* (the name recently given to *Scindapsus* or *Pothos*) is a strong climber and will thrive even in quite a dark hall, as will *Cissus rhombifolia*.

Many plants need a rest period during the winter and must be kept in cooler conditions than may prevail in the living room. Those which like as much light as possible will be better wintering in a bedroom, but some can get by with little light and can be successfully placed in halls or corridors. Among these are *Azalea*, *Chamaedorea*, *Cissus antarctica*, *Fatsia*, × *Fatshedera*, *Howeia* and other palms, *Pteris*, *Schefflera* and *Tradescantia*. These make such a decorative crowd that you might well prefer to keep them in their winter quarters all the year round where possible.

A single *Sparmannia africana* (left) stands in welcome at the door of a glass and tile entrance porch.

An imposing *Nephrolepis* (right) becomes the focal point of a long cool corridor, whose only other decoration is a haze of dappled light.

Fittingly placed on a solid wooden fern-stand, *Nephrolepis* (above) emphasizes an archway.

A procession of *Asparagus sprengeri* (above) gracefully highlights a handsome wooden spiral stairway.

Sharp lines are softened by *Ficus benjamina, Cyperus, Sparmannia africana* and *Asparagus* (above).

The iron spiral (below) fades into a mass of green *Zebrina, Howeia, Cordyline, Dracaena, Sparmannia* and *Maranta.*

Plants in the office

It is a sad fact that a large percentage of people spend most of their lives in offices or workrooms. It is therefore important that these be as pleasant as possible, and nothing gives a room more life and spirit than a healthy row of plants. In fact plants harmonize very successfully into most offices. The formal design of modern offices, the severity of their furniture and equipment, wall-charts, filing cabinets and drawing boards make an effective backdrop for the softer contours of plants. The plants themselves can counteract the often too severe aspect of a place of business, without making it any less business-like.

Essential plant requirements are of course the same in the office as the home. Light, clean air, regular watering and an undisturbed spot are the prerequisites of most plants. Offices score over the home environment as plant settings in so far as temperatures are usually kept constant all year round, there is often plenty of space for expansive display, and, thanks to air-conditioning, there is little pollution of the air. There is also usually plenty of light, both natural and artificial. With a reasonable supply of artificial light, plants can even be successfully grown in a windowless room. Of course there are disadvantages, such as the weekends and public holidays, when the plants are left unattended and without nourishment. These difficulties can be overcome by growing the plants hydroponically so that they are self-watering, detailing a member of staff to be responsible for the plants and choosing the most suitable species.

Plants should be positioned with care. Ensure that they are out of the way of the main office traffic, placed safely on a high cabinet, or securely and permanently settled on a large, but little-used, desk or table. Large arums such as *Philodendron hastatum* and the good tempered *Fatsia japonica* are very suitable desk-top dwellers. Hallways and reception areas look very inviting when decked out with plants, and are usually well placed for plants needing a lot of light. But watch out for draughts. Climbing plants such as *Cissus antarctica* will form a leafy screen to disguise partitions in open-plan offices, and ivy will trail down satisfactorily from high shelves hiding the more hideous aspects of filing systems.

Long-lasting, undemanding plants must be the first choice. *Sansevieria* is a genuinely indestructible plant, and palms which prefer a shadier spot such as *Chamaedorea* should also do well. The *Ficus* family are good choices, as are *Schefflera*, *Syngonium* and the arums such as *Monstera deliciosa* and *Philodendron scandens*. *Aglaonema*, *Aspidistra*, *Cissus antarctica* and *Cissus rhombifolia*, *Dieffenbachia*, *Dracaena*, × *Fatshedera*, *Pandanus*, placed where its sharp leaves will not be in the way, and *Tradescantia* are all office veterans.

Unless the plants are very large it is usually best to group them in troughs or bowls. Whether bedded in compost or grown hydroponically most plants seem to grow well when surrounded by other healthy specimens. The more mature a plant is, the better it adapts to office life; smaller, younger plants will need more care.

Foliage plant groupings such as *Monstera*, *Ficus benjamina* and *Chlorophytum* can always be augmented in season by flowering plants to give glowing spots of colour; white flowers against green foliage are always effective. For summer displays the annuals are useful, and *Ipomoea* can be made to climb strings and make a curtain of leaves with bright blue, though short-lived, flowers. *Exacum affine* has tiny blue, sweet smelling flowers, and some of the flowering begonias and *Sinningia* (*Gloxinia*) bring splashes of colour that last for quite a long time. For temporary display flowering plants will give long service in good light but keep them away from direct sunlight.

Even the market garden can encroach on office life, and office workers can successfully grow tomatoes, green peppers and even melons on their high, light window sills, or a date palm can be grown from a stone. Herbs, like basil, grow well in pots and respond to a position on a sunny window sill.

A final point to remember is which plants *not* to choose for your office. Cacti and succulents will flourish on a summer window sill, but could pine and die in the uncomfortable heat of an office winter, when they should be enjoying their period of cool retirement. Ferns too would be disastrous in an office which is too light, warm and dry for them, and they should only be considered as extremely temporary inhabitants.

The undemanding *Dracaena* (right) complements a modern decor and fits in well with the timetable of a busy staff.

A profusion of ivy (below) that crept in from outside sprawls over walls in an unconventional display.

Sparmannia, *Pelargonium*, begonia, *Cyperus* and *Philodendron* personalize a characterless office (right).

Food plants like this young forest of aubergines (below) thrive in the sunny, air conditioned environment of a highrise office.

The handsome proportions of this charming, old-fashioned office area (left) are enhanced by *Nephrolepis*, *Crassula*, *Polypodium* and *Rhoicissus*.

The elegant yet easily maintained *Dracaena fragrans* 'Massangeana' grows to nearly 2 m (6 ft) in height and makes a superb addition to any large reception area.

Where to place your plants

There are very few places in a house which will not make a suitable home for one kind of plant or another. However, not all positions suit all plants and it is important to discover which spot will best accommodate the plant you have in mind before you set off to the nursery or seed merchant. Also, remember to bear in mind the light and temperature schema when filling up unused areas with plants. It is a good idea to analyze the amount of direct light available at each window in the rooms where you plan to display your plants. The size of the window is important but remember that, however large the window, the plants will only get about one quarter of the light indoors that they would receive if they were outside. You must also take into consideration the different temperatures that occur at different times of the day and year in various parts of the house.

Although light is important, very few plants enjoy being baked dry on a sunny, south-facing window still. On the other hand, none except perhaps the indomitable *Aspidistra* will survive in a cool, dark corner, and even that is doubtful. The majority of plants flourish best when placed in a good light but shaded from the direct rays of the sun, and well away from other sources of direct heat such as fires, cookers and refrigerators. Remember that many plants do not thrive in the same position all the year round. Some plants such as *Drejerella, Ceropegia, Euphorbia milii, Impatiens, Iresine, Zebrina* and most cacti like a warm, sunny spot in the summer, but must be cooler in winter. During the winter resting period, the light should still be quite good and the temperature should be maintained at approximately 5–15°C (41–59°F).

As each room and window differs there is bound to be some overlapping and firm dividing lines cannot be drawn. If you are in any doubt, the best thing to do is to draw up a small plan of your interior and then check the plants that you already have or are contemplating buying against the lists provided here. You will soon see whether your plant is in the right place by monitoring its growth and health; if the position seems right, yet the plant still languishes check the state of the pot, how wet or dry the compost is and whether the plant is pot-bound.

In this broad guideline to plant positioning, the rooms of a house have been divided according to temperature and lighting into moderate, warm and cool, light, semi-light and shady. The north-facing wall of the house is at the top of the picture, the south-facing wall at the bottom, and west and east are left and right respectively. The window area in a south-facing room is warm and light, while the same area in the north-facing room is cool with less light. East and west-facing windows have similar lighting and temperature at different times of the day, according to the position of the sun, and fall into the categories of moderate and light or semi-light.

Moderate/light
Asparagus
Begonia 'Gloire de Lorraine'
Begonia semperflorens
Begonia × tuberhybrida
Citrus
Coleus
Dracaena marginata
Echeveria
Exacum affine
Gynura
Hoya carnosa
Impatiens

Moderate/semi-light
Aechmea
Begonia rex
Billbergia
Chamaedorea (Neanthe)
Cryptanthus
Drejerella
Ficus benjamina
Ficus elastica
Howeia (Kentia)
Maranta
Monstera deliciosa
Peperomia
Philodendron scandens
Pilea
Schefflera
Zygocactus

Moderate/shady
Araucaria
Aucuba
Asplenium

Platycerium
Pteris
Palms and other ferns

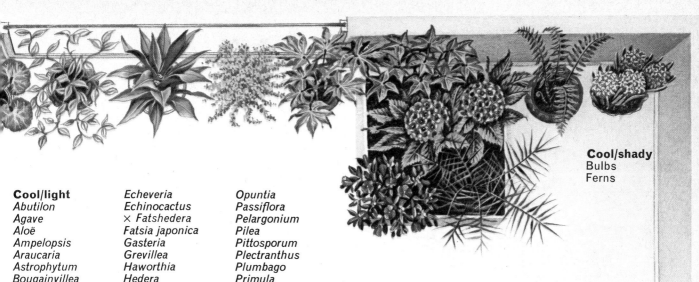

Cool/shady
Bulbs
Ferns

Cool/light
Abutilon
Agave
Aloë
Ampelopsis
Araucaria
Astrophytum
Bougainvillea
Cacti (winter)
Cereus
Ceropegia
Chlorophytum
Citrus
Crassula
Cyclamen

Echeveria
Echinocactus
× Fatshedera
Fatsia japonica
Gasteria
Grevillea
Haworthia
Hedera
Helxine
Hibiscus
Impatiens
Kalanchoë
Lithops
Nephrolepis
Nerium oleander

Opuntia
Passiflora
Pelargonium
Pilea
Pittosporum
Plectranthus
Plumbago
Primula
Rebutia
Rhoeo
Saxifraga
Sedum
Tetrastigma
Tradescantia

Cool/semi-light
Aspidistra
Araucaria
Aucuba
Azalea
Chamaerops
Chamaedorea
Cissus antarctica
Cyrtomium
Epiphyllum
× Fatshedera
Fatsia japonica

Ficus pumila
Hedera
Howeia (Kentia)
Hydrangea
Phoenix
Polystichum
Pteris
Rhoicissus capensis
Saxifraga
Schefflera

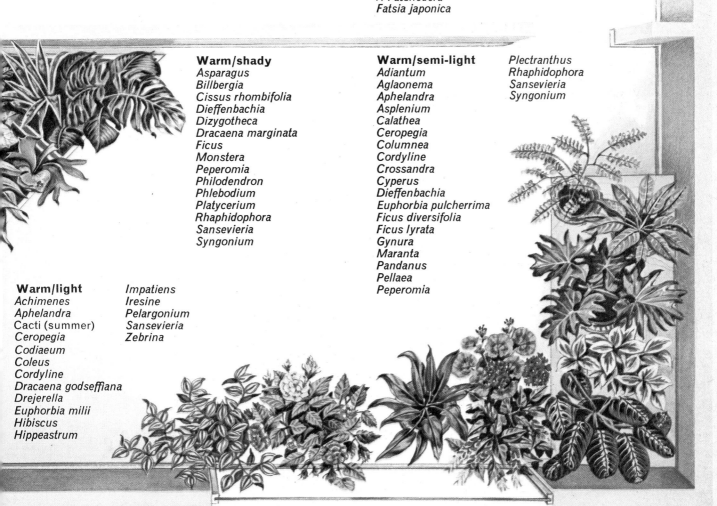

Warm/shady
Asparagus
Billbergia
Cissus rhombifolia
Dieffenbachia
Dizygotheca
Dracaena marginata
Ficus
Monstera
Peperomia
Philodendron
Phlebodium
Platycerium
Rhaphidophora
Sansevieria
Syngonium

Warm/semi-light
Adiantum
Aglaonema
Aphelandra
Asplenium
Calathea
Ceropegia
Columnea
Cordyline
Crossandra
Cyperus
Dieffenbachia
Euphorbia pulcherrima
Ficus diversifolia
Ficus lyrata
Gynura
Maranta
Pandanus
Pellaea
Peperomia

Plectranthus
Rhaphidophora
Sansevieria
Syngonium

Warm/light
Achimenes
Aphelandra
Cacti (summer)
Ceropegia
Codiaeum
Coleus
Cordyline
Dracaena godseffiana
Drejerella
Euphorbia milii
Hibiscus
Hippeastrum

Impatiens
Iresine
Pelargonium
Sansevieria
Zebrina

Choosing, buying and transporting plants

Obviously it is best to go and look for your plants at the nursery or garden centre of a reputable grower. When there, look into the greenhouses to get an idea of the conditions in which the plants have been growing happily, the degree of heat and humidity, light and ventilation, and thus get an idea of the best way to treat the plants at home. Also you should get as much information as possible from the grower about suitable compost for repotting and the type of food the plant will benefit from. Many plants are sold with much useful information on their labels. Naturally the plant you select should be healthy, glossy and strong, the soil should be moist and the plant not covered with moss.

It is important to have an idea of where you are going to put your plant before you buy it. Otherwise you may get enticed by a particular specimen without knowing what you are going to do with it. If you need a group of plants for a shady corner it would be a mistake to be seduced by the pale grey-green of succulents; and the cool arching fronds of ferns should be resisted if your only available plant space is on a sunny window sill. Think carefully about your interior, its warmth or coolness, the type of heating and amount of light. To begin with concentrate on those plants which have proved themselves the most congenial rather than starting off with tender subjects needing daily attention.

The same general rules apply when choosing plants as presents. Some people may not want to be bothered with a difficult plant such as an African violet. Some people will not want a plant that tries to become a forest giant in a small room, like African hemp. Think first about what sort of room your plant will inhabit, then choose a suitable one.

It is not usually necessary to pack and move plants from one home to another very often, but when you bring them away from a nursery, or move house, or take a young plant as a gift to someone, there are certain things to bear in mind.

Obviously the plant must spend the least possible time travelling. It must not become wind blown and damaged. Tender plants must not be chilled; plants needing cool temperatures must not be roasted on the journey. If possible take into account the temperature when travelling with plants. Many plants are easy-going. They have probably had to travel to get to your local nursery or garden centre. Even large chain stores have healthy looking arrays of houseplants which have travelled in cardboard boxes. If the plant is small enough, the pot can be placed in damp compost and carefully wedged

around with newspaper to keep it firmly in place.

Ideally plants should only be moved in their dormant season to lessen the possible damage to both leaf and flower buds. Plants that are not in pots, seedlings from friends, for example, should have as much earth around the root ball as possible, dampened and kept damp by being placed in a plastic bag. A large plastic bag over the whole plant will also help keep it from being upset by a journey. Delicate leaves or flowers are protected by the plastic bag being held away from them by canes and sticks.

Plants which die right down, cyclamen in summer or *Hippeastrum* in winter, will be no problem to move. The cool conditions needed in the dormant season should be kept up in transit. Obviously plants will not be sent alone on a long road or rail journey unless it is absolutely necessary. When wrapping a delicate plant, see that the plastic paper does not constrict the foilage. With large tough plants you can tie the leaves together before wrapping.

Finally a plant's ideal dwelling place should be ready for it when it arrives at its destination. The temperature at the place of arrival should be as close as possible to that which the plant has been enjoying.

Having chosen a healthy plant be careful not to damage it in transit. Large leaves can be loosely tied to their supporting stick.

For added protection carefully cover your plant with a plastic bag. This will maintain an even temperature and humidity level.

The rich scent of leaves and moist compost fill the air and entice you to buy as you wander through the rows of plants in a nursery (left).

In response to growing demand, indoor plants have become increasingly available in markets (above) as well as specialist nurseries.

Plants bought from a nursery usually have a long journey ahead of them. Little ones can be transported in a box with a layer of damp compost.

Lay the plants on their sides and neatly pack newspaper around them to keep them from shifting about during the journey.

A crowded display (left) of dozens of different little pots and their occupants, each labelled with an unfamiliar name, can make choosing and buying a perplexing business. Beware the temptation to simply close your eyes and take a pick at random. Think first about where you will put your plant.

All plants need to be packed and transported with a good amount of earth around the root ball. The worst damage occurs when the roots are broken off. With larger specimens like the spruce in this picture (right) a piece of sacking cloth can be firmly tied around the root ball to keep it intact.

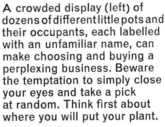

Pots and containers

For centuries house plants have been planted in flower pots and until the late 50s these were usually earthenware or clay. Then plastic pots began to be manufactured. Now these are on display everywhere while clay pots are more and more difficult to find outside specialist shops.

To some people clay pots are more attractive than plastic, and there is no doubt that their earthy colour goes well with all types of foliage and flower. However, clay pots soak up moisture through the porous texture of their walls and in clay pots plants need more watering. Clay pots hold less soil than their plastic equivalents and the soil is more likely to show white on top from salt deposits.

Plastic pots, though perhaps less attractive, do have their advantages: they are cheaper than clay and less likely to break. The thin, rigid, less expensive pots may become brittle and snap, but polythene pots which are soft and rubbery will last forever. Plastic pots are preferred by nurserymen. They are so light that numbers of plants can be easily transported. Plastic pots are bigger yet need less watering. When they first arrived people tended to use them like clay pots and many plants died. Therefore at first they earned themselves the title of 'murderers'. If you are used to watering plants in clay pots and acquire one in a plastic pot, or if you pot on to a plastic pot, remember to water much less frequently, otherwise you may find yourself surrounded by dying favourites.

Different soil mixtures are available for each kind of pot. The plastic pot mixture is more open and quick drying. With the correct attention and care most plants survive happily in both plastic and clay, and there are no rules about which pot to use for which plant. Some plants needing a lot of watering, such as African violets, may be easier to look after in plastic pots, but most plants will be as happy in one as the other. Ultimately, if clay pots disappear, there will be no choice. For the meantime you have to decide whether the undeniably more pleasant look and feel of clay outweighs the virtues of plastic with its less earthy texture and crude colour. However, modern advances in the design of plastic pots are making such objects increasingly more attractive and desirable.

Whatever the substance of your pot, it must have good drainage. Most basic clay and plastic pots have a drainage hole or several holes. Pots for planting bulbs need especially large holes. Depending on the texture of your pot, it is possible to enlarge holes using a small drill or handrasp. You may want to plant your plant in a pot which has no drainage: a beautiful bowl or porcelain urn, even a copper casserole. This is possible, but it is really only suitable for a large plant in a large container, since there must be a considerable depth of gravel in the bottom of the container and a layer of coarse fibrous peat to ensure passage of the water through the soil. A small pot may not have sufficient space for the necessary drainage. The soil will clog up with water and harm the plant. However, you can always use your pretty pot without drainage as a container.

For centuries the unattractive appearance and uniformity of pots led to the use of pot holders known as *cache-pots*. These used to be of glazed pottery in various colours, and they can still be picked up in antique shops. Nowadays, *cache-pots* are usually of plastic, but in fact you can use almost any container you have in your home or any pretty object you find in the shops. Containers may be of glass, pottery, basketware, china, wood, stainless steel. They range from exquisite, expensive objects to interesting old copper teapots and saucepans. They serve a dual purpose: they look attractive giving colour and variety to your display of plants and they can be functional. The space between flower pot and container can be packed with damp peat or moss to conserve moisture. Your container may even have a small drainage hole of its own. This extra layer of peat is especially good for ferns, who favour a moist atmosphere at all times.

A Chinese ginger jar, an antique wash basin, an art deco jug or a bright perspex container, anything that will hold a plant can be used as a plant pot. If you feel understandably wary about planting directly into a very beautiful and maybe rather fragile piece of china, then place a terracotta or a plastic pot directly inside it, and use it purely for its decorative effect. Your taste might be for something extravagant but it will also depend on the location you have chosen for your house plant. Exotic and flamboyant foliage plants, ferns, and palms in particular, often demand to be complemented by the container they stand in, and even the word 'container' seems far too hum-drum for those extravagant objects that show them off so well. It is always interesting to experiment with the contrasts made between the one-dimensional decorative designs on pottery and the natural organic patterns of leaves and stalks.

Whatever your choice of container do remember that drainage is an essential feature which must not be ignored at the expense of appearance. All pots made for growing plants have drainage holes. For this reason it is often wise to place a clay or plastic pot inside your decorative container which may not have holes. Kitchens are popular sites for plant display and old-fashioned kitchen utensils, such as copper kettles and saucepans, or rustic earthenware pottery make ideal containers. For those who prefer modern, streamline designs there is now available a wide range of brightly coloured plastic pots which come in all shapes and sizes. These have both advantages and disadvantages over the traditional clay ones, and your choice ultimately depends on the style of your interior.

Potting up, potting on and repotting

Potting up is the process of removing rooted cuttings and seedlings from seed compost in which they have begun their life and planting them in the compost in which they may live for the rest of their lives. Seed compost has no nutrients; it merely acts as a vehicle for root formation. Once the roots are formed and the plant is large enough to handle, it is ready to be moved into its own pot with its own potting mixture. A plant's first pot should be quite small, about 8 cm (3 in) in diameter. Do not overwater; let the roots fight for moisture. This will make them strong. Place the seedling in the compost which you should then build up around it. Treat rooted cuttings in the same way. With correct attention your cutting and seedling should now grow into healthy plants.

After a while your plant will grow too large for its first pot and will need potting on, moving into a larger pot. You will know when it is ready for this: either it will have obviously grown too large for its pot or its growth rate will have slowed down; in some cases the roots may even be escaping from the drainage hole. Always pot on in the spring or early summer. To disturb your plant during its late dormant period could cause unnecessary harm. When you have removed your plant from its pot examine the roots carefully. If they are thick and solid around the edge then the plant is potbound and needs a larger pot. With seedlings and cuttings in their first small pots it is usual to pot on to a pot about 5 cm (2 in) larger in diameter. With plants in larger pots over 18.5 cm (7 in) it is best to pot on to one 2.5 cm (1 in) larger. Remember to soak new clay pots in water overnight and wash old clay and plastic pots thoroughly. If you use a loam-based compost it is important to cover the drainage holes with crocks. This is not necessary with a peat-based or soilless compost where the water drains away more slowly.

It is useful to pot on into a compost similar to the one originally used. Therefore, you should find out when you buy your plant whether it is growing in a loam-based or soilless compost. The two are quite easy to tell apart: the loam-based one is light in colour, the soilless, peaty one is a dark, rich colour, lighter in weight. However, it is not essential to use the same compost; and if your plant has grown so large that even in its new pot it is top heavy, then regardless of original compost it is best to use a loam-based one which will weigh down the pot.

Repotting is the process of potting into a new pot of the same size. It is usually for older plants and should be carried out only as a last resort. Check everything else first. If your old, well-established plant stops growing this could be for a number of reasons: it may just need feeding, in which case you can buy a feeding mix from your local garden supplier. If this doesn't work, remove the plant from its pot and examine the roots. If the roots are healthy and growing freely then it may merely mean that your plant has reached maximum size. So check the maximum size in a book. If the roots are brown and rotting and few in number and the compost wet and nasty, it means that your pot is too large for your plant and you should pot down to a smaller size pot. However, if the roots are healthy and merely need space then it is time to repot. Repotting at the wrong time could slow down growth and damage your plant, so ensure that your plant is pot-bound first.

A flower pot is measured from inside the rim across the top. It is usual to plant seedlings or cuttings in a pot of 5 cm (2 in). When they grow too large for their first pots they are ready to be potted onto pots about 5 cm (2 in) larger. Never pot on to a pot which is too large for the plant because in an area with little root activity the soil will turn sour. Large well established plants will need repotting into a pot of the same size.

Take the rooted cutting or seedling from its bed of seed compost. Hold cuttings gently by the stem and seedlings by the leaves. Avoid bruising the plant.

If you are going to plant in a clay pot, soak it for several hours in a bucket of water before using it. A plastic pot should be well washed out before use.

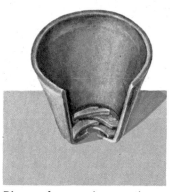

Place a few crocks over the drainage hole. This is not so important with plastic pots and peaty soil, but is essential for loam based soil, since it prevents soil particles from being washed away.

Sprinkle some potting mixture over the crocks and then plant the cutting being careful not to damage the roots. Press the mixture gently but firmly around it.

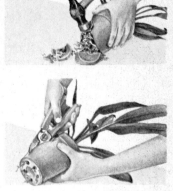

The visible growth of a plant is less important to its health than what is happening under the surface of the soil. If you pot on or repot too soon there is the danger that the insufficiently rooted soil ball

will break up. Only pot on when the plant has become so cramped in its pot that the roots are escaping out of the drainage hole. The plant is then 'potbound' and may be difficult to remove.

Holding your fingers round the base of the stem with the palm of your hand covering the soil, turn the pot upside down and give it a sharp tap on the base.

If the root ball doesn't slide out easily, don't attempt to prize it out as this may damage the roots. Break open a clay pot with a hammer. Use secateurs or scissors to cut open a plastic pot.

In preparing the new pot first place the crocks over the drainage hole and then put in the compost, making sure that your plant will be at the same level, neither too high nor too low, in its new pot.

If a large decorative pot is to be the new home for your plant, place a fairly deep layer of gravel at the bottom. This will compensate for the lack of drainage. Then proceed as usual with the compost.

Gently shake out the loose soil from the roots and lower the plant into its new pot.

Sprinkle new soil around the plant and over the surface, bringing the level in the pot to about 2·5 cm (1 in) below the rim.

Use a wooden dibber to fill in compost between the pot and the root ball. This is necessary when potting on to a pot only 2·5 cm (1 in) larger.

Tap the pot gently on the table surface to help the plant and compost to settle.

A layer of compost can be sprinkled over the surface to fill up new spaces. Water the plant well and allow to drain.

The roots will quickly spread out to fill up the new areas open to them, and the plant will soon look more healthy and start into new vigorous growth.

69

How to pot bulbs

When we speak of bulbs generally we mean the bulbous plants which herald the spring each year. But a bulb is technically a swollen underground bud covered in scales, which are the storage organs of the plant containing almost all the nourishment it will need.

Hyacinths, single and double early tulips, narcissi (including daffodils), large flowered crocus, scilla, dwarf iris and *Chionodoxa* are the best bulbs to choose for planting in bowls. Specialist producers prepare them for early growth which is called 'forcing'. Bulbs are stored at controlled temperatures so that they will flower at a specified time. Most of these hardy bulbs can be grown in a balanced potting compost in bowls or pots whether there is drainage or not. Or they can grow in bulb fibre (a mixture of peat, ground oystershell and charcoal), or in water. Bulbs cannot be forced a second year, and should be planted out after flowering. They will then usually flower again the following season.

Put planted bowls or pots in the coolest, darkest place you can find at a temperature of 5–7°C (40–45°F). This growing in the darkness encourages root and leaf formation. Check every two or three weeks to see that the bowls have not dried out. If they have, your dark cupboard is too warm.

When the tips of the leaves show yellow-green above the soil, move the bowls to a cool greenhouse, conservatory or room where the temperature is 10°C (50°F). When the buds are showing move the bulbs to a warmer place, 16°C (60°F). If planted in late summer or early autumn some early narcissi like 'Soleil d'Or' and 'Paper White' will flower in early winter. Tulips and hyacinths should be in flower at Christmas. Remove the flowers as they fade, and when they are over put the bulbs in a cool room or conservatory; water till spring and then remove them and plant them out in a garden.

Hyacinths and tazetta narcissi will grow in water alone. Special bulb jars in various colours of glass are available 15–23 cm (6–9 in) tall and very decorative. Plant them in late autumn. Place the jars in a cool place until the roots are 7.5–10 cm (3–4 in) long and the leaves 2.5 cm (1 in) above the bulb. Hyacinths should be kept in semi-darkness but narcissi can stand on a normal window sill. Top up the water from time to time so that the roots are kept completely submerged.

Tender bulbs which can only be grown indoors include *Freesia, Nerine, Vallota* and *Lachenalia*. These are grown in good composts in well-drained pots. Place crocks in clay pots over the drainage holes or if you are using plastic pots add your compost. Plant the bulbs firmly, tucking them well in. Water well and keep in a light place at a steady temperature. Most tender bulbs can stay in the same pot for several years.

After flowering cut off the faded flower. Leave the green stalk to help feed the bulb. Increase water and feed the bulb for next year. Dry off deciduous bulbs like *Lachenalia* and *Freesia*, stopping the water when the leaves yellow. Keep bulbs with evergreen leaves, *Clivia* for example, moist all the year.

'Forcing' is the process of encouraging hardy bulbs to flower during the bleak months of winter, instead of in their normal spring season. Daffodils, tulips and hyacinths are the most popular bulbs to choose, but the smaller ones like crocuses produce good results too. You can force bulbs in pots of all shapes and sizes, as well as in the specially designed bulb jars. The tangle of white roots is attractive to look at and is also a quite startling reminder of just how much root is produced and how fast it grows. In using this method be careful not to let the bulb base actually touch the water.

If you are using a clay pot then put crocks in the base. A plastic pot can have a layer of peat, and a round bowl should either have a drainage hole made in it or a layer of gravel placed at the bottom.

Put in a layer of compost or special bulb fibre, and press this down quite firmly. Fibre should be watered immediately but compost must stay dry until after the planting.

Arrange the bulbs shoulder to shoulder (pointed end upwards). They should be made to nestle firmly in their bed, but do not screw them in.

Water thoroughly by standing the pot in a bucket of water and draining it afterwards.

The planted bulbs should be stored in a cool, dark place like a cellar or cupboard, and left there for a period of between 6 to 12 weeks, or even longer.

In a moderately cold climate the pots can be left outside in boxes packed with straw or dry peat, and well covered. Keep them cold but do not let them freeze.

During this period the bulbs are developing a strong root system and preparing to produce leaves. To check if they are ready, remove them carefully from the pot and examine the root ball.

Small bulbs are well suited for growing in crocus pots which have holes all round the sides. Several small bulbs can be fitted into the holes with perhaps a large one at the top.

Glass bulb jars are a popular way of growing and displaying larger bulbs like hyacinths (left).

A bulb is the fleshy base of leaves protecting a flowering bud. Daffodils, hyacinths and lilies grow from bulbs. A corm is a thick underground stem base with food stored in its centre. Cyclamen and gladiolus are corms. A rhizome is a root-like underground stem from which leaves and flower buds arise. Irises and orchids grow from rhizomes. Rhizomes are usually found on or just below the surface of the ground.

Hyacinths (below) 'forced' to flower in December fill the air with their sweet scent during the bleak days of winter.

In order to produce a really abundant display of flowers in one small pot you can plant the bulbs in layers, which will make them grow and flower at different heights.

Add more compost or bulb fibre so that only the tips of the bulbs show above the surface.

When the tips of the leaves are pale green points above the surface, the plants are ready to be moved to a cool light place such as a window ledge or conservatory.

When the leaves are opening up, the plant should be brought to a warm place at a temperature of about 18°C (64°F). The bulbs can now be expected to burst into a blaze of flowers.

Troughs and trays

Many plants look and live well when grouped together. Pots can be simply grouped on a table or shelf, or more decoratively arranged on a tray. Better still you can display your pots in a trough deep enough to cover them, leaving a colourful array of flowers and foliage above. You may even decide to actually plant your tray or trough.

A tray is any shallow container of any shape or material but it should be at least 8 cm (3 in) deep. Troughs also come in varying shapes and sizes: some on legs, some designed to stand on window sill or floor. They can be made of stoneware, earthenware, wood, pottery, plastic, copper. Before standing your pots in the container of your choice, layer it with a damp floor of gravel and keep this permanently moist. It is the evaporated moisture from this damp lining that creates the microclimate plants need. In deep troughs the spaces between the pots may be packed with peat, creating a constantly damp atmosphere which is particularly necessary for almost all ferns and arums. Stand larger pots directly on the gravel; small pots can stand on inverted pots or saucers to bring them up to the required height. Be careful not to overwater your grouping; plants growing close together tend to need less water than free standing plants. Lift out the pots from time to time to ensure that no water has gathered at the bottom of the container.

If you decide to do away with pots in troughs altogether and actually want to plant one, remember that only plants requiring similar conditions can live happily together. It would be foolish to plant a fern who likes shade with a chrysanthemum who needs sunshine. Plants should also have practically the same rate of growth. If not, one could swamp the rest, plunging its neighbours into darkness and drawing all the moisture and nutrients from the soil. Apart from this the selection of plants is a matter of personal choice. It is attractive to group together plants of the same family: a trough full of ferns is always a good choice. It is also pleasant to select plants which give contrast in colour, texture and form such as an elegant, trailing *Ficus pumila* with a tall, pointed *Sansevieria trifasciati laurentii* and a full-bodied green and silver *Fatsia japonica* or a wrinkled dark *Begonia rex* with a bright, decorative dumb cane. For small bowls slow-growing plants should be chosen such as African violets.

Your container should have drainage holes. If it doesn't, drill holes if possible or make a false bottom using a sheet of perforated zinc. You can buy this from any ironmonger: he will cut it to size. Plant your plants in a coarse, open soil: 1 part loam, 2 parts peat and 1 part sharp sand is a good mixture. Plant with a reasonable space between each plant to allow for growth and spread. It may look a little thin to start with, but it will soon settle down. You can decorate the top of the soil between the plants with pebbles or marbles and granite chippings. Do not overwater, since overwatering in this instance would damage not just one plant but many. A moisture meter is helpful here, especially one which can bury deep into the soil of a trough. Your plants will grow rapidly and will need pruning from time to time. This is best done during the early spring period. Replanting should be done in spring or early summer when the quick growing plants look as if they are outgrowing their neighbours, or if the plants stop growing unexpectedly and you want to examine their roots. Take the bowl to some place where a certain amount of earthwork does not matter. Allow your trough to dry out a little. This makes it easier to free the mass of tangled roots. Tip the contents out gently. Tidy the plants up, remove dead leaves and re-plant in damp soil, adding new plants and removing any that look unhappy.

A variation of the trough and tray grouping is the *pot-et-fleur* arrangement. Plant your container with your chosen plants leaving a space for a small vase and pinholder. Fill the vase daily with fresh cut flowers.

This well-matched double begonia, multifloral begonia and foliage begonia (*B. rex*) look good grouped in a tray with pebbles.

A geranium, a *Fittonia* and a dumb cane can live happily together in a deep trough with a layer of gravel at the bottom. Shorter pots can be stood on an upturned saucer to bring them up to the same level.

Peat packed around the pots creates a well-balanced microclimate which is especially suited to certain plants like the *Aspidistra*, the spider plant and the shrimp plant that have been chosen for this grouping.

Planting directly into your trough means that you must choose plants in need of similar conditions. The

Pilea cadierei, ivy and *Sansevieria trifasciata* selected here all grow well together (below).

A *Philodendron, Vriesia splendens* and *Chlorophytum comosum* make up this elegant display (above).

A wickerwork basket makes an ideal decorative container for this delicately flowering *Campanula.*

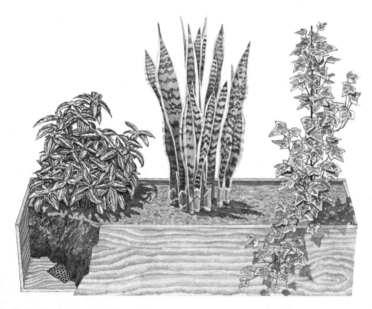

Hanging baskets

When space is scarce and every sill and floor has its decorative burden of plants, hanging baskets come into their own. Inside the home they hang from high ceilings and extend from wall railings. Outside they enliven the exterior, while still being visible from indoors. However they are difficult objects to site. They should not be placed so high that a mountaineering effort is required every time they need watering, which will be frequently; nor do you want them dripping on chairs, tables or passersby. Baskets outside must not give unwanted shade to windows nor must they hang so low so as to constitute a hazard for visitors. Despite their undeniable attractiveness, hanging baskets can be impractical. For this reason begin in the conservatory or outside, provided you live in an area where there is little or no frost.

Baskets were traditionally lined with a layer of sphagnum moss, which, if you are lucky enough to find it, does look very pretty and natural. However, in many countries this is now difficult to come by and baskets are more commonly lined with a plastic sheet.

Baskets need constant vigilance. They must be kept damp at all times and watered twice a day in hot weather. From time to time the whole basket will need to be immersed in a bucket of water until the bubbles stop rising. This will keep your display looking fresh. Your basket will also need constant pruning. Remove all dead flowers immediately.

Prune straying shoots, and use hair pins to hold shoots and vines close to the wire container. Repot with new soil when necessary. When your basket eventually grows old, or frost rids it of its beauty, take it outside and turn it upside down. Perhaps you can salvage your plastic or sphagnum moss lining and, if it's still in good condition, you can start afresh with new plants and new compost.

Traditionally baskets are made of wire. They are usually round or semi-circle in shape. Nowadays you can avoid the problem of drainage by planting attractive glass containers, and specially designed plastic containers which come with their own drip tray.

Hanging attachments must be firmly fixed since large and well watered baskets are very heavy. Ordinary ceiling hooks and wall brackets can be used together with specially designed attachments like the fisherman's swivel, which allows for freedom of movement.

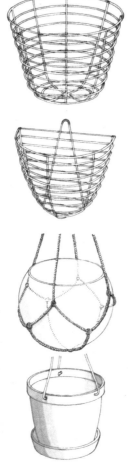

Planting Your Basket

A hanging basket is not difficult to plant. Plastic is often used as a lining in areas where sphagnum moss is not readily available.

1   Line your basket with plastic. A horticultural grade is best.
2   Make small drainage holes in the base of the lining.
3   Fill one-third of the basket with a good compost mixture. Do not use crocks.
4   Make slits in the side of the plastic large enough to insert the plants.
5   Gently poke each root ball or cutting into the slits in the lower part of the basket.
6   Add enough compost to cover the roots of the plants.
7   You can prevent the plastic lining from slipping by building a cement collar. Mix equal portions of cement and soil in a bucket. Add enough water to make a thick clay-like consistency.
8   Roll the cement into a collar and fix it around the rim of the basket.
9   Spray the collar to keep it damp and prevent cracking.
10   Repeat the planting procedure until your basket is filled. Immerse the whole basket in a bucket of water, drain and hang up.

1

6

When making a hanging basket display it is a good idea to experiment with all sorts of plants. A lot of unexpected species suddenly come into their own when they are seen suspended in front of a window, or fixed against an expanse of white wall. Trailing plants are the traditional choice because their long leafy stems or fronds can cascade down freely. Often they spray out in such profusion that nothing can be seen of the basket or pot which holds them. A good basket display always looks as if it is overflowing on all sides, and to achieve this luxuriant effect it is important to shape the young plants regularly so that they do not become straggly. Vividly flowering fuchsias (left) always make a striking focus point in any interior, while the delicate fronds of the *Columnea* (centre) are seen at their best in a hanging display. The trailing ivy and *Peperomia* (right) make a dramatic contrast to the tall and stately cyperus whose dominant lines are highlighted against a stark white wall.

2

3

4

5

7

8

9

10

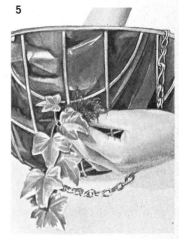

String containers and how to make them

Instead of buying a hanging basket made out of metal or wood, why not make one yourself! This way you can decide which container suits the plant of your choice, and fits in with the decor of your home. Some of the prettiest plant holders can be made quickly and easily using the macramé method, for materials such as twine or fine hempen rope have a direct affinity with plants.

Macramé holders are light, they are easy to hang in places where space is limited, and they are easy to store when they are not being used. They make ideal temporary holders for summer flowers or for a fern which wants to be moved to a cooler place during the winter months.

The holder illustrated is made upside down, beginning with the end which will eventually form the fringe and ending with the loop from which the basket will hang. To make the holder with its bead decorations, you need six lengths of 6.5 m (7½ yards) of jute and twenty-four bamboo beads 5 cm (2 in) long. The finished holder is 120 cm (47 in) long and designed to hold a pot 15 cm (6 in) diameter, although these measurements can be adjusted to your own requirements.

For working the macramé you will need a piece of light-weight wood or cork board approximately 120 cm (47 in) × 15 cm (6 in). You will also need some drawing pins (thumb tacks) and some spare string.

Cut a piece of spare string approx. 25 cm (10 in) long. Pin in a horizontal line near the top of your working board. Fold each cut length of jute in half and mount on the pinned string as shown, thus forming twelve hanging lengths.

Divide the lengths into three groups with four hanging lengths in each. Leaving 10 cm (4 in) from the mounting knots and working on each group in turn, work 12·5 cm (5 in) of spiral half-hitch knotting. To tie the knot, make a loop with

the left-hand strand and pass the end behind the centre two strands. Make a loop with the right-hand length and pass it under the end of the left strand, over the centre two strands and through the left loop. Start the next knot with

the strand now on the left in the same way as the first knot. The cord will spiral automatically when you have worked a few knots.

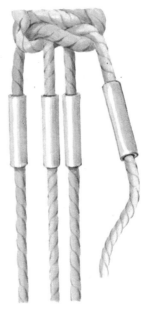
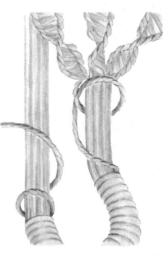

Cut off a short length of spare string and tie the three cords together. Work two flat knots on each group.
To tie a flat knot, work one knot as for the spiral cord. Start the next knot by forming a loop with the strand now on the right, pass it under the centre two strands. Make a loop with the left-hand strand, pass it under the end of the right strand, over the two

centre strands and through the right loop. Continue working these two knots alternately.
Leaving 5 cm (2 in), or more for larger pots, take two lengths of jute from each group and tie a flat knot. Work an extra half flat knot on each group.
Leaving 7·5 cm (3 in), or more for larger pots, re-group the lengths as for the original spiral cords and work a further 23 cm (9 in) spiral half-hitch knotting (you can adjust the total length of the holder here).

Thread a bead on to each length of jute. Work a further 12·5 cm (5 in) spiral knotting, thread a bead onto each length, work a further 15 cm (6 in) spiral knotting.

Leaving 10 cm (4 in) from the last knots worked, hold eleven tengths together and wind the twelfth length round them lightly for 15 cm (6 in). Bend this part round to make a loop.

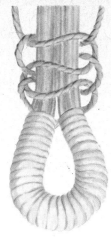

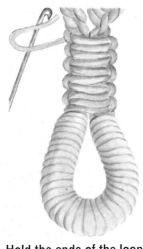

Hold the ends of the loop level with ten of the jute lengths in a group. Use the two remaining lengths to work flat knots over the ten held lengths back to the spiral cords. Use a crochet hook to thread the ends of the two lengths into the spirals. Finish off the base by cutting through the mounting knots at the top of the macrame to make the fringe.

The natural colouring of the holder is highlighted by the *Spathiphyllum* within (right)

Window boxes from inside

Window boxes are usually planned to work well and give pleasure from outside the house, their colours being thought out in relation to wall colour. But they must obviously be designed to please the occupants of the rooms whose sills they decorate, too. Colour is important: you do not want your begonias to clash with your curtains, nor do you want to spend too much time gazing at the row of dark green miniature cypresses that make such a good backdrop for the daffodils seen clearly from the road; you must see the daffodils too.

Any dismal view or grey day has a less depressing aspect if is seen across or through golden marigolds or pink and white geraniums. A hot window overlooking a sun-baked wall or part of the 'concrete jungle' may well be the ideal place for climbing plants – bright blue *Ipomoea*, *Thunbergia alata* or beans. Sweet-smelling heliotrope, wallflowers and flowering tobacco will fill rooms with scent, and so will the scented leaves of plants such as rosemary, geraniums and *Artemisia*. A hanging plant container could be suspended from the ceiling in front of a window (firmly attached to a joist), filled with trailing begonias, petunias, geraniums, lobelias and asparagus fern.

You will not want a dense plant screen outside a window, taking away all light and air, but a box of mixed annuals, regularly deadheaded to keep them flowering, a miniature field of daffodils, or a tiny grove of silver, yellow and green evergreens in winter will add much to a room as well as to the view outside.

Boxes of plants should go where they will give the greatest pleasure, perhaps the window of a bedroom, where someone is ill or bed-ridden, or a study window for the desk-bound, or a kitchen window, where someone can take pleasure in both flowers and herbs.

There are plants for every aspect of window, but the least suitable place is a window facing the prevailing wind. The best aspect is probably a window facing west.

A window box on the sill of a child's window may well be the beginning of a lifetime's interest in plants. Children can be encouraged to sow the quick growers such as verbena, nasturtiums, beans and radishes, for example, and they can be put in sole charge of the plants.

A shallow box can be the ideal place for a collection of *Sedum* and *Sempervivum*. Use a gravelly compost with pebbles decorating the spaces between the plants, or a group of miniature conifers. An empty box in winter can be a good feeding place for birds, but only so long as it is well out of the range of prowling cats.

Seen from inside, a traditional box of geraniums, ivy and the colourful foliage of *Coleus* pleasingly lead the eye to an enclosed tiled yard containing a splended *Aucuba japonica*.

A collection of annuals including geraniums, lobelias and fast-growing *Impatiens*, climbing *Ipomoea* and asters, the full perennials, turn a small box into a cheerful sight for occupier and passer-by

If you have a generous window area, you can have the best of both worlds, with scented-leaved geraniums outside and a bank of chrysanthemums within (below).

Framed by shutters, a free standing trough of petunias and geraniums with ivy (left) makes an attractive picture from within and without. A *Howeia* fills the foreground.

The logical extension of a window box is a balcony (right), which also reaches a wider audience. Contained in suitable troughs, geraniums, lobelias and varieties of ivy can be moved around to suit the weather or the owner's whim.

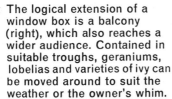

Window boxes from outside

The special thing about window boxes is that they work many ways: they brighten, soften and generally decorate the outside of a house, giving pleasure to visitors and passers-by, and for everyone inside the house they create a miniature landscape.

It is always best to let all the colour come from the plants alone: bright boxes and other containers are a mistake. Natural wood, terracotta, white, cream, stone and faded blue-grey are the best background colours for flowers and foliage. A lot depends on the colour and texture of the walls of the house and on whether you want the box to stand out (white on red brick, for example) or blend with stone or stucco.

If you cannot have a window box proper, you can fill containers or pots with plants and stand them on a wide sill or a balcony or at the top of a flight of steps. The inspiration behind this idea comes from the pavements, balconies and steps in France and Italy which are covered with every kind of box and container, from oil drums and petrol cans upwards, spilling over with brilliant flowers.

In boxes and containers you can have a blazing mixture of colours which would be too much, too overwhelming, on a larger scale, in a garden bed or border. This is because the colours are contained in a framework of stone or wood and the scale is small. A restricted use of colour is always successful too.

Background colour is important: obviously a red brick facade will not be best decorated by a mass of shocking pink and vermilion geraniums, but they will look beautiful against white or grey stone or brick. In all colour combinations white and silver grey add contrast and lightness.

You must have the right kind of window and sill for a window box. Casement windows are fine if they open into a room and have shutters which will open outwards. Clearly you cannot have a window box if the contents are going to be given a smart slap every time you open the window. So, with casements that open outwards, a window box is not possible.

Sash windows are ideal. Wide sills are a help as the box will have a solid base. If there is no sill but only some decorative ironwork, be extra careful about attaching the box to the wall. Stout metal brackets will be needed, rawl-plugged to the wall and to the box, and, in addition, restraining rods will have to be hooked into the sides of the box and into the wall. If you are in doubt about doing this consult a builder: the importance of firm, safe fixing cannot be overstressed.

At ground-floor level, of course, a box can be fixed well below a window that opens outwards, and all the watering, dead-heading and other maintenance jobs that have to be taken care of can be done from outside.

Window boxes are ideal for displaying coloured flowering plants like these begonias.

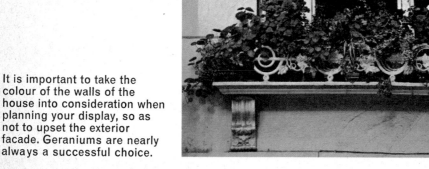

It is important to take the colour of the walls of the house into consideration when planning your display, so as not to upset the exterior facade. Geraniums are nearly always a successful choice.

Petunias and lobelias have long been window-box favourites, and their bright presence on the window sill (above) reinforces the old fashioned character of the window.

An orderly collection of geraniums are shown off to their best advantage in this stylish box. The addition of trailing plants or plants of different heights would spoil the balance.

For summer displays, the colourful blooms of begonia, geraniums, lobelia and petunias, are all deservedly popular. Each window box, brimming with colour, gives its own individual stamp to a house, and there are many ways of organizing them to make particular effects. Plants can be so arranged that they appear to be growing straight out of the wall (above) or trained to follow the contours of a window (left), while the formal, traditional style (right) has a charm of its own.

Keeping an interesting window box

A three-part scheme will keep your window box looking beautiful for most of the year. Of course, no window box can be in full bloom all the year around: there must be fallow times. However, a peat-filled box will give you extended flowering time since you can stand pots of plants in it at almost any point in the year, except when it is extremely cold.

Window boxes are usually at their loveliest in summer, but in spring there can be a show of bulbs and in winter a display of evergreens and miniature trees.

Plants, bulbs and seeds are planted in boxes as they are in the garden: hardy plants in winter and spring, seeds for annuals in spring, bedding plants in late spring and bulbs in late summer and autumn.

Plants in boxes have rather a hard life compared with garden plants; often they have little protection from high wind or shelter from the sun and so they have to withstand draughts and drought. A number of tough, good-tempered plants are the best to choose for this somewhat spartan life: geraniums, begonias, marguerites, lobelias, petunias, and French or African marigolds (*Calendula*) for example. Where there is a lot of sun petunias, verbena, marigolds and lobelias will thrive; a shadier window makes a more suitable home for begonias and pansies. Climbers such as *Ipomoea* (morning glory) and *Cobaea scandens* can be trained up strings, and trailers such as trailing begonias, nasturtiums and ivy grown to fall softly over the front of the box.

One spring scheme: bulbs – daffodils, hyacinths and crocuses, or *Chionodoxa*, grape hyacinth and scilla – and bushy wallflowers, all planted in autumn. Plant the wallflowers first. Another spring scheme is bulbs with forget-me-nots, later replaced by *Nicotiana* (flowering tobacco): plant the white variety for scent and the green for colour. Plant nasturtiums (from seed) at the beginning of summer to give bright, trailing flowers in late summer.

Bulbs can either be left in for next year or taken out. One reason for removing them is that their leaves take a long time to die and can look untidy. Give them to someone to plant in their garden. Dwarf daffodils, however, will do well again the next year and are a good choice for small boxes.

Take out wallflowers and put in the summer bedding plants antirrhinums, marigolds, petunias, geraniums, lobelias, alyssum for example. (Whatever you plant, remember to keep the tallest plants to the back of the box and the small ones – or the trailers – to the front.) At the end of summer these could be replaced by chrysanthemums.

For winter the dwarf conifers and variegated ivies give a surprising amount of colour. Shrubby veronicas (*Hebe*), *Euonymus* and heathers are tough plants for cold or exposed places, but where it is very cold it is better to empty the box until spring.

There are, of course, many ways to plan your planting. One scheme is based on a restricted use of colour, which is often more attractive and harmonious in a small area than too much variety. It is also very enjoyable to work out a colour plan: perhaps yellow, orange and white, red, pink and white, white and dark green, or blue and purple. Another beautiful and unusual scheme could be based on gradations of one colour.

In all planting plans remember the beauty of white and grey. The silver-grey leaves of *Cineraria maritima*, for instance, are a perfect foil for bright, hot colours, and white flowers always give a feeling of cool freshness.

The planting plan need not be concerned with flowers at all: herbs for cooking can be grown very successfully in boxes, and their scents are an additional pleasure. In a vegetable box small tomatoes and peppers and a wide variety of other edible crops grow well and decoratively, and it is only in such an outdoor position that they can get all the sunlight and fresh air that is essential to their growth.

Spring

No spring window box is complete without bulbs, as shown in this box (above) of daffodils, crocuses, *scilla*, wallflowers, forget-me-nots with the addition of trailing ivy.

Hyacinths (below) are set off by the dark green background of the little conifer *Juniperus horizontalis*. Also included are tulips, *Chionodoxa*, *Muscari*, crocuses and *Tradescantia*.

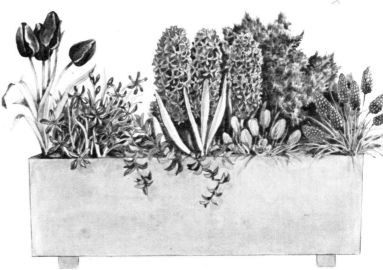

In spring time the window box needs lightly forking over to aerate the soil. Some fertilizer should be added as well.

Plant bedding plants in carefully prepared holes, taking care not to damage the roots.

Seeds of hardy annuals for a summer display can be sown directly in the box.

Summer

Winter

The reds and golds of the summer are reflected in this display (above), dominated by a begonia and zonal *Pelargonium,* Lobelia, alyssum and pansies complete the picture.

The ivy-leaved geranium (below right) is a lovely addition to any window box. Marguerites, petunias, marigolds and the fluffy blue *Ageratum* are also good for the summer.

A good winter display is shown in this grouping (above) of *Aubretia, Cotoneaster, Sempervivum, Chamaecyparis lawsoniana* 'Ellwoodii' with *Erica* and *Sedum spurium*.

A *Rhododendron* dominates this bright winter window box (below), which also includes *Hedera helix* 'Glacier'. *Erica carnea, Chamaecyparis* and *Saxifraga.*

Summer is the peak time for window box displays, but it is important to keep the box in good condition. All flowering plants including the petunias shown here, look very untidy if they are not treated to regular dead-heading to remove all withered and dead flowers.

Geraniums thrive in window boxes with a good exposure to sunlight. However once they have flowered they do tend to overreach themselves and grow too tall and straggly. They should be pruned back to a height of something like 23 cm (9 in) towards the end of the summer.

All dead foliage must be cut right back to tidy up the box for the winter.

Every two or three years it is a good idea to completely empty your box and fill it with fresh compost.

Towards the end of autumn plant your bulbs such as daffodils and hyacinths.

How to make and plant a window box

Window boxes can either be made to fit a given window or bought. There are ready-made fibre-glass boxes, pottery boxes of terracotta, cast cement boxes, polystyrene, plastic and wooden ones. Hard wood is best, and teak, oak, ash and elm are traditionally used. Once made they can be painted or left to weather. You can treat them with a preservative against rot; but be sure it will not harm the plants.

A box should be at least 23 cm (9 in) deep: the soil in anything shallower would dry out too quickly. Raise the box on tiles or strips of wood to allow for circulation of air and drainage, and make drainage holes in the base.

Any box above the ground-floor level of a house must be securely attached to the wall. Consult a hardware or garden store about the safest method of attachment. The usual one is to fix two strong metal brackets underneath the box, with metal tie bars holding it to the wall on either side to ensure extra safety.

When the box is safely and securely in place, it is ready to be planted. At the bottom of the box put an inch or so of drainage material, broken clay flower pots, pieces of brick or small stones, to help to keep the soil sweet (fresh) and wholesome. Above the drainage layer should go a layer of peat, or a well-rotted mixture of leaf mould and a little organic manure. A layer of turf with the grass side face downwards is a good alternative. The compost to fill the box can be a ready-made mixture containing fertilizer obtainable from garden shops.

The compost should be firm in the box, reaching to within about 2.5 cm (1 in) of the top. Check its condition regularly, making sure that it is neither dusty or clay-like. The surface should be forked over regularly, once a week or so, to keep it aerated and sweet. And whatever its composition, the compost should be changed once a year; winter is the usual time for doing this.

It is vital to remember that a box full of soil is very heavy, weighing about 25 kg (56 lb) on average, and it must be firmly attached. If it fell, it could cause a serious accident.

Into the box you can put seeds, bulbs or plants. Hardy annuals (plants that grow, flower, set seeds and die in season)

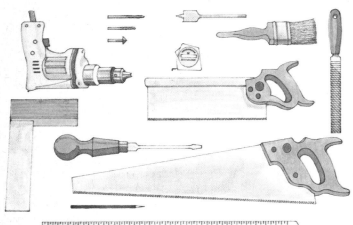

You don't need a particularly well equipped tool box, or a large work table to make yourself a practical and attractive window box. You may have the necessary tools already except, perhaps, the drill attachment needed for making the 2.5 cm (1 in) holes. A wood file is useful for giving a smooth finish to the surfaces. The box can be made out of soft plywood or traditional hard wood.

Cut the planks and the battens to size. This box was made to fit an average window ledge length of 0·9 m (3 ft). For a longer ledge it is advisable to make two boxes in order not to put too much strain on the whole structure. A width of 24 cm (9 in) ensures enough room for a good display of plants. The depth of the box should also be 24 cm (9 in) which is sufficient for the roots to develop fully.

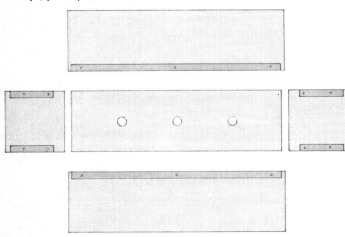

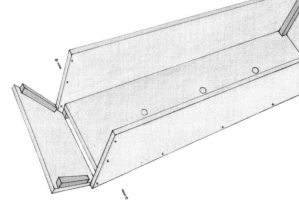

The battens are an essential feature in construction. They strengthen the box, so that the screws can be inserted, and they keep the structure rigid, making it a firm and solid base. Glue the battens to the wood as shown, using a good wood glue, and screw them in with brass screws. For drainage make three 2·5 cm (1 in) holes in the centre of the base, allowing one hole for each 30 cm (1 ft) of length.

You now have a ready prepared kit. Glue the edges of the base and hold it in place resting on the battens between the two long planks. Repeat the procedure with the two end sections using the battens as supporting struts inside the box. Screw the sides firmly with brass screws. Paint the wood with an undercoat and two coats of oil-based top coat. Line the box with a layer of polythene.

are grown from seeds planted in spring; bedding plants are put in in early summer and bulbs in autumn. Sow seeds thinly covering them with a sprinkling of fine soil. When the seedlings are large enough to handle, thin them out, following the instructions on the seed packet. Even in a box annuals must have room to spread their roots, otherwise they become weak and spindly. When you put in plants, first moisten the soil, then make spaced-out holes with a trowel. As each plant goes into its place, press the soil round it firmly.

Water with care: soil that is too wet can kill plants, so it is best to underwater slightly. In hot, dry weather water twice a day, but not when the sun is high; in cool or overcast weather water less, and in rainy weather even less or not at all.

Give the soil a general fertilizer in spring and a little liquid manure when plants are budding; in autumn a sprinkling of bonemeal is excellent. Dried farmyard manure or a seaweed fertilizer crumbled on the surface of the soil will keep up its humus content. Hop manure and leaf mould are good organic fertilizers, too.

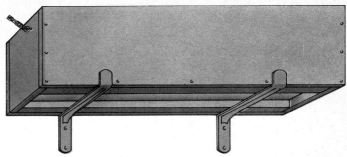

Window boxes when filled with compost and plants can be very heavy objects. Outside on the window sill they are exposed to winds and rain. It is essential that they be firmly fixed and never merely be placed unattached on the ledge. The simplest form of attachment is using metal angle brackets with ends bent upwards to hold the box in place.

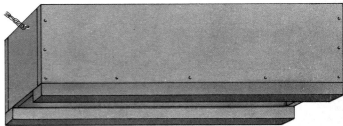

If you have a strong window ledge with a metal railing around it the only problem is drainage. Two wooden battens screwed along the bottom of the box will lift it up sufficiently to save the box from standing in a puddle. A plastic drip tray should be used to catch excess water.

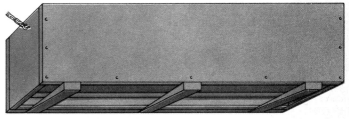

If your window ledge is not set at a perfect right angle to the wall, it is sensible to fix wedge shaped pieces of wood to the base of your box. For safety's sake it is always better to have the weight of the box leaning towards the house wall. As with all boxes attach side hooks.

This attractive display makes good use of the different types of plants which can be effectively grouped together. Ivy and *Campanula* trail down the sides, while the top is dominated by the stately *Chamaecyparis* conifers. To these are added geraniums, coleus and *Impatiens*.

Drainage is one of the key factors in making a successful window box. Each hole should be covered with crocks or perforated zinc to prevent the soil washing away with the water. If you are using a plastic sheet, then pierce holes through the sheeting. Add a layer of gravel, followed by a layer of turf. Then build up the compost in layers to a level of about 2·5 cm (1 in) from the top of the box. Make holes in the turf, remove plants from their pots or seed beds, and plant them.

Temperature, light and shade

Photosynthesis

Photosynthesis, which means 'putting light together', is especially crucial to house plants, as they have less access to a direct source of light energy than plants outside. It is the process whereby a plant turns carbon dioxide and water into the starch and sugar that it needs for its food. Light rays from the sun or from an artificial light source are assimilated by the green parts of the plant which contain chlorophyll, and used as a source of energy. The most important role in this process takes place in the chlorophyll pigments which are called the *chloroplasts*. The energy decomposes the carbon dioxide into carbon monoxide and oxygen, which then combine with the water taken up from the roots to make sugar. If it is not used at once for active growth then this sugar is converted by the plant into starch which is stored in the roots. Photosynthesis can only take place during the daytime, unless the plant is growing under artificial light conditions which can be manipulated to achieve the desired growth-rate.

The chloroplasts contain the green pigment which is the mechanism central to the photosynthesis process.

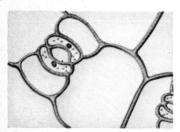

The stomata are the tiny pores in the plant's epidermis which absorb sunlight and through which the gases pass.

Respiration alone occurs in the hours of darkness.

Photosynthesis and respiration take place in daylight.

Respiration

Respiration is the breaking down of the sugar foods which the plant has produced through the process of photosynthesis into the fats, proteins and other nitrogen containing components essential to its life. This releases the energy that the plant needs in order to grow and carry out all other energy consuming cellular activity. At the same time the plant gives off carbon dioxide and water via its leaves. The respiration process is continuous both night and day although photosynthesis occurs only in daytime.

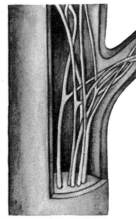

The stem supports the leaves so that they can receive the necessary light. The tiny capillaries carry water and food collected by the roots.

The root holds the plant in the soil. The necessary water and mineral nutrients are taken in by the root trains and diffused through cells to the capillary tubes in the stem.

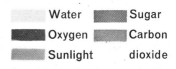

Water	Sugar
Oxygen	Carbon
Sunlight	dioxide

House plants have a difficult part to play in our interiors. We expect them to be living sculptures, always looking their best regardless of the circumstances. The ideal house plant must be strong and amenable, and if not forever flowering, at least forever green. It must remain undisturbed by dryness and smoke, steam, draughts and changes of temperature. It must survive and thrive in the air-conditioned, central-heated, often sunless climate of modern houses, flats and offices. The plants which have been most successful for centuries are those which originally came from jungles and forests, for they have been able to adapt to the often sunless rooms of our houses.

All house plants need as near possible the conditions they enjoyed in their place of origin. Above all they need light. Photosynthesis, the process by which the energy-giving foods are manufactured from water taken in through the roots and carbon dioxide from the air, cannot go on without light. Chlorophyll, the green pigment in the plant cells, absorbs the radiant energy in sunlight. Lack of light results in a weak pale plant, unable to flower. No light at all will kill it. It is difficult to ensure that all plants will receive the light they need. Therefore, as a beginner, it is safest to choose plants that are used to shady conditions in their native habitat. Arums, ferns and palms fall into this category. Later you may want to experiment with artificial lighting which overcomes the plant's need for sunlight and works well for almost any plant.

Light and shade needs vary enormously from plant to plant. *Araceae*, *Aspidistra* and palms all do well in a warm but north- or east-facing room, which does not receive very much direct light. Begonias, bromeliads, *Chlorophytum*, *Dracaena*, *Fatsia*, *Ficus*, *Fittonia* and *Tradescantia* thrive when placed reasonably near the source of light. A bright place is ideal for flowering begonias, *Euphorbia* and African violets, and an extremely bright place will make crotons, *Impatiens*, *Pelargonium*, *Sinningia* (*Gloxinia*) and all succulents and cacti very happy.

Turn all plants from time to time. Otherwise they will grow in a lop-sided fashion, and you will be forever gazing at the back of the leaves as they strain towards the light. If your plant looks unhappy try moving it nearer or farther from the light. But remember to adjust the water accordingly, since a great deal of moisture is evaporated by the heat of the sun.

Apart from good lighting, the essential needs of your plant are: good soil mix and correct feeding, the right temperature and the correct amount of moisture. Temperature varies according to the season, your country's climate and the climate of your home or office. With so much variation in temperature, each plant or group of plants needs to be studied separately. Knowledge of where the plant grows wild is essential. Humidity is of the utmost importance, especially for large-leaved plants which lose a lot of water through transpiration. In general a constant room temperature of 18°–21°C (64°–70°F) is satisfactory for most plants sold for the house. Plants needing cooler places can thrive in halls and bedrooms. No plant will manage for long in a temperature over 24°C (75°F), unless it is in a greenhouse where there is plenty of light.

Light decreases in intensity as you move away from a window. It is important to know how much direct light your plant needs when deciding where to place it. Some plants such as *Codiaeum* and *Impatiens* need direct light, others such as African violets need a lot of light but it does not have to be direct. *Fatsia*, *Ficus* and *Dracaena* need a medium amount of light, while ferns and palms are happy in shady corners.

No plant should be placed in a position where it is subject to attack from draughts. Cold streams of air come in from obvious sources: from under doors and through badly fitted windows. Less obvious places such as air conditioning vents can also be a hazard. Plants should be kept away from indirect heat sources, a refrigerator, a central heating system, a washing machine and a cooker, as well as from direct heat supplied by an open fire.

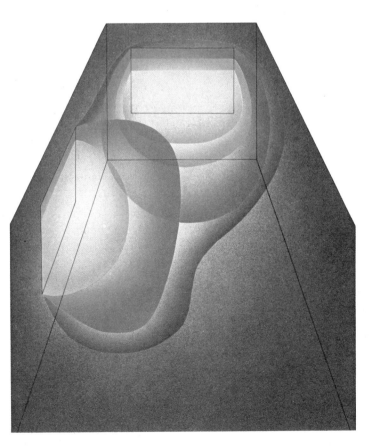

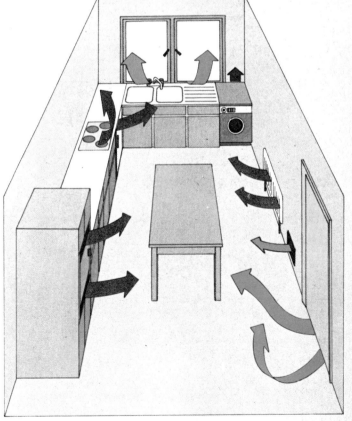

Watering

A watering can or bottle is the most basic piece of watering equipment you will need. A spray is useful for added moisture. A bucket is a good idea for plunging dried-out pots and dampening peat.

Water is life or death to a plant. It is absorbed from the soil by the roots, carrying with it the essential mineral nutrients. It is also absorbed by the leaves, which is why a spray is an important adjunct.

More plants die from overwatering than from any other cause. It is impossible to be dogmatic about the amount of water a plant must have or when to give it, since this must be dictated by the immediate surroundings. Plants will be affected by the kind of pot and the soil used, the temperature, time of year and their positioning.

Plants in clay pots need more water than those in plastic. Plants in a loam-based compost need more than those in a peaty or soilless compost, and plants growing hydroponically have their own indicator telling you when to add water.

Your plant does not grow at the same rate all through the year; in spring and early summer when it is rapidly making new leaves above the soil and new roots below it will need a lot of water. In the winter when lack of light slows down growth water should be reduced to a bare minimum. However, the dryness of a centrally heated room means that your plant will still need quite a lot of water.

Plants on a sunny window sill need more water than plants in a shady corner. Plants outside in pots, boxes and hanging baskets need more water than plants in humid bathrooms and kitchens.

Examine your pot daily. If the surface of the soil looks dry it may need watering, but check the undersurface first. A tap on the side of a clay pot will tell you: a ringing sound means the soil is dry, a dull thud means there is still moisture present or your pot is cracked. If your pot is plastic you can poke a pencil or knife into the soil and see if it emerges sticky, or you can use a moisture meter.

Don't let your plants dry out and wilt, but don't water too soon. Plants need to fight for moisture in order to encourage growth of their roots. When you do water, water to the brim. Little drips now and then are not sufficient. If your plant does become so dry that the soil ball shrinks and water runs straight through the pot, immerse pot and plant in a bucket of water. Leave them there to soak until air bubbles stop rising. Be sure that the water covers the top of the soil, especially if the pot

It is sometimes difficult to be sure that the compost is at the correct state of humidity, neither too dry nor water-logged. When in doubt a water meter is a useful means of finding out precisely what its condition is. Meters come in several easy-to-use designs.

When a plant dries out the root ball shrinks. Watering from a can is not enough as water poured from above simply runs down the sides of the pot. The whole pot must be plunged into a bucket of water. Prick the soil with a fork and leave submerged until bubbles stop rising.

is plastic and the soil peaty. Otherwise there is little chance that the water will actually get into the pot. Your plant should recover quite quickly. Take out the pot and firm down the soil round the rim.

You place saucers and trays under the pots to collect the moisture that drains through the soil. However, do not let a pot stand in a saucer of water. This can lead to root rot. Plants needing a constantly humid atmosphere such as ferns and arums are best plunged into a second container packed with moist peat. Or you can stand them in a trough or tray lined with moist gravel and pebbles. Spray often with water. This creates humidity in the air round the plants and provides the atmosphere in which they thrive.

Some plants with delicate, easily damaged leaves and flowers should be watered very carefully. Either use a long-necked watering can which can reach under the foliage direct to the soil, or water them from below. Place the pots in a basin of water until the top of the soil shows moist. Then stand them on a layer of pebbles or gravel which is always moist. This method of watering can be used for *Sinningia* (*Gloxinia*), cyclamen and African violet.

Cacti and some succulents need to be kept very, very dry in the winter resting period. Water them occasionally to prevent them from shrivelling up and dying. Move them out of a warm living room into a cooler room or hall. Remember that their home the desert can be a very cold windy place in the winter.

Watering when you're on holiday is always a problem. The ideal solution is to have a reliable friend or neighbour who will look after your plants. Failing this there is the well known remedy using a dampened lamp wick of glass fibre or cotton, or the clay-pot method using a bandage attached to a dripping tap. Nowadays there are many more reliable self-watering methods. They require a small expense, but this can turn out to be a long-term saving particularly if it is difficult for you to water your plants regularly.

There are a number of self-watering systems which can maintain your plant while you are away on holiday. A length of bandage with one end in a bowl of water and the other pushed into the soil draws up water by capillary action.

In this variation of the wick method water travels up from the bowl and comes into contact with the root ball in the base of the pot. The plant must be removed first so that the wick can be inserted and splayed out over the base.

A bandage attached to a dripping tap and draped over a row of pots standing in an empty bath tub creates a very odd visual effect but is a useful method of ensuring adequate water supply when the house is empty.

By placing your plant in a plastic bag made airtight with a rubber band you create a makeshift terrarium. The plant produces humidity by the process of respiration and this will keep it moist and healthy for some time.

A number of self-watering containers can now be bought from garden shops. They come in a variety of simple and modern designs in bright coloured plastics. They are especially popular in offices, and with people who cannot give their plants the regular watering they need. They are ideal for people who are regularly away from the home for long periods of time or at holiday time. All you have to do is keep the reservoir topped up, and this automatically keeps the soil at its correct level of moistness. The tank needs refilling every three to four weeks.

There are many designs of automatic water diffuser available on the market today. You can buy a porous 'frog' which sits decoratively beside the plant, and which allows a regulated amount of moisture to drain out into the soil. This method lasts 2 to 3 weeks.

Troughs and trays and hanging baskets can be rather awkward to water regularly, or be placed in such a way that you tend to forget about them. This terracotta 'porous irrigator' can be inserted among your plants and then filled and refilled with water which will slowly seep into the soil.

Artificial lighting

In the modern office buildings and apartments of our cities we no longer see rows of pot plants competing with each other for their daily dose of sunlight from the window; and large stately plants can be seen standing way back in a corner of a room which before would have been considered too dim for anything other than a shady fern. This new boost to indoor plant growing is all thanks to the use of artificial light. For the professional gardener this can mean growing exotic plants like orchids in nothing but artificial light, but for the amateur enthusiast it is usually a question of supplementing the light available in a room or growing small illuminated gardens of flowering plants in specially designed light-fitting boxes.

Before, the easiest and longest lived house plants were those that needed least light, coming as they did from shady jungles and forests, where only a little light filtered through onto their broad leaves. In the last thirty years the changes in architectural design, the trend towards large picture windows and the growing need to compensate for the lack of outdoor greenery, has led to the houseplant boom, and an increased inventiveness in ways to make up for the lack of sunlight available in city interiors. You must remember that even a plant standing right by a window pane gets only a quarter of the light that it would enjoy outside, while one in the centre of a room gets perhaps a tenth. Without adequate light a plant cannot survive as it should. It will become pale and unable to flower and the process of photosynthesis will cease to work properly. About thirty years ago two New York gardeners experimented with growing pot plants under a normal light bulb to give extra light when daylight had gone; and twenty years of experimentation has now proved that almost any plant can be grown in artificial conditions.

Any ordinary household lamp can help to boost plant growth, but there are certain rules to be followed and certain principles which must be understood first. Artificial light has nothing of the intensity of sunlight, and much fewer of the red and blue wavelengths which are absorbed in photosynthesis. But although it is weaker, it produces much more heat and can easily scorch the leaves of a plant. Ordinary spot-lights or floodlights directed at a plant make a decorative focus in the room, and they do help the plant's growth by giving it extra warmth and light, but this is only suitable for foliage plants which do not need very much light. A much better daylight substitute is found in fluorescent tubes, especially when a 'daylight' and a 'cool white' tube are used together. Leaves

may touch these tubes without being damaged. You can buy specially designed Gro-Lux tubes from gardening shops and they can be used both for your foliage plants and for propagation from seeds and cuttings.

A handyman can easily make a container for artificially lit plants. Bookshelves and room dividers make good places for them, where the plants can be easily seen but the light does not shine into your eyes. The woodwork should be painted white for maximum light reflection and a pelmet or strip of wood will conceal the tubes themselves. However, if you feel wary about making your own equipment you can choose from a wide range of manufactured light gardening fittings. Fluorescently lit panel squares and rings can be obtained in specially designed 'illuminated gardens' which are like inverted tables with a tray for a row of small plants to stand on, and one or two fluorescent tubes with a reflector suspended above them. There are also smaller versions like a table lamp with a circular tube above. Many have automatic watering devices and can be fitted with a time switch. Artificial lighting can indeed minimize many of the problems and pitfalls that have often been associated with indoor gardening and guarantee a large range of healthy-looking plants.

The cool and austere lines of this very modern interior make an ideal background for these three tall succulent euphorbias. A single spotlight directed on them makes them the dramatic focal point in the room, and brings out their natural sculptural beauty.

Artificial light enthusiasts can make use of specially designed fitted cabinets, in which their plants lead a healthy and well regulated life with no need ever to see the sun. Such cabinets can make attractive room dividers, and look as pretty as a display of ornaments. The plants shown (left) include *Episcia, Columnea, Kalanchoë* and geraniums on the top shelf and *Begonia rex* and *Streptocarpus* below.

Plants needing considerable exposure to light can have their daytime prolonged into the night by means of artificial lighting. Here a display of *Nephrolepis, Peperomia, Crassula, Ficus* and *Calceolaria*, all of similar height, benefit from the three low-hanging lamps.

When choosing your plants for artificial light systems it is necessary to know something about photoperiodism. This is the word that describes the relative length of light needed by flowering plants. It must be remembered that creating a partly or wholly artificial environment for a plant, with regulated heat, no seasons of the year, no cloudy days, is not necessarily ideal in its monotonous perfection. Given too much exposure to light miniature plants will be inclined to grow high and straggly, while too little light will stunt the growth of others. Foliage plants under artificial light only need enough light to promote healthy growth, but flowering plants are divided into three groups. 'Long day plants', of which tuberous begonias, *Aster* and *Calceolaria* are good examples, need between 12–16 hours of light in order to produce flower buds. 'Short day plants' need 12 hours or less light every day. Chrysanthemums, *Kalanchoë* and poinsettias are popular members of this group. The third category, sometimes known as 'the

indifferents' are not particularly affected by day length, and include the popular African violets, tomatoes and roses. As a general and obvious rule, winter flowers need less exposure to light than summer ones.

It is a good idea to select plants of the same or similar height otherwise you will find that the tall ones will get their full light requirements while the shorter ones 'starve', or the short ones will have enough and the tall ones will be burnt. Short plants with broad leaves are much easier to light than tall ones, as the light can reach all the leaf surfaces at the same time. This is why African violets and miniature begonias are such a popular choice for artificial light gardening. Plants grown wholly or partly in artificial light conditions are planted normally in a loam-based compost, a peat-based compost, or using a hydroponic system. The constant temperature and lighting means that the plant is not controlled or affected by seasonal changes, and has no winter dormancy period. The

growth rate of some plants like geraniums is speeded up; this means that regular pruning is necessary. All cuttings can be used for stem and leaf propagation, and you will find that all forms of vegetable and sexual reproduction can be managed with a far higher success rate by using artificial light propagators. Bulbs can also be forced artificially, and narcissus and *Amaryllis* have proved to be the most successful.

As with hydroponics, artificial light gardening is still in its infancy. It opens up so many possibilities both for commercial growers and for home enthusiasts that a lot of research is now being done. In the last year a new light unit has come onto the American market. It is called Verilux True-Bloom and it gives off a far more natural light. At the time of writing this product is still hard to obtain, but the demand is so great that it is bound to be answered in the near future. It seems inevitable that very soon artificial light gardening will become a common feature in many offices, showrooms and private houses.

The *Howeia* and begonias above are displayed to great effect with the aid of a light panel on the wall and ceiling spotlights. In this way these already conspicuous plants are given even larger and more dramatic personalities.

Much research has gone into finding ways of preventing artificial light from looking too artificial. Sometimes the fluorescent glow is distracting, but it can be incorporated into an overall design as with the group of *Schefflera* and *Monstera* (left) whose light intake is boosted by the pinkish glow from the fluorescent tube over them.

Given sufficient lighting, plants make attractive ornaments in a recessed wall unit. A pink azalea (far left), backed by cut narcissi, glows in the rosy light given off by fluorescent tubes.

A luxuriant jungle is created by this mixed grouping (right) of *Aechmea, Aspidistra, Ficus elastica, Maranta leuconeura*, chrysanthemum and *Ananas comosus*. The unit serves as a room divider, breaking up a large open-plan area without cutting off either side of the room.

Tools and equipment

With ten or twenty house plants in pots around the house you do not need many tools. Any old spoon and fork can be used to loosen the surface of the soil, and a sharp knife will serve for all your cutting and pruning work. A bottle or two will be enough to keep your water for watering. However, you might still prefer to make use of some of the equipment especially designed for looking after house plants.

A watering can with a long spout, deep set in the can, is an important adjunct. This can be in plastic for lightness, or in galvanized iron or brass; the fine rose at the top of the spout reaches into window boxes and onto the gravel base of plant troughs. A plastic bucket is useful for moistening peat or peat compost. If you are in doubt about the amount of water needed, then buy a moisture meter, which comes with a handbook giving recommended readings. A hygrometer will give you the moisture content of the air, and a thermometer will check the temperature.

In order to give plants like ferns the daily shower they like, a spray or syringe can be used to direct a fine mist of water over the leaves. These are usually plastic and light. Should you need to use insecticides and pesticides, then do be careful to use a different spray. Hairy or furry-leaved plants which cannot be sprayed can be dusted with a small brush with soft bristles, and large leathery leaves can be wiped over with cotton-wool or a soft cloth dipped in tepid water. There is also a special spray designed for this purpose.

As well as keeping a sharp knife for removing offsets and cuttings and a pair of secateurs for pruning and taking stem cuttings, a sharp pair of scissors for dead-heading and cutting twine and string might be useful.

A small hand trowel and fork can be used for working in a window box, for filling pots with compost and for keeping the soil regularly aerated, but this can just as well be done with your old fork and spoon.

You will need compost, seed compost and bulb-fibre, unless you grow your plants hydroponically. Canes for supporting plants, green or natural in colour will be needed, and bass string or plastic ties for attaching them to the stems.

1 Max/min thermometer
2 Supporting rings
3 Hygrometer
4 Self-watering device
5 Moisture meter
6 Leaf shine
7 Liquid fertilizer
8 Thermostat
9 Atomizer
10 Twine

Soils and feeding

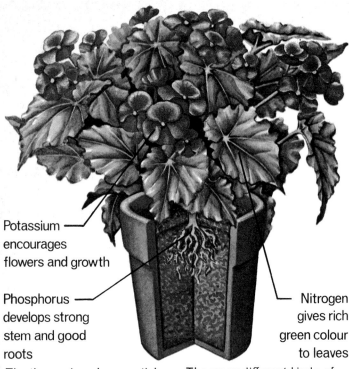

Potassium encourages flowers and growth

Phosphorus develops strong stem and good roots

Nitrogen gives rich green colour to leaves

The three minerals essential to healthy plant growth are: nitrogen, potassium and phosphorus. Nitrogen gives the rich green colour to the leaves. Potassium encourages flowering and general growth. Phosphorous develops a strong stem and root system. Soil also carries calcium, copper, iron manganese, sulphur, zinc and aluminium.

The many different kinds of compost and drainage materials available for indoor gardening include, from left to right, hydroponic granules, gravel, rocks, charcoal and grit (back row); dried blood, cacti compost, humus, potting compost, compost for seeds and cuttings (middle row); coarse silver, builders', Bedford and fine silver sand (front row).

The soil or compost in which a plant grows contributes a great deal to its health (or lack of it). It is not sufficient for any kind of container gardening to dig up a bucketful of earth from a friend's garden, fill a pot with it, put in a plant and hope for the best. Garden earth does not have the right consistency because it does not contain enough sand and humus. Sand with its large particles keeps soil porous and therefore well drained. Humus, vegetable and animal matter in various stages of decomposition, supplies many essential nutrients and has to be constantly replenished. In addition, the trace elements in garden soil, such as iron, magnesium and cobalt, may be unsuitable for some indoor plants. In compost for potting the two main ingredients are loam and peat. Loam is a rich mixture of sand, clay and humus. Peat consists of dead plant material, principally moss, which decomposes slowly and has a light, dry, fibrous texture. Compost mixtures also include fine sand to aid drainage, small amounts of chalk to counteract the acidity in peat, phosphates and potash.

Few people with pot plants or window boxes can easily obtain loam, garden compost or farmyard manure, and it is not easy to make the right mixture of necessary ingredients in a kitchen. In any case, different plants need different mixtures, for example, lime haters such as rhododendrons and ferns, cannot tolerate chalk. As a result horticultural scientists in Britain, the United States and elsewhere in the world have developed a wide range of seed and plant potting composts. These have the essential nutrients; they are free of weed seeds, pests and diseases and, since they have the right texture, they retain moisture without getting waterlogged.

A popular potting compost used mainly for slow growing plants, consists basically of 7 parts loam, 3 parts peat, and 2 parts coarse sand, with added chalk and fertilizer. A variation on this mixture has twice as much chalk and fertilizer; this makes a general purpose compost which is good for window boxes. Another mixture has three times as much chalk and fertilizer and is used for quick growers, such as tomatoes. Any good garden centre or nursery will tell you which compost suits particular needs. It is important to remember that even in the case of the best-known composts, the names are simply those of the formulae, not brand-names, and mixtures can vary considerably in quality.

Since the late fifties soilless composts based mainly on peat have been developed. Peat has almost no food value in itself but contains humus-forming salts, which enable it to take in fertilizers and store them for the plant in a form it can absorb. It can also store a great deal of water without becoming waterlogged and so allows a good supply of air to reach plant roots. The amount of fertilizer in a soilless compost depends upon the purpose for which it is to be used. In addition to light, water and air plants need food in the form of chemical substances in the soil. In a plant's natural habitat the proportion of nutrients it needs is to be found in the type of soil it chooses. This is why certain plants grow in certain places. In the natural world the humus in the soil is constantly replenished through the decay of vegetation and the fall of leaves. The humus keeps the soil soft, crumbly and porous, able to hold moisture and yet well aired. It also causes acidity in the soil which helps the roots of plants to absorb the nutrients. In indoor and outdoor gardens soil has to be fed with the substances which the plants need to keep them

All plants must be fed according to their particular needs and the time of year. *Do not* feed a seedling when the roots are not fully formed.

Do not feed a plant in the winter dormant or resting period, during which time there is very little growth activity.

Do not feed a plant when it is in full flower such as this *Allamanda cathartica* since it has already absorbed all the food required for flowering.

Do feed a plant such as this *Philodendron* if the leaves have turned yellow. Otherwise it only needs feeding 2 or 3 times a year.

Do feed plants like this *Monstera*, when new growth is apparent, such as a leaf unfurling.

Do feed a plant when it is about to flower, as with the *Nerium* shown here. This is the time when it needs to use all its energy resources.

Some flowering house plants, such as this Kaffir lily are known as 'heavy feeders' which means that they require a regular supply of nutrients to keep up with their growth rate. However this plant must be seen as the exception rather than the rule. Most plants only need feeding at regular intervals in their development, and it is never wise to try and 'build them up' unnaturally.

healthy. This has to be put into it in the form of fertilizers.

There are two main groups of fertilizer: organic and chemical. Rotting garden compost is an organic fertilizer, and so too are animal droppings (manure). Others in the organic group are dried blood, bone meal and fish meal. These are all available from garden centres. Well-rotted manure or garden compost contains a large number of plant foods and can be bought in sterilized packs.

Organic fertilizers have to be activated by bacteria in the soil and take longer to work than synthetic ones, which are easier to use for indoor and window-box gardening. They can be bought in small quantities and they contain all the nutrients plants need in the correct proportions. They come in liquid form as a soluble powder, and as pellets.

It is very important that you read the label on the bottle or packet of fertilizer with care and follow the instructions exactly. Never increase the amount of fertilizer recommended on the principle that the plant cannot have too much of a good thing. A plant can be damaged beyond remedy by overfeeding. Never give a fertilizer solution to a plant which is very dry, because it may harm the roots. First water it well and let it recover for a few days.

As a rule indoor plants need less feeding than their relatives in the garden or greenhouse, although it is always important during the growing season. Feeding generally ends at the close of this season, when winter is on the way and the plant's growth slows down.

It is a good idea to change the fertilizer you use from time to time: in that way, anything slightly lacking in one brand will be made up for by another.

Hydroponics

The modern trend in growing indoor plants takes us further and further away from natural organic garden materials, towards an entirely artificial means of cultivation. Hydroponics, which literally means 'water work', is a method of growing plants entirely without soil, using instead a sterile soil-substitute placed in a specially designed container.

Only in the last hundred years or so was it discovered that the roots of a plant do not in some mysterious way 'eat' the soil, but that they have three main functions to perform: they take in the essential nutrients with the water in the soil, they absorb oxygen which enables iron assimilation to take place, and they keep a plant anchored in its upright position. Hydroponics make it possible for all the root requirements to be answered artificially. It can be seen as the natural progression from growing indoor plants in a sterile peat-based (soilless) compost, enriched with artificial fertilizers, and is often used in conjunction with artificial light gardening.

Experimentation with hydroponics has been taking place for a considerable length of time. Around the turn of the century a tropical tree was grown in a nutrient solution in Switzerland; an American professor managed to grow giant tomatoes in such a solution in the twenties; and food crops have been produced in what seemed to be impossible or unsuitable climatic conditions. However, it is only quite recently that the hydroponic method has been developed as a viable commercial growing method, and only very recently did it become possible for anyone to set up their own small indoor hydroponic system. Soon this unfamiliar technical term will become a household word.

A hydroponic system is easy to use, but it is not so simple a process that you can grow happily flowering plants of all

Plants grown in a controlled hydroponic system glow with good health, like the *Syngonium podophyllum* below.

varieties by merely standing their roots in a jam jar or large pot filled with a well balanced nutrient solution. In fact, as many children have discovered to their disappointment, a plant subjected to these conditions will die rather speedily. This is because the roots also need oxygen, which enables iron assimilation to take place, and without which the plant will die of anaemia. Thus every hydroponic system needs an aeration system. For a long time the method of supplying oxygen to the submerged roots posed many problems. The pioneers tried installing huge machinery in their greenhouses, and on a smaller scale a bicycle pump was used to give the daily dose of oxygen to a lettuce plant. Commercially this was not a viable proposition, nor was it the end of the problem. A delicate light plant like a lettuce can easily be suspended in a wire frame, but something large and top-heavy like a rubber plant needs support as well as oxygen. After much experimentation with substances like pumice stone and natural gravels, a sterile aggregate was developed, which would hold the plant, allow a root system to develop, and also 'catch' the required amount of oxygen, just as soil does.

There are now several different varieties of man-made inert and sterile soil substitutes which can be bought in garden shops. The clean white 'popped' granite product called perlite is the most popular, but you can also use vermiculite or one of several similar substances.

Once you have made the decision to try out hydroponics the next step is easy. You can buy a hydroponic unit at a garden centre. This comes complete with plant, instructions and very often a guarantee of success for the first six months. During this time your plant will need very little tending. It will obviously need the correct lighting, surrounding temperature and general routine attention; and apart from this you will only have to keep the water level topped up to the point marked on the indicator. On the other hand, and at the other

The home-made system above comprises a tray with holes at one end standing on a slope. Fill the tray with a sterile soil substitute and add a nutrient solution daily. This drains away and is used again.

The wick fed system below uses wicks of synthetic fabric. The soil substitute in the top tray is fed by capillary action with nutrient solution from the tray below. Replace this solution every two weeks.

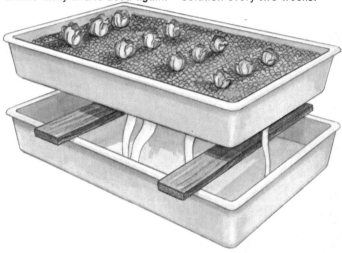

This air pump system below uses a simple aquarium pump to circulate a nutrient solution from the airtight reservoir into the growing tray. An automatic timer enables the system to operate for two hours daily. The solution is pumped quickly, then the pump aerates the growing medium. When it switches off the solution drains back into the reservoir.

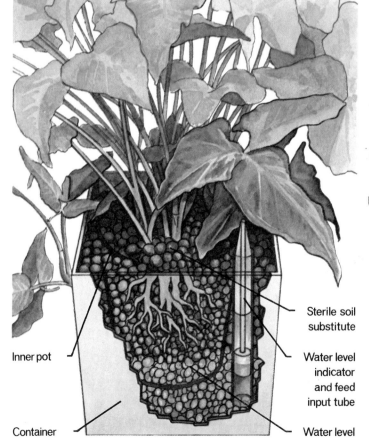

Inner pot

Container

Sterile soil substitute

Water level indicator and feed input tube

Water level

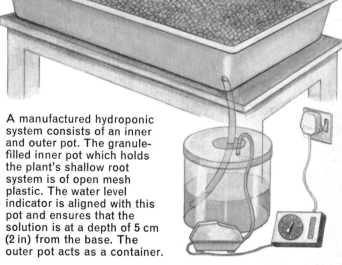

A manufactured hydroponic system consists of an inner and outer pot. The granule-filled inner pot which holds the plant's shallow root system is of open mesh plastic. The water level indicator is aligned with this pot and ensures that the solution is at a depth of 5 cm (2 in) from the base. The outer pot acts as a container.

extreme, if you are a dedicated, adventurous gardener you can convert an old plastic bowl into a hydroponic garden, and with daily care and attention produce a concentrated and high yield vegetable patch in an absurdly small space, or a splendidly flowering group of decorative plants. Whether you choose the 'lazy' or the 'dedicated' method all depends on your way of life and the kind of indoor environment the plant is to be grown in.

The ready-made systems are ideal for offices and showrooms which are empty over the weekends, as well as for houses where the plants need to fend for themselves for a lot of the time. These systems are almost always used for growing decorative plants. The hydroponic containers are usually made of plastic and come in a variety of modern styles in different sizes ranging from small ones for table display to large ones fitted with castors for easy movement. As long as you read the instructions carefully and obey them to every detail, it is unlikely that any problems will arise. Any failures will probably be due to upsetting the delicate balance of the fertilizers. Remember to use only tap water, and never add any additional nutrients.

Plants growing hydroponically do not develop the same rooting system as those grown in a compost or potting mixture, so they are most unlikely to become pot bound. A very large plant can get all the root space it needs in a relatively small container. The one danger is that it might become top heavy and be liable to topple over. When this happens potting on to a larger, more stable container is necessary. The process is simple, but do follow the instructions when you are setting up the new container.

If you are a dedicated indoor gardener, or even a dedicated experimenter, fascinated by the possibilities of hydroponics, then you can set up your own hydroponic garden. And you can choose from several different systems which can be made quite easily at home. A plastic bowl, a flower pot, a cat litter tray, almost any container that can be given adequate drainage can be adapted.

Plants grown hydroponically need exactly the same conditions as those grown in compost. Dryness, exposure to draughts, lack of sufficient lighting or too much direct sunlight, will affect them in exactly the same way as they do other house plants. There is however a minimal risk of infestation from soil-borne pests and diseases, since the sterile conditions do not encourage foreign bodies of any sort.

The greatest attraction of hydroponic gardening lies in the fact that by feeding the plant with such a well-balanced and constant supply of nutrients and oxygen, you speed up its development considerably. A lettuce which usually takes eight weeks to grow will be ready in forty days. Flowers bloom more quickly and a crop yield of vegetables is increased four or even five times. Plants can be grown in seemingly ridiculously small and cramped spaces; a tomato plant 1 m (3 ft) high can be raised in an adapted flower pot, as long as there is a stick to support the weight of its fruit.

It is advisable to use plants that have themselves been propagated hydroponically, either from seed or from a cutting that was rooted in water such as *Impatiens* (busy lizzie) or fuchsia. A plant grown in a loam-based or soilless compost can be used, but its roots must be really thoroughly washed, since even the tiniest trace of compost will upset the whole hydroponic system by turning the water stagnant.

There are several different systems which you can choose from in making your own hydroponic system, ranging from the very simple wick method, to the more complex automatic pump systems. No matter whether you choose to make your own home-made system or buy one ready-made, you must give your plants daily attention; two days of neglect could ruin your efforts. It is demanding but rewarding work.

Hydroponic systems are well suited for growing indoor vegetables like capsicum.

An unobtrusive container allows a splendid *Philodendron scandens* to come into its own.

The design of hydroponic units tends to be fairly unobtrusive, so that they can easily be placed among antique or modern objects without a clash of character.

In spite of its lofty height, this palm tree grown hydroponically needs a relatively small container rather than a tub.

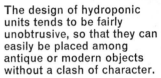

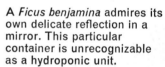

A *Ficus benjamina* admires its own delicate reflection in a mirror. This particular container is unrecognizable as a hydroponic unit.

Small, compact containers, with *Aglaonema* and *Philodendron*, make an attractive pair arranged neatly on a bamboo plant table.

Hydroponic containers come in many shapes and sizes, and each has its own prominent water-level indicator (left). This container houses the broad leaves of an *Aglaonema*.

Propagation

Once you have some houseplants the likelihood is that you will want many more. It is expensive to be forever buying new ones for friends, and a pleasure to be able to give plantlets which you have grown yourself as presents. It is also a fact that many of the most attractive plants cannot be easily obtained from shops when you want them, but can be easily obtained by other means. All this takes one into the world of propagation, a term which means quite simply reproducing or making more.

In the plant world there are two forms of reproduction: vegetative and sexual. Vegetative reproduction comprises all forms of cutting from the stem, leaf and root of a parent plant; it also includes air layering and the division of roots, tubers and bulbs. The result is the production of a miniature version of the parent plant. Sexual reproduction takes place through the sowing of seeds or spores. Some plants such as Christmas cherries and peppers grow best from seeds, and this is the only way to obtain new varieties, instead of imitations of the parent plant. However there are relatively few house plants that can be grown from seed, and as a rule it is advisable to propagate from cuttings whenever this is possible. Vegetative propagation is much quicker and more dependable than sexual propagation, and very easy to do.

Both seeds and cuttings have the same basic requirements: they need an atmosphere which is constantly warm and damp, in order for the cuttings to root and the seeds to sprout. As a result a wide range of ingenious 'miniature greenhouses' has been invented, which makes it possible to provide the ideal conditions in a house, regardless of the room temperature or humidity. These devices go under the general name of propagators. Covering any small container with glass or plastic does away with the need to buy special equipment. The simplest form of propagator is a seed box or tray standing in a warm light place, but not in direct sunlight, with a sheet of glass placed over it. Seed trays can also be covered with plastic domes in various shapes and sizes, which are easily obtainable from garden suppliers. If you are propagating from a cutting and wish to concentrate on only one area in the box, then simply stand a jam jar over your cutting. You can grow cuttings in a flower pot covered with a polythene bag, propped up with fine wires or sticks, and you can even use a plastic bag on its own in some instances. An ordinary aquarium makes an obviously adaptable propagator as well, while for growing more difficult seeds a heated propagator is advisable.

If you don't want to have your rooms cluttered with all kinds of strange makeshift contraptions of your own design, and you have no conservatory or greenhouse to keep your fledgling plants in, then you can make or buy an electrically heated propagator. A propagator is simply a heated box, and is a simple construction job for any handyman. The best ones, obtainable from all good garden centres, are thermostatically controlled at 15–27°C (59–81°F) and can be adjusted to the right temperature for the particular conditions needed. They are powered by ordinary household electricity, and they can be very useful.

The compost you use in the propagator can be a mixture of equal parts of sand (or gravel) and peat, or vermiculite and sterilized soil, or an ordinary seed compost bought from a nursery or garden centre. This acts as a medium and has no nutrients in it.

Neither cuttings nor seeds should ever be planted in ordinary potting compost, because at this stage they are busy making their roots and they have no need of the added nourishment present in all potting composts. Only when you are sure that they have rooted, can they be transferred to an ordinary potting compost. The compost for growing seedlings needs some nourishment in it. You can make a suitable mixture by 'thinning' ordinary compost with an equal amount of sharp sand and adding a handful of peat fibre.

The pop-up propagator is ideal for germinating a large number of seeds.

A plastic dome fitted over a plastic or clay pot.

A plastic bag filled with seed compost, planted with seeds and tied at the top creates a warm, humid atmosphere.

A wooden or plastic seed tray covered with a sheet of glass makes a simple propagator.

A jam jar over a saucer of damp compost creates the right conditions.

An ordinary aquarium covered with a sheet of glass creates a natural miniature green-house.

Another improvization is a polythene bag tied over a pot with a wire frame to keep it in shape.

An electrically heated propagator tray ensures quick germination and an even soil temperature, ideal for seeds.

There are several ways to grow the roots on a cutting. Some soft stemmed plants like this flourishing *Trade-scantia* are easily propagated. All you need do is cut off a healthy leafy stem and put it in a glass of water. This will produce roots quickly and easily.

Geraniums can be propagated from cuttings of healthy shoots taken when the parent plant is pruned. Insert the cutting in a small pot of compost. It will need good light, but not direct sunlight.

A plant cutting is a piece of the parent plant which has been cut, nipped or pulled off from the parent. A stem, a leaf, a rhizome can all have cuttings taken from them. The best time to take them is between spring and late summer. It is not advisable to use the flowering part of the plant but take the cutting from the most vigorous growth of a healthy plant. Some plants such as geraniums and fuchsias can have cuttings taken when they are being pruned into shape before the winter season.

For stem cuttings remove the cutting from the parent plant with a pair of sharp secateurs or a knife. It should have three or four nodes, and be between 7 to 15 cm (3–6 in) long depending on the size of the parent plant. Strip off the leaves and buds from the lower half, leaving only about four on the stem.

African violets, begonias and *Cissus* plants are most frequently rooted from leaves. A good healthy leaf will produce a small flowering plant in about ten months. Some plants like *Sansevieria* and *Streptocarpus* can be grown from leaf sections which have been cut widthways across and then planted in a rooting medium. Leaves of succulents like *Echeveria* and *Crassula* must be left to 'callus', dry out, for a day or so before being planted. They must be planted in a dry rooting medium and must not be covered by a dome or plastic bag since this would create a too humid atmosphere which could destroy them.

Hairy-leaved plants are well suited for leaf cuttings. Begonias, and the African violet shown here, are especially easy to leaf root. Remove a leaf from the parent plant and place it in compost.

Another form of leaf cutting is leaf vein cutting. Good plants for this method of propagation are *Begonia rex* and *Sinningia* because they have thick and prominent leaf veins. Taking a full grown leaf you make little incisions on the most prominent veins on the underside. The leaf is then put shiny side up on damp compost and held in place with small pebbles, hairpins, or anything that does the job. The pot is covered with a sheet of glass. The roots form where the incisions were made, and new little plants grow from them. When they are large enough to be handled without damaging they can be potted separately.

Another method of propagation is by root division. Plants which form clumps such as African violets, some ferns, *Sansevieria* and *Cyperus* can be split up into as many sections as there are individual crowns. The roots must be gently teased apart, keeping some top growth attached to each separate piece. If they are very matted, they can be cut into sections with a sharp knife but this could damage the roots. The best time for root division is in early spring, just at the beginning of the new growing season.

Very few houseplants can be propagated by root cuttings,

Long-leaved plants like *Sansevieria* can be propagated by cutting the leaves into sections with a sharp knife or razor blade and planting the sections. They are subject to rotting, so water with caution.

but the tuberous begonia is one of them. The tuber is cut into pieces just when it has started to shoot, with a shoot to each section. The cut surface needs to be dusted with a fungicide as a precaution against rotting. Some bulbs and corms also produce what are called offsets, a cluster of little tiny bulbs, which grow around the parent. These can be removed and potted, but it will take them a year or more to produce flowers.

Some plants obligingly reproduce without either cutting or seeds by producing offshoots, miniature versions of themselves, which can simply be cut off with a knife and potted. The spider plant forms young plants at the end of its long curving runners, as do *Saxifraga sarmentosa* and *Episcia*.

Soil layering is a good method of propagation for climbing and trailing plants such as some *Philodendron* and ivy. Make a small incision in one of the longest trailing stems, or take off a small piece of outer skin. Lay this exposed part across a pot of the rooting medium and weigh it down with small pebbles.

Once roots have formed the new plant can be cut away from its parent, and potted on into potting compost.

Air layering is the method you use when your rubber plant and *Dracaena* are masquerading as feather dusters, getting closer and closer to the ceiling. It is also a way of propagating the taller types of begonia, croton, and *Pandanus* plants. With this method the plant is induced to develop roots in the middle of its stem, or at whatever level you want to reduce it to. The procedure is started by making a diagonal cut in the stem, which is prevented from healing, by inserting a splinter or matchstick. It is then covered with damp moss and wrapped up in plastic, tied at the top and bottom. A kind of propagator is created attached to the plant itself. The air layering is complete when you can see a well-developed root system in the package. The parent stem is then cut just below the roots; the new and improved plant is now ready for potting, and the parent plant begins to grow again.

Plants that form tight clumps, including ivy and many ferns, can be propagated by root division. When breaking the clump of roots be careful to keep the root ball intact as far as possible.

To take a leaf bud cutting remove a section of stem which has a bud nestling in the axil of the leaf as on the *Philodendron* shown here. Plant the stem horizontally just below the surface of the propagating medium. The stem will root and a new plant grow from the bud.

Spider plants send out long runners with baby spider plants at the end. These can be potted directly alongside the parent plant and then separated once they have rooted.

Ivy and other trailing plants can be propagated by pinning down the long tendrils with hairpins or pebbles over a pot of compost. When roots develop the plantlets can be cut free.

105

Woody stemmed plants like *Dracaena* and *Ficus* are suitable for air layering. Make a slanting cut in the stem.

Dust the cut with charcoal powder. The cut must be held open slightly but not allowed to heal, so insert a match in it.

Tie moist sphagnum moss around the cut. Peat fibre can also be used, but this is more difficult to manipulate.

Place a plastic wrapper over the moss and tie it firmly at the top and bottom to retain moisture and make airtight.

In anything from two to nine month's time the new root formation will have appeared, although it might be difficult to see it through the condensation on the plastic. Remove the wrapper taking care not to damage the delicate roots.

With a very sharp knife, cut the plant's stem just below the new root system, thus making two separate plants. It is important to deal with the new plant first because it is far more sensitive and liable to be damaged.

Remove the matchstick and any excess moss. Put the plant in its own pot, being very careful with the young roots. Cover the plant with a polythene bag to create a warm and humid atmosphere which will prevent wilting.

The much reduced parent plant, still in its own pot and compost, will start into new growth. Air layering in effect creates two new plants from one that was possibly overgrown and too top heavy for its own good.

Propagating house plants from seed demands more perseverance and patience than growing from cuttings or bulbs, because you are starting your plant right from the beginning with no short cuts. As a rule it is wise to experiment with the easy plants first, before attempting to produce anything sophisticated. *Coleus* seeds sown in the spring will be flowering six months later, but a specialist might have to wait five years to see if he has produced a really good flowering plant.

Growing from seed is sometimes the only way to obtain a special plant which you cannot find in the shops. It is an inexpensive way to produce a whole batch of young plants which you can give away to your friends and relations. Cuttings give you a miniature version of the parent plant, while with seed propagation each new plant is a new individual, and one packet of geranium seeds can give you single and double flowers and all the variations of colour from white to bright red.

Always buy seeds from a recognized dealer; these will have been developed as a selected strain. Seeds from your own plants will be unlikely to produce good stock. The packet will give you instructions about when and how to sow the seeds, but there are some general rules which can be followed. Most seeds should be sown between early spring and late summer, because the rest of the year is not so good for germination. The

two essential requirements are moisture and warmth, and this must be carefully regulated during the two or three week period when the seeds are germinating. Choose a shallow tray or seed box, and make sure that it has adequate drainage; a soggy soil will kill the seeds. The seed compost must be a sterilized medium, either vermiculite, or some other manufactured preparation. The finest seeds should not be covered with compost at all, and larger ones should have a light covering of seed compost shaken over them through a sieve. Either use a specially heated seed propagator, or choose a warm place like the top of a refrigerator.

The tray needs to be covered with a sheet of glass to keep the moisture level, and since the seeds germinate in the dark they must either be placed in a dark cupboard or covered with a sheet of newspaper to keep out the light. They must be kept in a quiet place where they are not going to be shifted about.

When the seedlings appear, they can be brought out into the light, but not into direct sunlight. At this stage the glass is removed. The seedlings are ready to be transplanted, when they are big enough to be carefully handled and before the second pair of leaves, the *true* leaves, have formed. They can be gently dug out, and either put into separate pots of potting compost, or planted in lines in seed boxes to grow on before the final planting.

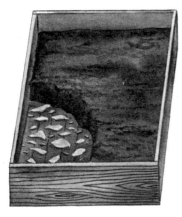

To grow seeds, first clean the plastic or wood seed tray thoroughly. Ensure that it has adequate drainage and cover the bottom of the tray with a layer of broken crocks.

There are many seed composts to choose from. Sterile vermiculite can be added to your compost as a rooting medium or you can use a specially prepared organic mixture.

Water the compost well and drain. Further watering will not be necessary while the seeds germinate. Once the seedlings have appeared, too much water can cause damping or disease.

Make rows in the compost 5 cm (2 in) apart. Scatter the seeds in the rows tapping the seed packet lightly. Sprinkle with a fine layer of compost shaken through a sieve.

Cover the tray with a sheet of glass to retain the humidity level. Protect germinating seeds from the light by placing them in a dark cupboard or covering the glass with a sheet of newspaper.

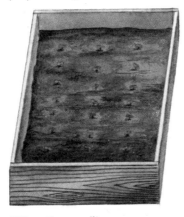

When the seedlings appear bring the tray into the light, but do not expose them to direct sunlight yet. A few days after germination has occurred remove the glass covering from the top of the tray.

Do not disturb the seedlings until the secondary leaves have formed. Then prick out the seedlings holding them very gently by a seed leaf either with the hand or with tweezers.

Plant out the little seedlings either in separate 7·5 cm (3 in) pots or in trays, allowing space of at least 4 cm (1½ in) between each one to prevent overcrowding from occurring as they grow.

What went wrong

This African violet is suffering from overwatering and also from watering in the wrong way. Plants with hairy leaf surfaces should be watered only very carefully from above. Drops of water landing on the leaves cause light patches to appear which can lead to leaf rot. Watering from below prevents this, but care must be taken to do it correctly. This plant has been left standing in a dish of water and as a result the base of the clay pot has become permanently water-logged. Root rot is beginning to set in. The plant is drooping and not as brightly coloured as it should be. To cure the problem allow the plant to dry out for a couple of days and then stand it not straight into a saucer of water but onto a bed of pebbles in water. Within a short time your plant will perk up again.

It is always painfully obvious when a plant has not had any water for a long time and is dying of thirst. In the case of flowering plants such as the *Primula vulgaris* shown here it is the leaves and stems which show signs of collapse first and become too limp to support the flowers. Then the flowers themselves begin to wilt and eventually drop their petals. It will not help to water the plant from above because the root ball has shrunk and the water will simply run down the inside of the pot and out of the drainage holes. Plunge the whole pot into a bucket or basin of water and leave it completely submerged until air bubbles no longer rise to the surface. Drain well before putting the plant back in position. Although a dried out plant can look as if it is beyond help, you will be amazed at how quickly it revives.

Some of the problems that afflict your plant might be due to very subtle mistakes that you have made. Such mistakes can often be easily and gently rectified without any need for drastic action. When a plant looks sick with no obvious cause it is unwise to assume that it has been inflicted with pests or struck down by some dreaded virus. First check whether it is getting the correct amount of water and then look at the lighting. The *Dracaena marginata* shown here is a plant that doesn't need direct sunlight, but will nevertheless suffer if it is left in too sombre a corner of the room. Without sufficient light the spiked leaves begin to droop and the lower ones yellow and eventually fall off. Move the plant nearer to the light source, but not into direct sunlight. The plant will gradually improve and regain full health.

The *Monstera* shown here is a classic case of the large plant in a pot that is too small for it. The roots are compressed into a tight package twining round and round themselves and, if you look at the underside of the pot, you will see the roots escaping and realize at once that the plant is pot-bound. A pot-bound plant is unable to get sufficient nourishment. The tips of the leaves are affected first. They turn a pale, yellow colour. The growth rate of the plant slows down or stops altogether. The plant needs potting on to a larger container. Do not try to force it out of its pot as this will severly damage the roots. If the plant does not slide out easily when turned upside down, break open a clay pot or cut a plastic pot open with sharp secateurs. In its new pot the root system of your plant will soon spread out and the plant will recover its health.

Coleus is one of the group of brightly coloured foliage plants which need about fifteen hours of light a day. Crotons and *Dieffenbachia* also belong to this group. If these plants do not get sufficient light then the distinctive markings on their leaves fade; they become rather drab and unattractive specimens in sharp contrast to their usual flamboyant beauty. Before resorting to feeding the plant or giving it more water do check that it is getting sufficient light. Traditionally these plants belong in a sunny window box or standing in bright array by a window. This tradition was established with good reason and it could be detrimental to your plant if you ignore it.

The leaves of the *Hydrangea* are particularly delicate and need to be treated with care. This plant has been standing in a south-facing window, and its leaves have become scorched through receiving too much direct sunlight. It could also be that it was watered carelessly, so that water falling on the leaves was quickly dried up by the sun's rays. Heat from the sun is much fiercer when reflected through a pane of glass on to water. The brown paper-thin patches and the wilting appearance of the leaves are a clear sign of what is wrong. The immediate action needed is to place the plant in a position where it still gets plenty of light but is not directly in the sun's path. *Hydrangea* can also lose the delicate blue tint on their flowers and take on a faded green colour. The simple remedy for this is to spray special blueing fertilizer directly onto the flowers.

The *Tradescantia* is a succulent plant that stores water in its thick stems for a considerable length of time. It is a resilient plant, which may sometimes be left untouched for many months until it is completely dried out, simply because it is so slow in showing what is wrong. The plant shown has been left without water. Rather than drooping and wilting in the manner of most plants, the stems slowly become thin and shrivelled. Close to the leaf they turn a pale brown colour. The leaves themselves go greenish pink at their tips. It seems to be in a fatal condition. *Tradescantia* is famous for its powers of recuperation. Take cuttings from the most healthy stems with about five or six leaves on each shoot. These will root quickly and easily in ordinary potting mixture and you will soon have several new plantlets.

This *Pelargonium zonale* instead of growing into its usual compact bushy shape has become a tall, straggly and altogether unsightly plant. It has reached the height of roughly 75 cm (2 ft 6 in), which is much too tall for a *Pelargonium*. This plant was left standing on a bright sunny window sill all through the summer. It was watered regularly, but was not given any fertilizer food to make up for the huge energy output needed for vigorous summer growing. As a result it overreached itself and now must be pruned back dramatically. Many people are nervous about pruning their plants. With some types like *Pelargonium*, fuchsia and many other flowering plants, annual pruning is essential for strong healthy growth. This plant should be cut right back to a height of not more than 23 cm (9 in). It will start into new growth and be ready to flower the following year.

Pests and diseases

A pest is any one of the many creeping, crawling, flying and burrowing creatures of various shapes and sizes who consider your treasured house plants as their staple diet and a future home for their myriad children. They are always brought into a house from outside. Perhaps they were present in a new plant given by a friend or bought from a shop, or they may have settled on a plant while it was temporarily outside on a verandah or a window ledge. They could even have made their own way in through an open window.

The larger garden pests rarely ignore a pot plant left outside. They belong to the category of pests called 'chewers', and even if you don't notice a caterpillar or beetle or snail on the plant, it would be hard to miss the great holes or scoops that it has eaten out of the leaves.

Such pests are a problem in a large garden area, but in the house they are easy to see and remove. Trouble occurs when your plant is infested by the tiny and even microscopic insects, that are often only noticed when they have severely damaged your plant. These pests are mostly 'suckers'; they clamp themselves to the selected portion of a stem, leaf or bud and then suck the plant juices. A number of these pests excrete a substance known as honeydew, which leaves a sticky coating on the plant, and often attracts a light black mold to its surface if left undisturbed. Aphids, commonly known as greenfly, and blackfly are the most familiar of this variety. There are however many other pests that attack the plant in even less obvious ways: the first sign of trouble might be when the leaves turn yellow and then brown (red spider mites), or are covered with greyish flecks (thrips), or seem generally sad and unhealthy (root aphids), though this might also be caused by root rot or a virus.

Obviously the best way to control pests is not to allow them near your display of house plants in the first place. This preventative method demands regular attention. When you buy a new plant you should inspect it carefully for any sign of sickness, and leave it in quarantine for a couple of weeks before putting it in with the others. During this period any pests that are around will show themselves. Frequent washing or misting of the leaves with a mild soapy solution is a good idea and you should examine the leaf joints and stems regularly for any signs of habitation. The places which are inaccessible and hard to see are usually just those chosen by pests for egg laying or settling.

Once you have pests, you must take very quick measures to get rid of them. The larger ones can simply be removed by hand or with tweezers, and the smaller ones can be annihilated by swabbing them with a piece of cotton wool soaked in methylated spirits, alcohol or a soap solution. This will rid you of a mild case of attack but won't be sufficient if you're infested by a real blight. The final and most drastic method is the chemical one, which involves spraying infected areas with a specially prepared pesticide or insecticide. This method is attractive because it has such quick and devastating results, but it should be used with caution and discrimination. All pesticides are potentially harmful, especially to children and pets. The instructions must be followed very carefully, and a

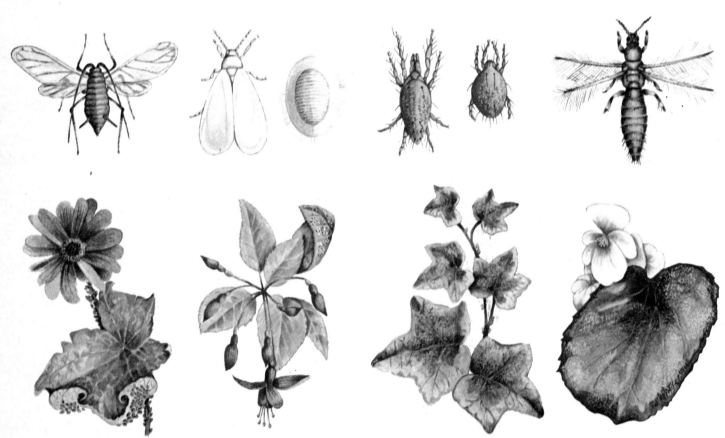

Aphids are green, black or red, winged or wingless. They accumulate on the underside of leaves and young shoots, and attract ants. Wash them off with a soapy solution followed by clear water or use an insecticide.

These tiny white flies settle on the underside of leaves making them mottled and sticky with 'honeydew' which attracts ants. They multiply at a great speed. They and their eggs and larvae should be sprayed with insecticide.

These almost invisible red spider mites appear in hot dry conditions, so regular mistings are a preventative. They suck sap turning the leaves yellow, brown and shrivelled. Rinse in a soap solution or use an insecticide.

Thrips are small, black, flying insects which suck buds, flowers and leaves, leaving a silvery sheen and speckled markings. Shake the plant over paper and the thrips drop onto it. Destroy with soap solution or an insecticide.

spray recommended for one purpose should never be used to deal with another. It's a good idea either to spray pot plants out of doors, or to shield the afflicted plant with a piece of paper, so that the spray is kept away from its neighbours and the furniture.

It can be that your plant is sick, yet has no visible pests on it. Perhaps it has a fungus or rotting disease. Or its leaves may be covered with white, powdery mildew. These conditions are most common outside, and a pot that has been left out all summer, sometimes carries its problems into the house in the winter. It is generally advisable to spray all plants with a mild fungicide before bringing them back in.

Diseases do not hunt for a plant, they are always caused by unhealthy conditions. Roots that are too cramped in a pot may start to rot, and a plant that is in a damp and unventilated place will be liable to develop mildew. Very often a change of position and air will cure a mild fungus or mildew, but it is always necessary to remove the affected areas very quickly, before they spread the disease.

Your plant can be spared from most diseases if you look after it carefully. Regular cleaning of leaves is a good idea, because dirty leaves do collect the spores of fungus. If all attempts to cure a wilting, yellowing and generally sick looking plant fail, then it might be necessary to destroy it. Perhaps it has a virus, which is hard to identify and impossible to treat, or some other unamiable and unseen pest or disease which could endanger your whole collection. Before giving it the final verdict, keep it in quarantine for a couple of weeks.

Grey mold or botrytis attacks the leaves and stems of many indoor plants including the tomato shown here. It is usually caused by too much humidity and inadequate ventilation. Fuzzy grey patches appear and then rot sets in. Remove and destroy the infected parts and spray the whole plant with a fungicide.

Rusts are a powdery mass of orange coloured spores which develop on the leaves and stems of plants such as the geranium shown here. They are often caused by humidity and bad ventilation. To cure the plant, remove and destroy the infected parts and spray with fungicide.

A virus disease can effect some indoor plants including daffodils. The leaves become blotchy and mottled with a yellowish colour. They might also be distorted. The only treatment is to try and save the rest of your collection. The infected plants must be destroyed immediately.

Mildew is a white powdery coating which appears on the leaves and stems of plants such as the chrysanthemum. It is usually the result of too much water and not enough ventilation. Cut away the infected parts, spray the plant with a fungicide and place in a more congenial position.

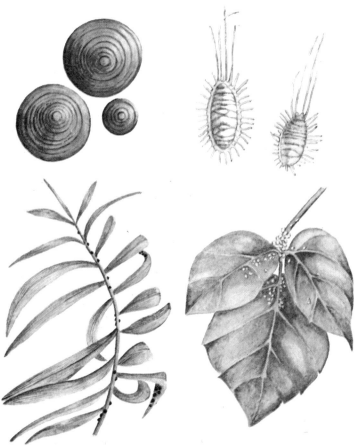

Scale insects attack stems and leaves. They are virtually invisible because of their brown colouring and their immobility. Knock them off the plant with an old toothbrush or swab with cotton wool soaked in alcohol.

Mealy bugs are like specks of cotton. They are easily controlled if checked when they first appear. Remove them with a cotton wool swab dipped in alcohol, or dip the whole plant in a bucket of prepared malathion liquid.

Common garden pests do sometimes appear on house plants, usually carried in on a pot from outside. They are conspicuous for their size and the trail of chewed leaves they leave behind them. Remove them by hand.

111

Dictionary of houseplants

The dictionary of house plants describes the habit and origin of over 200 house plant genera and their most popular species, giving details of how to cultivate them and, where possible, how to propagate them in the home. In most cases the description is accompanied by a photograph of one of the species mentioned. The plants are arranged alphabetically under their latin names within five groupings—foliage plants, ferns, flowering plants, bulbs and corms, cacti and succulents. Common names for genera are given after the latin name. To look up plants under their common name it is necessary to refer to the glossary of common names and index.

Most of the plants grown as house plants came originally from tropical or subtropical regions but the specimens bought by the individual indoor gardener have usually been grown in nurseries. These often represent a hybrid, not found in the wild at all, but developed in cultivation either for particular features or to increase its suitability for room cultivation. The naming of plants reflects both the existing knowledge of plants in their wild state and also their debt to the professional grower. The latin genus name (eg *Ficus, Blechnum, Thunbergia*) refers to a group of plants found in their natural habitat which have several features in common, although they may be scattered over a wide area of the earth's surface. For example the genus *Blechnum* is found throughout the floristic realms of the world while *Ficus* is found in Africa and the East Indies, and *Thunbergia* is restricted to the Neotropical realm of Central and South America. Within the genus particular species, distinguished according to their characteristic structure, are given a second latin name. *Ficus elastica* has a single straight trunk and large ovate glossy green leaves; *Ficus deltoidea* has smaller rounded leaves and a branching structure. Occasionally a third name is given preceded by the abbreviation *var.* which indicates that this is a naturally occurring variety of the original species. More commonly a third name indicates a hybrid which has been produced in cultivation, for example, *Dieffenbachia picta* 'Exotica'. The third name is called the cultivar and is always printed in Roman and placed between quotes.

Foliage plants

Foliage plants make the most popular indoor plants, outnumbering flowering plants by about ten to one. Given the right treatment they can become permanent room features with the added advantage that they look good all year round. The most successful house plants are evergreens, which have a growing season and a dormant season but never lose their leaves. Many are semi-shade lovers, making them adaptable for room decoration and in addition slow growers so that there is little danger of them getting too large for a room too quickly. Above all foliage plants are valued for their robustness and their ability to survive in normal interiors.

Perhaps the most striking feature of the foliage plants now available is their variety. Whereas previously *Aspidistra*, palms or *Ficus* have all had their special periods of fashion, advanced methods of transporting plants and breeding them in nurseries to create hybrids suitable for room cultivation have made a much larger range of plants widely available. At the same time changes in house design which ensure a higher light level in room interiors have helped to ensure that the average plant buyer has a wider choice. Many foliage plants, among them the old favourites mentioned above, are extremely easy to grow. But others like *Dizygotheca* require spraying to maintain a high level of humidity or like *Fittonia* survive best in a plant window or terrarium. One group, the ferns, are discussed in their own section.

Aechmea rhodocyanea

Aechmea

This beautiful member of the Bromeliad family grows as an epiphyte in the rain forests of Central and South America. The star-shaped rosette of leaves surrounds the central cup from which the plant takes water. *Aechmea rhodocyanea* has a large rosette of leaves 60 cm (2 ft) in length with grey-green transverse stripes and a central inflorescence composed of pale pink, spiny bracts and small, mauve flowers. *A. fulgens var. discolor*, which is slightly more difficult to grow, has thinner, olive-green, sword-shaped leaves 30 cm (1 ft) long with purple undersides. The flowers are purple and the bracts and flower stem bright scarlet.

Light and situation: a good light without direct sunlight indoors or in a plant window.
Temperature: warm, 16–24°C (60–75°F).
Moisture: pour water into the central funnel in summer and keep the root ball moist at all times, spraying on very hot days. Empty the central funnel in the dormant period unless the temperature exceeds 20°C (68°F).
Soil: equal parts loam, leaf mould, peat and sand.
Propagation: remove young rosettes with some roots of the parent plant when they have reached half its size. Pour water into the central funnels two weeks before doing so.

Aglaonema
Chinese evergreen

This genus of small herbaceous perennials with leathery, usually variegated leaves comes from the Malay Archipelago and the islands of the Pacific and Indian Oceans. *A. crispum* has large, pointed oval leaves, mainly silver with dark green streaks and is often sold under the name 'Silver Queen'.

Light and situation: a roomy position in a tropical plant window.
Temperature: warm.
Moisture: water freely in the growing period; more sparingly in winter. Use tepid, softened water.
Soil: a loam-based compost.
Propagation: by division of mature plants or by stem-tip cuttings in an indoor propagator.

Aglaonema crispum

Ampelopsis

Many species of this genus of trailing or climbing plants (often sold as *Vitis* because it is a member of the vine family) are well suited to home cultivation since they are insensitive to a warm, dry, living-room atmosphere in winter. *A. brevipedunculata*, however, a beautiful, variegated form, requires a cool winter. It is ideal for trailing around columns or screens in an unheated part of the house or in a conservatory. The leaves are white, green and pink and the stems tinged with red.

Light and situation: a half shady position without direct sunlight.
Temperature: warm in summer; warm or cool in winter according to the species.
Moisture: keep moist in the growing period; water more sparingly in winter.
Soil: a loam-based compost.

Ananas comosus
Pineapple

Ananas comosus, the pineapple, has thorny leaves up to 1.2 m (4 ft) in length growing in a rosette about 60 cm (2 ft) in diameter. The purple flowers appear among a sheaf of bracts and are followed by the edible fruit. Dwarf forms are now widely cultivated as

Ampelopsis brevipedunculata

pot plants. The flowers are small and, together with the spiny bracts among which they grow, form a thick-set central spike. *A.c.* 'Variegatus' has attractive narrow leaves with a clear green central stripe and creamy edges. It grows to 60 cm (2 ft) across.

Light and situation: a good light with some shade in summer.
Temperature: warm.
Moisture: water well; maintain a humid atmosphere.
Soil: a loam-based compost.

Anthurium crystallinum

Propagation: from newly formed rosettes.

Anthurium
Flame plant, flamingo flower, flamingo plant

This genus, usually grown for its flowers, includes one species, *A.crystallinum,* grown for its decorative foliage. The leaves are heart-shaped and a velvety green with silver ribs.

Light and situation: in a tropical plant window.

Temperature: a steady 18–20°C (64–68°F).
Moisture: maintain a high degree of atmospheric humidity.
Soil: a peat and sphagnum moss mixture.

Aphelandra squarrosa
Zebra plant

Aphelandra squarrosa is an evergreen plant about 30 cm (1 ft) in height with broad, glossy, dark green leaves with white or yellow veining. The inflorescence, which appears in winter in terminal spikes, consists of small, yellow tubular flowers which emerge from a multi-faceted column of brilliant yellow bracts. *A.s.*

Ananas comosus 'Variegatus'

Aphelandra squarrosa 'Louisiae'

'Louisiae', a low-growing hybrid, makes a particularly good pot plant. Its yellow flowers are carried on red stems. Remove dead flowers with a pair of leaves.

Light and situation: a good light without direct sunlight.
Temperature: warm.
Moisture: water very generously in the growing and flowering periods, spraying every few days. Water more sparingly after flowering. Use Soil: a rich humus-based compost.
Special points: cut back hard after flowering and repot in spring before the plant starts into growth. Take cuttings from new shoots in spring.

G. Smith
Zebra.   Take 1½ in stem with two leaves - split down middle and insert in sandy potting compost.

Araucaria
Norfolk Island pine

An evergreen coniferous tree from eastern Australia and New Caledonia, *Araucaria excelsa* reaches over 60 m (200 ft) in its natural habitat but will grow as a pot plant up to 1m (3 ft) high for many years. The needle-like leaves closely follow the shape of the trunk and branches creating a light, feathery appearance and the sheaves of foliage grow at right-angles to the trunk like those of a cedar.

Light and situation: a well ventilated position from spring until autumn, near a north-facing window and away from other plants. Shade from the hottest sun.
Temperature: cool; in winter 5–10°C (41–50°F).
Moisture: water moderately in summer; hardly at all in winter. Use lukewarm softened water.
Soil: a loam-based compost.
Propagation: from seed in autumn or spring.

Araucaria excelsa

Asparagus

The *Asparagus* is a foliage plant whose fine stems are covered with needle-like 'leaves', strictly phyllocades. *A. densiflorus* does not flower and has relatively widely spaced, slightly glossy 'leaves'. *A. setaceus* (syn. *A. plumosus*) has finer, much divided 'leaves' growing at right-angles to the stems creating a flat sheaf of feathery foliage. The plant produces red berries when young and after several years becomes a climber. *A.s.* 'Nanus' is the most commonly grown cultivar. It is smaller than the original species and has denser fonds.

Light and situation: a good light.
Temperature: warm. *A. setaceus* requires a resting period in winter at 8–10°C (46–50°F).
Moisture: water moderately throughout the year with softened water taking care not to let the root ball dry out.
Soil: a loam-based compost.
Propagation: from seed or by division in spring.

Asparagus setaceus

Aspidistra
Cast-iron plant

This adaptable evergreen foliage plant grown for its broad, glossy, dark green leaves comes from the mountains of Japan. It will tolerate a wide range of temperature, light and humidity and is standard decoration in parlours, restaurants, hotel foyers and shops.
Light and situation: shady.

Temperature: cool.
Moisture: water moderately and maintain a humid atmosphere. Avoid excess water in the bottom of the pot.
Soil: a loam-based compost.
Propagation: by division in spring or summer.

Aspidistra elatior

up to 30 cm (1 ft) long ranging in colour according to strain from metallic silver and pink to rich crimson purple, green and dark brown. 'La Pasqual' has enormous, nearly black leaves with a silver and purple stripe and purple undersides; 'King Henry' has a dark centre, a stripe of silver, a band of dark green with silver spots and a purple edge; 'Silver Queen' has silvery leaves with purple undersides. *Begonia masoniana* has pale green leaves, deeply textured with a brown cross in the centre which gives the plant its name of 'Iron Cross'. *B.*

manicata has leaves covered in red scales on their upper surface and frilled edges.

Light and situation: a shady position in a north-facing room.
Temperature: moderate; 15–20°C (60–68°F) in winter.
Moisture: water generously with tepid, softened water in the growing period; slightly less after flowering. Spray occasionally but do not allow drops of water to fall on the leaves.
Soil: a peat-based compost. Use shallow, wide pots.
Propagation: from leaf cuttings in summer.

Aucuba japonica

Aucuba japonica

Aucuba japonica, a hardy, evergreen shrub from Japan which reaches 2 m (6 ft), has slightly dentate, pointed elliptical leaves, leathery and dark green in colour. The cultivars 'Variegata' and 'Maculata' are flecked with yellow and develop attractive red berries.

Light and situation: a shady situation in a showroom or on a staircase landing.
Temperature: cool; 4–6°C (40–43°F) in winter or slightly higher.
Moisture: water moderately in summer; sparingly in winter.
Soil: a loam-based compost.
Propagation: by cuttings or from seed.

Begonia

In its wild state this forest plant is found in the subtropical regions of the world, for example, in the foothills of the Himalayas. Flowering and shrubby begonias are covered under 'Flowering plants' though many shrubby forms may also be grown for their foliage. Among foliage

begonias the best known is *Begonia rex* and its hybrids which have succulent stems and asymmetrical, ovoid leaves

(above and below) A selection of *Begonia rex* hybrids

below for starting into growth.
Moisture: in spring and
summer water generously;
more sparingly from late
summer onwards until the
leaves shrivel.
Overwintering: dry the plant
out. Start into growth again
after repotting one to three
tubers to a pot in spring. The
plant should be given a warm
situation, 24–26°C (76–79°F),
and kept damp. When the
leaves have sprouted move to
a slightly cooler place.
Soil: a rich, humusy mixture.
Propagation: from small offsets which can be removed
once they have put out their
own leaves.

Caladium

Caladium, a genus from
tropical South America, is
with *Begonia rex*, *Coleus* and
Dracaena among the most
spectacular and best known
decorative foliage plants. The
large, arrow-head-shaped
leaves hang delicately on long
stems and are of a papery
texture varying in colour from
pale tints of cream and green
to pink or crimson. In
most cases the patterning on
the leaves follows the leaf
veining and spreads outward
from the centre. The many
varieties available are largely
the hybrids of two particular
species, *C. bicolor* and
C. schomburgkii.

Light and situation: a shady
position in a tropical plant
window.
Temperature: warm; 21–24°C
(70–75°F) in spring and
summer; overwinter tubers
at 18–20°C (64–68°F); see

(above and below) A number of *Caladium* hybrids

(right) *Calathea makoyana*

Calathea

Calathea, a genus of shrub
with variegated foliage related
to the *Maranta*, has 150
species occurring in their
natural state mainly in the
islands of the Indian Ocean
and the Malay Archipelago.
The long, narrow, spear-
shaped leaves grow directly
from the roots with markings
in several shades of green. *C.
backemiana* has pale green
leaves with dark green bands.
C. lancifolia has leaves with
scolloped edges and delicate,
oval spots of a darker green
on the upper surface. The
undersides are deep maroon
in colour and the plant may
reach 60 cm (2 ft). *Calathea*

makoyana, the peacock plant, has silvery green leaves with splashes of a deeper green radiating from the central vein. The patterning is repeated beneath the leaves in maroon.

Light and situation: a shady position in a tropical plant window.
Temperature: warm; in winter 16–18°C (60–64°F).
Moisture: maintain a high degree of atmospheric humidity in spring and summer.
Soil: a loam-based compost.
Propagation: by division in early summer. Place new plants in small pots.

Callisia

This creeping foliage plant resembles the *Tradescantia* to which it is related. It has bright green leaves striped with white on the upper side and reddish-purple below which fold round the stem at their base.

Care: as for *Tradescantia*.

Carex
Sedge

Carex, a genus of foliage plant with over 1000 species, grows in the wild in an enormous range of habitat. It has stiff, grass-like, often glossy leaves growing in tufts. *C. morrowii* 'Variegata' has leaves with fine white stripes which grow

(above) *Callisia elegans*

in a fountain-like swathe 20–30 cm (8–12 in) high.

Light and situation: a well ventilated position shaded from the hottest sun.
Temperature: moderate or cool; 8–16°C (46–60°F) in winter.
Moisture: keep moist but not too wet.
Soil: a loam-based compost.
Propagation: by division or from seed in spring. Seeds will produce all green plants.

(right) *Carex morrowii* 'Variegata'

119

Chamaedorea elegans

position outside in summer if possible.
Temperature: warm in summer; very cool in winter, 4°C (40°F).
Moisture: water well in summer; very sparingly in winter.
Soil: a loam-based compost.
Propagation: by suckers taken from the base of the plant in summer.

Chlorophytum comosum
Spider plant

Chlorophytum comosum is a decorative vigorous creeping and trailing plant from South Africa and one of the least demanding of house plants. It has narrow, strap-like, curving leaves 20–40 cm (8–16 in) long and trailing flower stems from which grow the rosettes of young plants. *C. comosum* is plain green. Its cultivar *C.c.* 'Variegatum' has finely striped green and white leaves.

Light, situation and temperature: this plant tolerates a wide range of light and temperature.
Moisture: water freely in the growing period; less in winter depending on the temperature.
Soil: use a somewhat loamy mixture or grow in soilless cultivation.
Propagation: by removing young plants or by division.

Chamaedorea

This genus of small palms from Central and South America has in most species neatly paired stemless leaflets growing on either side of the tubular stems, thus creating the familiar palm frond. *C. elegans* (also sold as *Neanthe bella*) grows to 1.2 m (4 ft) and has fine, narrow, leathery leaves 13 cm (5 in) long and tapering at both ends. It is an ideal house plant. *C. tenella* is a smaller species usually growing to 80 cm (32 in.)

Light and situation: a good light without direct sunlight.
Temperature: moderate in summer; cool in winter, 12–14°C (54–57°F).
Moisture: water freely in summer, spraying on warm days; water sparingly in winter. Use softened water.
Soil: a loam-based compost.
Propagation: from seeds sown in spring at a soil temperature of 24–26°C (75–79°F). Sow in threes and prick out with care to avoid damaging the delicate roots.

Chamaerops humilis
European fan palm

This species of palm from the temperate regions of Europe and Asia is sold small as a house plant. The 45 cm (18 in) semi-circular, fan-shaped leaves are divided at the base into many fine segments and carried on 1–1.2 m (3–4 ft) stalks.

Light and situation: a well-lit

Chrysalidocarpus lutescens
Areca palm, butterfly palm

This delicate palm from Mauritius and the tropics has feathery foliage composed of leaves divided into a fan of long, narrow, pinnate leaflets. It can grow to 6 m (20 ft) but young plants make good pot plants 1.2–2.5 m (4–8 ft) tall.

Light and situation: a slightly shady position.
Temperature: very warm: a daytime temperature of 24–29°C (75–84°F); a night-time temperature of 16°C (60°F).
Moisture: water well and maintain a humid atmosphere.
Soil: a loam-based compost.
Propagation: from seeds in spring or when ripe.

Chamaerops humilis 'Elegans'

Cissus

This large, varied genus of tropical plants can be roughly divided into the rare, succulent species cultivated for their unusual forms and the more woody, climbing species which are most frequently used as house plants. *C. antarctica* is a climber with pointed, slightly dentate, glossy leaves.

C. discolor is a climbing plant with red stems and long arrow-shaped leaves marbled in green and white with brilliant mauvy-red veins and edges and a red underside. This erect shrub is best suited to a tropical plant window.

C. antarctica
Light and situation: a well-lit

Cissus antarctica

Chlorophytum comosum 'Variegatum'

but not sunny position indoors.
Temperature: a wide range of temperature is tolerated—12–24°C (54–75°F).
Moisture: water moderately and avoid excess water in the bottom of the pot.
Soil: a loam-based compost (avoid peat-based mixtures).
Propagation: from cuttings 3–5 cm (1–2 in) in a special compost with a soil temperature of 25–30°C (77–86°F). This is best done in an indoor propagator.
Special points: repot yearly retaining the old soil and allowing the plant adequate drainage.

Keep stem to act as anchor

Citrus

This genus of evergreen shrubs and small trees from East Asia includes the well-known commercial fruits oranges, lemons and grapefruit. Young plants make good house plants but will usually require a greenhouse to flower and bear fruit. The fine, glossy, dark green leaves

are pointed oval in shape and are borne on woody stems. *C. mitis*, the Calomondin orange, is the species most commonly grown as a house plant. The leaves are 5 cm (2 in) in length and a narrow oval. The plant flowers fairly easily when small producing white flowers which appear almost all the year round.

Light and situation: a good light, outside in summer if possible.
Temperature: warm in summer; cool in winter, not above 4–6°C (40–43°F).
Moisture: water freely in summer; keep the root ball just moist in autumn and winter.
Soil: a loam-based compost.
Propagation: from seeds in spring (see House plants for Children, p. 224).

(below) *Citrus mitis*

Cleyera japonica

Cleyera japonica comes like the *Camellia*, to which it is related, from East Asia. It is a small, evergreen, slow-growing shrub which reaches 1 m (3 ft) as a pot plant and has fine, glossy, pointed oval leaves 6–8 cm (2½–3 in) long. *C. j.* 'Tricolor' is a variegated form with an uneven border of creamy yellow and two shades of green.

Light and situation: a semi-shady position outside in summer if preferred.
Temperature: cool; in winter 10–12°C (50–54°F).
Moisture: keep the soil moist throughout the year using softened water. Spray the foliage occasionally to remove dust.
Soil: a loam-based compost.

(right) *Cleyera japonica* 'Tricolor'

Codiaeum
Croton

Codiaeum, a handsome evergreen with variegated leaves in a range of shapes and patterning, came originally from Polynesia. Most strains are marbled, veined or spotted in shades of green, red, white, pink, yellow and brown. The hybrids in cultivation are referred to as *C. variegatum var. pictum*. *C. v. p.* 'Disraeli' has yellow patches on the upper surface of the leaves and red undersides. *C. v.p.* 'Volcano' has large oval pointed leaves suffused with yellow when young and gradually turning pink.

Light and situation: a good light without direct sunlight.
Temperature: an even air and soil temperature; 16–18°C (60–64°F) in winter.
Moisture: keep moist in spring and summer; water more sparingly from autumn onwards. Do not allow the root ball to dry out and spray occasionally if the air is dry.
Soil: a loam-based compost.

(left) *Codiaeum variegatum var. pictum* hybrids

Coffea arabica
Arabian coffee

Coffea arabica, one of the smaller species of a genus of shrubs and trees from the tropical regions of Africa, will reach 3 m (10 ft) in a botanical garden and 2 m (6 ft) as a pot plant. Indoor plants are usually 60–80 cm (24–32 in) tall and bear mid green, very glossy, wavy leaves in opposing pairs along the stems. The dwarf form 'Nana' is also cultivated as a house plant.

Light and situation: a half-shady position out of bright sunlight with slightly more light in winter.
Temperature: warm; cooler in winter, 15–20°C (59–68°F); a soil temperature of not below 16°C (60°F).
Moisture: spray occasionally in summer and water freely but avoid leaving excess water in the pot; water sparingly in winter but do not allow the root ball to dry out. Use softened water.

Soil: a loam-based compost.
Propagation: from seed in spring or cuttings of side-shoots with a heel in late summer.

Coleus

Coleus is a genus of remarkably beautiful shrubs from Asia and Africa grown for their foliage or flowers. The latter species are described in the flowering section. *C. blumei* hybrids, the types most renowned for their foliage, vary in the colour of their leaves through combinations of yellow, red, green and dark brown. The colours suffuse the leaves spreading from the centre outwards and often picking out the veins and stippling the edges. The plants are usually bought in spring and thrown away when the leaves die down although they may be overwintered if kept in a warm and light position. Pinch out the flowers in summer to ensure a good shape. The best

colours are only achieved in a good light and lack of light causes the foliage to revert to green.

Light and situation: a light situation, eg on a sunny *)No* window sill but shaded from the hottest sun.
Temperature: warm.
Moisture: water freely in spring and summer, spraying frequently on warm days. Use softened water.
Soil: a lime-free compost.
Propagation: from seed in spring, or from stem-tip cuttings in spring or late summer. Root the cuttings in a mixture of sharp sand and peat fibre or place in water in a dark bottle.

C Smith says loam based: keep them hungry. Allow to get pot bound

(left) *Coffea arabica*

(below) *Coleus blumei* hybrids

Cordyline
Cabbage palm

Cordyline is a varied genus of small shrubs or trees from South East Asia and Australia. *C. australis* has long, narrow, pointed leaves which grow in a fountain shape and are dark green or variegated. Older plants may grow so large that they are suitable only for large, high-ceilinged rooms or for offices. *C. terminalis* has broad, glossy, pointed oval leaves in a dramatic range of colours. Those with red patterning are suitable for room cultivation. *C.t.* 'Firebrand' has mid green leaves loosely edged with brilliant red. *C.t.* 'Tricolor' has striking leaves in a combination of crimson pink, cream and dark green.

Care: as for *Dracaena*.

(above) *Cordyline terminalis*

umbrella plant, which has many dark green stems up to 80 cm (32 in) in height, each topped with a group of long, leaf-like bracts radiating outwards at right angles like the spines of an umbrella. The greenish-white flowers grow in a rosette above the bracts. *C. argenteostriatus* is a dwarf species which does not grow beyond 30 cm (1 ft). It is in general more compact with broader, tapering leaves.

Light and situation: a fairly well-lit position.
Temperature: the plant tolerates a temperature range of 10–12°C (50–54°F) to 20°C (68°F). It prefers the cooler temperatures in winter, however.
Moisture: place in a water-filled bowl or saucer.
Soil: a mixture of clay or loam with leaf mould and some manure or blood meal.
Propagation: by division in spring or from young shoot tips cut to 5 cm (2 in) with shortened leaves and rooted in sand.
Special points: because it grows rapidly this plant should normally be repotted once a year.

Cyperus argenteostriatus

(above) A variegated *Cryptanthus*

Cryptanthus

Cryptanthus, an evergreen belonging to the Bromeliad family, comes from South America. The sharply pointed, usually variegated leaves are borne in a slightly flattened rosette. *C. bivittatus* has wavy leaves up to 23 cm (9 in) long with a mid green central stripe on an olive green background tinged with pink. *C. zonatus*, the zebra plant, has 15–23 cm (6–9 in) waxy, scaly leaves with veneer-like, toothed transverse bands in coppery brown and grey above with silver-grey colouring beneath.

Cyperus
Galingale, umbrella plant

This genus of grass-like plants which includes the papyrus and the ground nut occurs in the wild in tropical, subtropical and temperate regions. The species most often cultivated as a house plant is *C. alternifolius*, the

Both species come from Brazil.

Light and situation: a good light without bright sunlight.
Temperature: warm; in winter 20–22°C (68–72°F) for the variegated forms mentioned. Other species will tolerate slightly lower temperatures.
Moisture: water very sparingly but do not allow the root ball to dry out.
Soil: a peat-based compost.
Propagation: from small plants produced in the axils of the rosettes. When large enough these will detach themselves and should be potted in very shallow bowls.

124

Dizygotheca
False aralia, spider aralia

Dizygotheca, an elegant tropical shrub from the New Hebrides, has delicate leaves divided into 7–10 radiating leaflets. In the case of *D. elegantissima*, which may grow to 1.2m (4 ft) the leaflets are deeply indented to give an arrowed effect. *D. veitchii* 'Gracillima' grows to 60 cm (2 ft) and has spear-shaped, slightly wavy leaflets which create the appearance of an open hand.

Light and situation: a good light without direct sunlight preferably near other plants to maintain humidity.
Temperature: warm; not below 15°C (59°F) with a constant soil temperature of 18–20°C (64–68°F).
Moisture: water moderately in the growing period, spraying frequently; more sparingly in autumn and winter taking care that the root ball does not dry out. Use softened water and maintain a high degree of atmospheric humidity.
Soil: a loam-based compost.
Propagation: from seed in early spring.
Special points: pinch out new shoots in the dormant period.

(above) *Dizygotheca elegantissima*

Dieffenbachia
Dumb cane

Dieffenbachia is a robust, slow-growing, evergreen shrub from tropical America with clusters of large, ovate, variegated leaves growing from thick, somewhat fleshy stems. Mature plants may reach 2 m (6 ft) in a green-house border. Young plants will grow to 1 m (3 ft) as pot plants in the house. *D. amoena* has dark green leaves touched with white and pale yellow. *D. bowmanni*, the largest species, has dark green leaves up to 75 cm (30 in) long flecked with a paler green. *D. picta* has 25 cm (10 in) blunt oval leaves with creamy white markings leaving the veins and margins green. *D. p.* 'Exotica' has liberal pale yellow markings on dark green background; 'Superba' thick, glossy leaves flecked with white.

Light and situation: a draught-free, slightly shady situation out of direct sunlight.
Temperature: warm; not

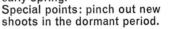

(above) *Cyperus alternifolius*

below 15–18°C (58–64°F) in winter.
Moisture: water generously in the growing period and maintain a humid atmosphere using tepid softened water. Water sparingly in autumn and winter and spray occasionally or rinse the leaves with lukewarm water.
Soil: use a rich, friable compost.
Pruning and propagation: cut back plants which have lost their lower foliage to 10 cm (4 in) above the soil. Propagate in an indoor propagator from cuttings with 2–4 leaves at a soil temperature of 24–26°C (75–79°F), providing plenty of moisture.

Dieffenbachia picta 'Exotica'

125

Dracaena deremensis

Dracaena hybrid

Euonymus japonicus

This hardy shrub from Japan will grow to 2 m (6 ft) as a pot plant. The leaves, which grow on branching stems, are leathery, glossy and oval, resembling those of the laurel but slightly softer. *E. j.* 'Microphyllus' has small, green and yellow or green and white, variegated leaves. *E. j.* 'President Gauthier' is a white-variegated form and 'Ovatus Aureus' has dark green leaves with yellow edges in an irregular oval shape.

Light and situation: a good light and a well ventilated position away from other plants.
Temperature: cool; in winter 4–6°C (40–43°F).
Moisture: water freely in summer; more sparingly from autumn onwards. Rinse the leaves in spring to remove dust.
Soil: a loam-based compost.
Propagation: green varieties can be propagated from shoot tips in spring.
Special points: cut back well in spring. Repot young plants yearly at the same time.

× Fatshedera
Ivy tree, tree ivy

× *Fatshedera* is a cross, or hybrid, between *Fatsia* and *Hedera* (ivy) made in 1912 which as × *Fatshedera lizei* has become one of the most popular foliage house plants. A tall, hardy shrub it has dark green, shiny, hand-shaped leaves up to 20 cm (8 in) wide with three or five pointed

Dracaena

This large genus of tree- or palm-like plants, usually with arching groups of lance-shaped leaves, growing in rosettes one above the other includes some of the most elegant plants for the living room. *D. deremensis* 'Warneckii' has a mass of slender, pointed leaves striped green, silver and grey; *D. fragrans* has broader leaves up to 50–70 cm (20–28 in) long, striped gold and green and curving downwards in a long arc. *D. marginata* has the narrowest leaves of all—a grass-like fountain striped green, cream and pink. *D. godseffiana*, the gold dust Dracaena, is a freely branching plant with laurel-like leaves flecked with yellow.

Light and situation: buy the plant in spring and place near a window with central heating. Protect from the hottest sun.
Moisture: water moderately in summer; more sparingly in winter. Avoid having excess water in the pot or allowing the root ball to dry out.
Soil: a rich, porous, humusy mixture.
Propagation: from suckers or 8 cm (3 in) stem sections in an indoor propagator in spring or summer.
Special points: repot young plants yearly in late spring.

Euonymus japonicus hybrid

lobes. It will reach 2 m (6 ft) if given some support. 'Variegata' has leaves with creamy white margins.

Care: as for *Fatsia*.
Special points: cut back slightly each year to encourage a bushy growth.

Fatsia japonica
False castor oil plant, Japanese aralia

This hardy plant, growing to to 5 m (16½ ft) in its native Japan, is an ideal house plant and will reach 1 m (3 ft) in a living room. It has glossy, leathery green leaves with seven or nine pointed lobes

× *Fatshedera lizei*
growing on stems up to 40 cm (16 in) tall.

Light and situation: a well ventilated, draught-free position in a good light near a north-facing window. Remove to a shady position out of doors in summer if possible.
Temperature: cool; 6–8°C (43–46°F) in winter.
Moisture: water freely during the growing period; less from autumn onwards. Avoid excess water in the pot or allowing the root ball to dry out.
Soil: a loam-based compost.
Propagation: raise from seed in an indoor propagator.

Ficus
Fig

Ficus is a very large genus of trees, epiphytic shrubs and climbers which have in common the milky white liquid that once made *F. elastica*, the rubber plant, of some economic importance. Of the erect species those most commonly grown in the home are *F. benjamina*, *F. deltoidea* (*F. diversifolia*) and *F. elastica*. *F. benjamina* has small, pointed oval leaves and a pale grey 'trunk' with

(below) *Fatsia japonica*

delicate arching branches giving it the name weeping fig. *F. deltoidea*, a smaller plant with small, leathery leaves, rounded in shape and held horizontally, and yellow berries, grows to 60–80 cm (24–32 in). *F. elastica*, the rubber plant, has a single perfectly straight stem and large, glossy, pointed oval, leathery leaves. It is a fast grower, reaching 3 m (10 ft) as a pot plant but if cut back can also be trained as a climber *F. elastica* 'Decora' has more rounded leaves and *F. e.* 'Variegata' has variegated foliage with drooping, elongated oval leaves. The creeping varieties include *F. pumila*, a small plant irregular, dark leaves not unlike an ivy, which can be used as a trailing or hanging plant or trained as a climber, and *F. radicans* which has larger, pointed oval leaves. The latter has extremely beautiful white and green variegated forms including *F.r.* 'Variegata'.

Light and situation: a well ventilated, well-lit position out of direct sunlight.
Temperature: moderate; 12–15°C (54–59°F) in winter.
Moisture: water freely in the growing period; more sparingly from autumn onwards. In winter keep only just moist.
Soil: a mixture of sand

and peat fibre.
Propagation: from eye cuttings in an indoor propagator at a temperature of 25–35°C (77–95°F).
Special points: Clean the upper surfaces of the leaves regularly with damp cotton wool.

(above) *Ficus deltoidea*

(right) *Ficus elastica*

(above) *Fittonia argyroneura*   (right) *Grevillea robusta*

Fittonia

These low-growing, creeping plants whose rounded leaves have a netted appearance because of their many conspicuous white or pink veins come from Peru. *F. verschaffeltii* has carmine red veins. *F. argyroneura* (considered by some a variety of the former) has silver veins. These plants are ideal for bottle gardens.

Light and situation: in a bottle garden or tropical plant window with a good light but without direct sunlight.
Temperature: warm, 18–20°C (64–68°F).
Moisture: keep moist from spring until autumn; water more sparingly in winter. Maintain a humid atmosphere and use softened water.
Soil: a proprietary peat compost.
Propagation: by division in summer or from cuttings in an indoor propagator in spring or summer.

Grevillea robusta
Silk oak, silk bark oak

Grevillea robusta, an evergreen shrub from New South Wales with feathery foliage, will usually grow to 1–2 m (3–6 ft) as a pot plant but can reach 3 m (10 ft). The finely

divided, mid green leaves, 45 cm (18 in) long, darken as they mature.

Light and situation: a half shady position in summer with more light in winter.
Temperature: cool: 6–10°C (43–50°F).
Moisture: water moderately.
Soil: a loam-based compost.
Propagation: from seed or cuttings of sideshoots in spring or late summer.

Guzmania

Guzmania is a bromeliad genus from Central and South America which like *Neoregelia* produces a brilliantly coloured central group of bracts when in flower. The leaves grow in the typical bromeliad rosette around a water-holding cup. *G. lingulata* has 45 cm (18 in) green, lance-shaped leaves suffused with purplish-red and produces a 30 cm (12 in) tall central flower spike of red bracts topped by yellow flowers. *G. monostachya* has a large rosette of light green leaves from which rises a 38 cm (15 in) flower stem carrying the small white flowers in crimson bracts.

Light and situation: a shady position in a tropical plant window.
Temperature: warm and

constant in summer; not below 16–18°C (60–64°F) in winter.
Moisture: pour water into the central cup in spring and summer and spray frequently. After flowering pour off the

Guzmania monostachya

water and keep just moist.
Soil: a mixture of peat and sphagnum moss.
Propagation: from offsets in summer.

Gynura
Velvet plant

Gynura aurantiaca, a semi-climbing shrub from East Asia growing to 1 m (3 ft), has long, pointed, dentate leaves covered with bright purple hairs giving the plant a velvety sheen. *G. sarmentosa* (considered by some a variety of the former) is a climbing plant of similar appearance requiring training on wires or canes.

Light and situation: a sunny position.
Temperature: warm.
Moisture: water freely in summer; more sparingly in winter.
Soil: a loam-based compost.
Propagation: from cuttings in autumn.
Special points: pinch out young flowering stems.

(right) *Gynura sarmentosa*

Hedera
Ivy

Hedera is a well-known genus of evergreen climbers, all of them hardy, with three- or five-lobed, undivided leaves and adhesive, aerial roots which enable them to cling to vertical walls. They can be used as hanging plants, trained on wires or canes as pot plants, or given a trellis or wall on which to climb. *Hedera helix* is the major species with glossy, dark green leaves up to 8 cm (3 in) across. The number of strains available for indoor cultivation is constantly changing. These include *Hedera helix* 'Pittsburg', a small form whose dark leaves have lighter green veins. A variegated type is also available with yellow-edged leaves. The leaf shape of both is a delicate triangle or five-pointed star. *H.h.* 'Golden Heart' has small leaves with golden yellow centres and a very dark green edge. *H.h. ssp. canariensis* has slightly lighter green, glossy foliage with leaves 13–20 cm (5–8 in) across. *H.h. ssp.c.* 'Gloire de Marengo' has very decorative leaves marbeled in green and cream.

Light and situation: allow to grow undisturbed in a half shady situation. Variegated forms are susceptible to direct sunlight but all forms will grow spindly if given too little light.
Temperature: moderate in summer; cool in winter (eg in an unheated room).
Moisture: keep moist in the growing period but avoid excess water in the pot; water more sparingly in winter.
Soil: a not too acid, loam mixture with some leaf mould and manure or blood meal.
Propagation: from cuttings ideally in autumn. Keep under glass or plastic at a soil temperature of 20°C (68°F) until well rooted.
Special points: ivy should be repotted once a year.

This group of *Hedera* shows some of the range of leaf shape, size and colour found in this varied genus.

Helxine
Mind-your-own-business,
baby's tears

This genus has only one
species, *Helxine soleirolii*
(*Soleirolia soleirolii*), a
creeping plant ideal for
ground cover or for hanging
baskets. The pink stems root
as they grow and the mass of
small round leaves are pale
green. *H. s.* 'Argentea' has
silver patterned leaves.

Light and situation: a good
light without direct sunlight.
Temperature: moderate in
summer; cool in winter, 4–7°C
(40–45°F).
Moisture: water freely in
spring and summer; more
sparingly in winter.
Soil: a loam-based compost.
Propagation: from rooted
stems in early summer.

Helxine soleirolii 'Aurea'

Hypoestes

Two species of this shrub
from Madagascar are suitable
for room cultivation—*H.
sanguinolenta* and *H. aristata*.
The former is low-growing
and has rounded leaves
flecked with pink and white,
and fragile, lilac flowers
which appear in summer.
The latter is a bushy plant
with ovate or oblong leaves
and tubular purple blooms
which appear in autumn.

Light and situation: a well
ventilated position without
direct sunlight in a plant
window.
Temperature: warm, 18–20°C
(64–68°F).
Moisture: water freely with
softened water and maintain
a humid atmosphere in
summer.
Soil: a loam-based compost.
Propagation: from young
cuttings in spring in an
indoor propagator.

Howiea belmoreana

Howeia

This genus of palm, a native
of Lord Howe Island in the
Pacific from which it takes its
name, has only two
known species, *H. belmoreana*
and *H. forsterana*, the latter
growing to a greater height in
its natural habitat but the two
hardly distinguishable in room
cultivation. The multiple
upright leaf stems 2 m (6 ft)
tall grow from the roots and
the elegant leaves are divided
into many long, slender,
arching leaflets which spread
outwards to give a fan-like
effect. Both are ideal for room
cultivation being very tolerant
of shade.

Light and situation: a shady
position.
Temperature: warm 14–18°C
(57–64°F) in winter.
Moisture: water sparingly
throughout the year using
softened water.
Soil: a heavy, humusy mixture.
Special points: remove the
dust from the leaves with
water occasionally.

Hypoestes aristata

Iresine herbstii

(above) *Jacaranda mimosifolia*

Iresine

This genus of decorative perennials from tropical South America includes *Iresine herbstii*, the beefsteak plant, and *I. lindenii*, the bloodleaf, both of which have deep purplish-red foliage and stems. *I. herbstii* has shiny, heart-shaped, dark purple leaves with crimson veins and undersides. *I. lindenii* has narrower leaves in a deep rich red with a lighter central stripe. They should be kept in sunlight to maintain the colour of the foliage.

Light and situation: a well-lit position in a tropical plant window.
Temperature: warm.
Moisture: water freely with lukewarm water and maintain a humid atmosphere.
Soil: a loam-based compost.
Propagation: from stem cuttings, in spring and autumn in an indoor propagator.

Jacaranda mimosifolia

This ornamental, semi-evergreen shrub from tropical Brazil reaches 3 m (10 ft) as a pot plant and has 45 cm (18 in) multiply divided, bright green, fern-like leaves. It will grow as a young plant in room cultivation but is best suited over time to a green-house or tropical plant window.

Temperature: warm: not below 16–18°C (60–65°F) in winter.
Moisture: water sparingly in summer; even less in winter. Use softened water and maintain a humid atmosphere.
Soil: a loam-based compost.
Propagation: from cuttings of half-ripe shoots in summer in an indoor propagator.

Maranta leuconeura 'Erythrophylla'

Maranta

This genus of low-growing, evergreen plants with hand-somely marked, broad oval leaves comes from the tropical rain forests of Brazil. *Maranta bicolor* has leaves with dark green upper surfaces and regular pale brown patches on either side of the central vein. The undersides are purple. *M. leuconeura*, a white-veined species, has a cultivar *M. l.* 'Erythrophylla', the red herringbone plant, with prominent, pale crimson veins and a pale green, herringbone stripe along the central vein. *M. l.* 'Kerchoveana' has grey-green leaves with brighter veins and dark brown patches on both sides of the central vein.

Light and situation: a well-lit position without direct light in a tropical plant window.
Temperature: a daytime temperature of 22°C (72°F) in summer; 18–20°C (64–68°F) in winter. At night maintain a temperature of 16–18°F (60–64°F) in summer; 16°C (60°F) in winter.
Moisture: water freely in summer but avoid leaving excess water in the pot. Water more sparingly in autumn and winter but do not allow the root ball to dry out. Use tepid, softened water.
Soil: a loam-based compost.
Propagation: by division when repotting at the end of winter.

Microcoelum
Coconut palm

Microcoelum, a small palm from Brazil, where it grows in tropical rain forests, is well suited to a warm greenhouse but may be cultivated in the home when young. *M. weddellianum* with its arching stems and long, slender, tapering pinnate leaflets will reach 1.2 m (4 ft) in room cultivation. It suffers most from dry, warm air in winter which will make the leaves turn brown.

Microcoelum weddellianum

Light and situation: a good light without direct sunlight.
Temperature: warm in summer; 16–18°C (60–64°F) in winter.
Moisture: water freely in spring and summer and maintain a humid atmosphere; more sparingly in winter but do not allow the root ball to dry out. To prevent this always leave a little water at the base of the pot.
Soil: equal parts loam, leaf mould and sharp sand.

Mimosa pudica
Sensitive plant

A spreading perennial from tropical America grown as an annual in the home, *Mimosa pudica* has deeply cut leaves consisting of four radiating groups of pinnate, elliptical leaflets. The plant is called the sensitive plant because the leaves will fold at the slightest touch but after a pause the leaves flatten out once more. Mature plants may grow to 50 cm (20 in) and the stems usually become woody. It bears pink, ball-like flowers in summer and early autumn.

Light and situation: a good light without direct sunlight.
Temperature: a constant temperature of 20–22°C (68–72°F).
Moisture: water freely in spring and summer. Maintain a humid atmosphere.
Soil: a loam-based compost.
Propagation: from seed during spring.

Monstera
Swiss cheese plant

Monstera, known as the Swiss cheese plant because the large leathery leaves of many of its species develop indentations and holes as they mature, comes from Central and South America where the plants grow to over 10 m (33 ft) in the jungle. *Monstera deliciosa* develops deeply incised leaves up to 40–70 cm (16–28 in) wide and 60–80 cm (24–32 in) long, and can grow to 2.5 m (8 ft) as a pot plant if it is given some support. *M. obliqua* is a smaller but otherwise similar species which especially in its hybrid 'Leichtlinii' develops holes in the leaves while the edges remain intact. *M. pertusa* is a climber with dense masses of foliage which also develops holes as the plant matures. These plants are particularly well suited for cultivation as house plants adapting to all but the lowest temperatures. As many as 25 species may be available for room cultivation.

Light and situation: shady.
Temperature: moderate; 14–16°C (57–60°F) in winter.
Moisture: water freely in spring and summer; more sparingly in winter. Use tepid water.

Mimosa pudica

Monstera deliciosa

Soil: a loam-based compost.
Propagation: from leaf buds or from cuttings of a growing point and one leaf in summer rooted in a mixture of peat and sand.

(above) *Neoregelia* hybrid   (below) *Nidularium fulgens*

Neoregelia

This genus includes some of the most striking epiphytic members of the Bromeliad family. The rosette of saw-edged leaves is patterned according to species but in each the leaves surrounding the central, water-holding cup turn red or reddish-purple at flowering time. *N. carolinae* has shiny, green leaves and produces a central core of deep reddish-purple bracts at flowering time surrounding the clump of purple flowers. *N.c.* 'Tricolor' has leaves with a central white stripe and at flowering time the whole plant is suffused with deep crimson and the central leaves are carmine red. *N. spectabilis*, the fingernail plant, has long, olive green leaves with a red spot at the tip. When the dense cluster of blue flowers is formed the central leaves turn deep red.

Light and situation: a good light without direct sunlight, if preferred in a tropical plant window.
Temperature: warm in spring and summer, 22–25°C (72–77°F); moderate in autumn and winter, 15–18°C (59–64°C).
Moisture: pour water into the central funnel in the growing period; empty in winter, but keep the root ball moist.
Soil: a special Bromeliad compost.
Special points: repotting is unnecessary as old rosettes die and new ones are formed.

Nidularium

This Brazilian genus is very similar to *Neoregelia* and for a time was combined with it. These are nevertheless more delicate plants. Like *Neoregelia* this plant forms rosettes of strap-like leaves which enclose a central water-holding funnel. At the time of flowering it produces shorter central leaves or bracts in red or orange which surround the flowers.
N. innocentii has narrow, saw-edged, green leaves flushed with purple above and dark red beneath. The white flowers are surrounded by short, burnt orange bracts. *N. fulgens* has long, shiny leaves and many blue flowers surrounded by red bracts.

Light and situation: a half-shady position in a tropical plant window.
Temperature: warm in summer; slightly cooler in winter.
Moisture: fill the central cup with water in summer and maintain a humid atmosphere. Leave a little water in the cup in winter and keep the soil moist.
Soil: equal parts loam, leaf mould, peat and sand.
Propagation: by severing side shoots which are produced when the flowers fade and the original rosette dies off. Cut off with a sharp knife, dry off for one or two days and plant in growing compost.

133

(above) *Pandanus veitchii*   (below) *Peperomia hederifolia*

Pandanus
Screw pine

This genus of evergreen trees and shrubs mainly from the Indonesian Archipelago has arching leaves up to 1–2 m (3–6 ft) long which grow in spiral formation round the stem. After four or five years aerial roots develop which serve to replace the lower stem. Runners or sideshoots develop which can be left or used for propagation. *P. utilis*, the largest species, has dark green leaves up to 1.5 m (5 ft) long edged with red spines. This plant is particularly sensitive to changes in temperature and is best suited by its size to large offices. *P. sanderi* is a smaller species with narrower, pale green leaves striped with white or edged and tipped with white or red and 80–100 cm (32–40 in) long. *P. veitchii*, a similar size to *P. sanderi*, is the species best known as a house plant and has leaves with fine dark green stripes between wider yellowy-green stripes.

Light and situation: a good light without direct sunlight. Temperature: a minimum of 20–25°C (68–77°F) in summer; in winter 18–22°C (64–72°F). Moisture: water liberally and spray occasionally in the growing period; water less in autumn and winter. Soil: pre-packed potting compost. Propagation: from runners.

Peperomia

Peperomia, a genus of low-growing, mainly succulent plants from Central and South America has foliage often delicately marked with white or lighter greens or deeply impressed along the vein contours. The flowers are generally pale yellow, long and tail like. The plants can be divided into three main groups—the variegated species, the green-leaved species, many of them with variegated cultivars, and those with trailing stems. The variegated species are the best known. In this group is found *P. argyreia* (*P. sandersii*) which has shield-shaped, whitish leaves with deep green veining on red stems and *P. caperata* which has thick, fleshy, dark green leaves deeply wrinkled and impressed along the vein contours. In

the case of *P.c.* 'Emerald Ripple' these are also edged with a silvery-grey gloss. *P. hederifolia*, a similar plant, has less deeply indented, rounder leaves with a slight silvery gloss. *P. magnoliifolia* is a freely branching species with oval, glossy green leaves on purplish stems. 'Variegata' the commonest form, has whitish leaves when young which gradually acquire different shades of green as they mature. *P. fraseri* is a green-leaved species with dark green, glossy leaves with clearly marked, reddish veins and red stems. The flowers are whitish-yellow and spherical. *P. glabella*, the wax privet, is a freely branching plant with green leaves shaped like those of the privet. *P.g.* 'Variegata' is the form most commonly cultivated. *P. scandens*, usually cultivated in the form 'Variegata' is a climbing or trailing plant well suited to a hanging basket. The leaves are pointed and heart-shaped and begin a creamy white gradually becoming light green as they mature but retaining their cream edges.

Light and situation: a good light without direct sunlight in a tropical plant window. Temperature: warm; 18–20°C (64–68°F) in winter for variegated species; 15°C (59°F) for green species. Moisture: water sparingly in summer and maintain a humid atmosphere; even more so in winter. Use tepid, softened water.

Soil: a loam-based compost.
Propagation: variegated species from tip cuttings; green species from tip or leaf cuttings.

Philodendron

The *Philodendron* is a genus of climbing and erect foliage plants with large, leathery leaves. *P. scandens*, the best-known climbing species, has shiny, heart-shaped, bright green leaves ranging in length from 8 cm (3 in) when young to 30 cm (1 ft) when mature. *P. erubescens*, also a climber, has large, glossy, coppery-green leaves, rosy-pink when young. *P. ilsemanni* is a slow-growing climber with arrow-head-shaped leaves, creamy pink when young and turning dark green and white variegated when mature which can grow to 20 cm (8 in) long. *P. elegans* and *P. lacinatum* are climbers with variously divided leaves. *P. elegans* has dark green, three-lobed leaves, deeply jagged and incised; *P. lacinatum* has large, incised triangular leaves. *P. andreanum*, yet another climbing species, has large, heart-shaped, dark olive green leaves which are pale pinkish purple on their undersides. The leaves may reach 60 cm (2 ft) in length. Erect species include *P. bipinnatifidum* which when mature produces deeply incised leaves with wavy edges up to 60–90 cm (2–3 ft) in length. *B. martianum* is a handsome,

Philodendron bipinnatifidum

erect plant with long spear-shaped, brilliant glossy, wavy leaves up to 65 cm (26 in) in length. The last two plants mentioned soon grow too large for all but the largest room or office.

Light and situation: a dark position.
Temperature: moderate: 14–16°C (57–60°F) in winter; variegated forms should be kept at 18°C (64°F) in winter. Keep the soil warm.
Moisture: water freely in spring and summer; from then on more sparingly. Use lukewarm water and maintain a humid atmosphere in spring and summer particularly for velvet-leaved or variegated forms.
Soil: a loam-based compost.
Propagation: from cuttings in summer or by division.

Phoenix
Date palm

Species of these palms with feathery leaves from South East Asia and North Africa make very handsome pot plants when young. *P. canariensis*, from the Canary Isles, the species most suitable for home cultivation, has semi-erect arching fronds divided into many light green, pinnate leaflets. *P. dactylifera*, the commercial date palm, a larger species, has similar bluish-green fronds with fewer leaflets.

Light and situation: a sunny position outside in summer if

(below) *Philodendron scandens*

possible. Shade from the hottest sun when young.
Temperature: cool: *P. canariensis* requires a frost-free position in winter at 4°C (40°F); *P. dactylifera* requires 8–10°C (46–50°F) in winter.
Moisture: water freely in summer and drain well; sparingly in winter. Use tepid water.
Soil: a loam-based compost.
Propagation: from seed in spring.

(below) *Phoenix canariensis*

(left) *Peperomia magnoliifolia* 'Variegata'

Pilea

This genus of evergreen perennials, usually treated as disposable plants, comes from the tropical regions of the world. *P. cadeirei*, the aluminium plant, grows to 20-25 cm (8–10 in), an erect, freely-branching species with perfect oval, fleshy leaves about 8 cm (3 in) long, covered between the veins with a silvery sheen. *P. involucrata* is a smaller plant with dark, bronze-green, heavily quilted leaves growing in pairs on short purple-brown stems. *P. involucrata* 'Norfolk', a striking plant, has paired purplish-green leaves with three prominent veins and longitudinal silver banding.

Light and situation: a well-ventilated, shady position.
Temperature: moderate to warm; 10–20°C (50–68°F) in winter.
Moisture: keep moist in summer and maintain a humid atmosphere at the beginning of the growing period; water more sparingly in winter.
Soil: a loam-based compost.
Propagation: from stem cuttings in spring or summer.

shades of green, it grows to 6 m (20 ft) in its natural habitat but will reach 60 cm–1·2 m (2–4 ft) as a pot plant.

Care: as for *Ficus*.
Propagation: from cuttings with an eye planted in sand and peat with a soil temperature of 25°C (77°F).

leaves growing in starred groups of five and produces sweetly smelling, pale yellow flowers in terminal clusters in summer. *P. tenuifolium* from New Zealand has pale green leaves on black stems and grows into a graceful tree up to 4.5 m (15 ft) high.

Light and situation: a very well-lit position.

A group of *Pilea* hybrids

Temperature: cool; 4–8°C (40–46°F) in winter.
Moisture: keep moist.
Soil: a loam-based compost.
Propagation: from seeds in spring or from cuttings of side shoots with a heel in summer.

Pittosporum tobira

Pisonia

This pantropical genus has only one species in home cultivation—*Pisonia alba*. A shrub with leathery, pointed oval leaves irregularly marked with creamy white and several

Pisonia alba

Pittosporum

This genus of evergreen shrubs and trees from East Asia has shiny leaves, usually growing in circles round the stem, and tubular flowers. *P. tobira*, the best-known species in room cultivation, has oblong, shiny, dark green

Plectranthus

This pantropical genus of erect or trailing evergreen plants has a variety of leaf forms and includes some species with cowslip-like flowers in pastel shades. *P. fruticosus* grows to about 1 m (3 ft) and has light green, pointed oval, dentate leaves growing in pairs, and spikes

of blue flowers in winter. *P. coleoides* is a low-growing plant with hairy, oval, dark green leaves with scolloped edges. *P.c.* 'Marginatus', a particularly beautiful form, has clear white, irregular margins to the scolloped leaves. *P. oertendahli*, a creeping plant which can be grown in a hanging basket or used as ground cover, has reddish

Plectranthus coleoides 'Marginatus'

stems with almost circular, rich green leaves with silver veins and tall flower stems bearing pink tubular flowers.

Light and situation: a sunny position on a window sill. Temperature: moderate; 12–15°C (54–59°F) in winter. Moisture: water freely throughout the year but slightly less after flowering when the plant should be cut back and kept at 10–12°C (50–54°F) for a few weeks. Soil: a rich, loam-based compost.

Rhaphidophora aurea
Devil's ivy, golden pothos

Rhaphidophora, a genus consisting mainly of large lianas unsuitable for home cultivation, now includes one species well-known as a house plant— *Rhaphidophora aurea.* This low-growing plant, until recently known as *Scindapsus aureus,* has slightly stiff, angular stems and irregular, glossy, pointed oval leaves streaked with white and yellow. *R.a.* 'Marble Queen' has white leaves flecked with green; 'Tricolor' is green marked with yellow and white.

Light and situation: a good light without direct sunlight. Temperature: warm; 15–18°C (59–64°F) in winter. The paler strains require slightly more warmth. Moisture: keep moist in summer; a little dryer in winter. Maintain a humid atmosphere in the growing period. Soil: a light, humusy soil. Propagation: from short stems sections with one or two nodes or from self-rooting runners.

Rhapis excelsa

This species of dwarf palm with divided leaves comes from China and Japan. The leathery segments have longitudinal veins and the stems are reed-like. *R. excelsa* (syn. *R. flabelliformis*) grows to 1.2–2 m (4–6 ft) as a pot plant in the home.

Light and situation: a good light. Temperature: warm in summer; cool in winter, 7°C (45°F). Moisture: water generously and spray occasionally in summer; water more sparingly in winter but do not allow the root ball to dry out. Soil: a loam-based compost.

(left) *Rhaphidophora aurea* (below) *Rhapis excelsa*

Rhoeo spathacea var. vittata

Rhoeo spathacea
Boat lily, Moses in the cradle

Rhoeo spathacea, the only known species of this genus closely related to the trailing *Tradescantia*, was discovered in Mexico. Its spear-shaped, fleshy leaves 20–35 cm (8–14 in) long are green above and have reddish-purple undersides. They grow in rosettes around the stem. *R.s. var. vittata* has leaves striped with white and yellow.

Light and situation: a half-shady position in summer and a good light in winter without direct sunlight. Temperature: water freely and maintain a humid atmosphere in summer; water more sparingly from autumn onwards and keep dry in winter.
Soil: a loam-based compost.
Propagation: from shoot cuttings or seed in spring.

Rhoicissus

This genus of climbing plants grown for their ornamental foliage comes from Southern Africa. *R. capensis* has brown haired, woody stems and vine-like, large, dark green glossy leaves 15–18 cm (6–7 in) across. It is a vigorous climber. *Rhoicissus rhomboidea*, an evergreen climber reaching 1·2–2 m (4–6 ft) as a pot plant, has glossy green, rhomboidal leaflets with dentate edges growing in groups of three.

Care: as for *Cissus antarctica*. It is unsuitable as a hanging plant because of its woody stems.

Schefflera

Schefflera, a genus of handsome, evergreen trees from Australia and New

Schefflera actinophylla

(above) *Rhoicissus rhomboidea*

Zealand is represented in room cultivation by the species *S. actinophylla* which grows into a 2 m (6 ft) shrub as a pot plant over several years. The shiny, drooping, long oval leaflets grow in radiating groups from the end of the leaf stems and number three or five when the plant is young but increase with age.

Light and situation: a well ventilated, well-lit position without direct sunlight. Place outside in summer if possible. Temperature: moderate: not below 12°C (54°F) or above 16–18°C (60–64°F).
Moisture: keep moist and maintain a humid atmosphere.
Soil: a loam-based compost.
Propagation: from seeds sown in spring.

Senecio

Senecio is an enormous genus containing over 1000 species and including shrubs and trees, succulents, flowering and climbing plants. *Senecio cruentus*, also known as *Cineraria*, is included in the flowering section under the latter name. *Senecio macroglossus* 'Variegatus' is a tall, evergreen climber with

dark, lustrous green leaves. *Senecio mikanoides* has succulent stems and leaves which are curled and sharply pointed also resembling those of the ivy. Both are fast-growing climbers best suited to the conservatory.

Light and situation: a good light without direct sunlight. Temperature: warm. Moisture: *S. macroglossus* 'Variegatus': water sparingly; *S. mikanoides:* keep moist. Soil: a loam-based compost with some sand. Propagation: from terminal cuttings.

Sparmannia africana
African hemp, window linen

Sparmannia africana, an evergreen shrub, will reach 2·5 m (8 ft) in a greenhouse border but will grow to 60 cm–1.2 m (2–4 ft) as a pot plant. It has pale green, large oval dentate leaves covered on both sides with soft hairs and bears white flowers with purple and yellow stamens in terminal clusters in summer. The dwarf form will grow to 80 cm (32 in) and flowers more profusely than the original species.

Light and situation: a well ventilated, sunny position away from other plants. Temperature: cool; 6–10°C (43–50°F) in winter. Moisture: water freely in the growing period and drain well; water more sparingly in winter but do not allow the root ball to dry out. Soil: a loam-based compost. Propagation: from cuttings of young shoots in spring.

Syngonium

This genus of trailing and climbing plants, closely related to both *Philodendron* and *Monstera*, come from Central and South America. The plants contain a milky white liquid and the leaves change their shape with age until they consist of 3, 5 or even 8 leaflets. The leaflets are long, pointed ovals in shape and a shiny, bright green with lighter green patterning when young. *S. auritum*,five fingers, has leaves divided into five leaflets with a long central leaflet, two medium-sized leaflets on either side and a final minute pair close to the stem. *S. podophyllum* has dark green, shiny, arrow-shaped

(above) A variegated *Syngonium*

leaves divided when mature and held on stiff stems. It has many variegated cultivars including 'Albovirens' which has shiny, white leaves with green margins.

Light and situation: a good light without direct sunlight. Temperature: warm. Moisture: water freely in summer and maintain a humid atmosphere; water more sparingly in winter. Soil: a loam-based compost. Propagation: from stem tip cuttings or leaf bud cuttings in summer.

Sparmannia africana

Tetrastigma
Chestnut vine

Tetrastigma, a genus of evergreen climbing plants related to the *Cissus*, comes from tropical East Asia. *T. voinierana*, a vigorous climber from the region of Tonkin, is cultivated as a house plant trained on strong canes and has shiny, dentate leaves growing in groups of three or five. Each leaf can grow to 25 cm (10 in) in length and the plant will reach several metres (feet) in one year. The plant produces small greenish-yellow flowers when mature.

Light and situation: a good light without direct sunlight.
Temperature: moderate: not below 12–15°C (54–59°F) in winter.
Moisture: water freely in summer; more sparingly in winter.
Soil: a loam-based compost.

Tetrastigma voinierana

Tolmeia
Piggy-back plant

This low-growing member of the *Saxifraga* family is a genus with one species, *Tolmeia menziesii*. The plant derives its common name, piggy-back plant, from the small plantlets formed at the base of the leaves which later drop into the soil. The plant grows up to 15 cm (6 in) high with a spread of 38 cm (15 in). The leaves are rounded, soft green and hairy with slightly indented edges. Flowers appear in early summer on long spikes and are green and white.

Care: as for *Saxifraga stolonifera*
Propagation: from leaves with well-developed plantlets.

Tradescantia
Spiderwort

The hardy species of *Tradescantia*, named after the gardener of Charles I of England and his son, both called John Tradescant, first made their appearance in Europe in the 17th century. The first non-hardy species came to Europe from tropical South America in the early 19th century and have since become some of the best

Tradescantia fluminensis

known creeping and trailing house plants. These have succulent stems and leaves pointed oval in shape and 2·5–4 cm (1–1½ in) long which surround the leaf joint at their base. Flowers appear from the axils of the upper leaves in winter or spring. *T. albiflora* is the only green species. *T. a.* 'Albovittata' has leaves longitudinally striped with mauve and white. *T. fluminensis*, a similar species, has green or purplish shorter stems with bright green, oval leaves often purplish in colour beneath. The cultivar 'Variegated' has yellow striped leaves. A smaller species, *T. blossfeldiana*, called the flowering inch plant, is a creeping perennial with leaves brownish red on the upper surface and red beneath and many pink and white flowers. *T. sillamontana*, white velvet, is a species with stiffer stems and leaves covered in soft white hairs and tinged with purple on their undersides. The flowers are deep red and open in summer and autumn.

Light and situation: a well-lit position.
Temperature: moderate: not below 10–12°C (50–54°F).
Moisture: water well in summer; more sparingly

plant, has fine pointed elliptical leaves 6 cm (2½ in) long, coloured green and purple above with two silver stripes and purple beneath. 'Quadricolor', a more exotic variegated form, has rose-purple, white, dark and light green striped leaves coloured purple beneath. The stems of these hanging plants reach 45 cm (18 in).

Yucca aloifolia 'Tricolor'

Light and situation: well-lit.
Temperature: moderate: not below 15°C (59°F) in winter.
Moisture: water well in summer; sparingly in winter. Use softened water.
Soil: a loam-based compost with some sand.
Propagation: from rooted cuttings in spring.

(above) *Yucca aloifolia*

during the winter months.
Soil: a loam-based compost.
Propagation: replace yearly from rooted cuttings in spring. Several cuttings should be placed in one pot.

Yucca

The trunk-forming species of the *Yucca*, a genus of plants from North, Central and South America, make good house plants. *Y. aloifolia* produces a scaly central stem and spiky, terminal leaf clusters 45–60 cm (18–24 in) long. It will grow to 1·2–2 m (4–6 ft) as a pot plant. 'Quadricolor' and 'Tricolor' are variegated forms.

Light and situation: a light, sunny position outside in summer if possible; a well-lit position indoors in winter.
Temperature: cool; 6°C (43°F) in winter.
Moisture: water generously in summer and drain well; keep dry in winter.
Soil: a loam-based compost.
Propagation: by division of the rootstock.

Zebrina

Zebrina, a close relative of the *Tradescantia*, is a genus of trailing perennials with fleshy stems from Central America. *Z. pendula*, the best-known species grown as a house

Zebrina pendula

Foliage plants: Ferns

About 10,000 species of ferns exist distributed throughout the world in damp, shady habitats but growing mostly in the humid tropics. Since the last century when the temperature in private houses was more suitable for growing ferns the number of ferns commercially available has dwindled but there is now a revival of interest in them. The delicacy of their leaves and the intensity of their green colouring make them very attractive house plants.

Most ferns like a cool, moist, undisturbed place away from the sun, and thrive in a Wardian case or plant window. A north facing conservatory, bay window or glass porch suits them very well but it may be necessary to increase the level of moisture and humidity around the plant by putting the pot containing the fern into a larger container and packing the space in between with damp peat or moss. If you place a group of plants together, pack a trough with damp peat for them all to stand in.

Ferns look good on their own or in groups. They can be used in hanging baskets and to trail down pillars, and are ideal plants for bathrooms.

There are several plants which look just like ferns to the layman but in fact are not. The best known of these are members of the *Selaginella* genus which come from tropical rain forests and should be treated like ferns.

(above) *Adiantum hispidulum*   (below) *Adiantum raddianum*

and the tropics has two distinct shapes. *Asplenium bulbiferum*, the mother spleenwort, has finely divided, lacy, mid green fronds bearing bulbils which in turn produce small plants. The fronds will grow to 60 cm (2 ft). *A. nidus*, the bird's nest fern, is an epiphyte from the tropics which, unlike other spleen-worts, has undivided, glossy, pale green, spear-shaped fronds which grow in an arching rosette. The fronds are 60 cm–1.2 m (2–4 ft) tall.

Light and situation: *A. bulbiferum*: a shady position away from other plants; *A. nidus*: a shady position in a tropical plant window.
Temperature: warm in summer; not below 18°C (64°F) in winter.
Moisture: *A. bulbiferum*: water well in summer and maintain a humid atmosphere; *A. nidus*: as for *Aechmea* except that it should be watered via the roots.
Soil: a peat-based compost.
Propagation: from spores or by division in spring.

Blechnum

This genus of ferns from the tropics has sturdy, arching fronds often with dentate, pinnate leaflets. *B. gibbum*, the species best-known as a

(above) *Blechnum gibbum*

Adiantum
Maidenhair fern

Species of *Adiantum*, a genus with delicate, feathery foliage, are found both in temperate zones and in the tropics. In *A. capillis veneris*, found in Europe and the USA, the fine, wiry, dark stems, or stipes, carry delicate, light green fronds of small, dentate leaflets and the plant will grow to 60 cm (2 ft). The fronds grow upright to a height of 15–25 cm (6–10 in) and then begin to arch. *A. hispidulum* has leaf fronds forked at the base giving the appearance of branching, and rounded, hairy leaflets, reddish-bronze when young. This plant also grows to 60 cm (2 ft).

Light and situation: a shady, draught-free position. This plant does well in a bathroom for a while.
Temperature: warm in summer; not below 18°C (64°F) in winter.
Moisture: water generously and maintain a humid atmosphere. Use tepid, softened water. If the plant gets too dry, soak in lukewarm water until the rootball is saturated.
Soil: a proprietary peat compost.
Propagation: by division or from spores in spring.

Asplenium
Spleenwort

This genus of decorative ferns from Australia, New Zealand

Asplenium nidus

house plant, grows to 1 m (3 ft) and has light green, glossy fronds. *B. spicant*, the hard fern, has dark green, leathery fronds and also grows to 1 m (3 ft). *B. capense*, the palm-leaf fern, is an erect fern with long narrow segments rounded or heart-shaped at the base. The spores are borne on separate fronds 15 cm (6 in) long. *B. discolor* has fronds coppery-coloured when young and glossy green when mature with brownish undersides.

Light and situation: a well ventilated, shady position away from other plants.
Temperature: warm; but not above 16–18°C (60–64°F) in winter.
Moisture: water generously in spring and summer; moderately thereafter. Maintain a humid atmosphere.
Soil: a proprietary peat compost.
Propagation: by division or from spores in spring

Cyrtomium falcatum

This handsome fern from India has glossy, evergreen fronds with pointed oval, pinnate leaflets and slightly woody stems growing to 30–60 cm (1–2 ft). *C.f.*

'Rochfordianum' the holly fern, has larger leaflets with wavy margins and very finely pointed tips. It is more compact than the original species and rarely exceeds 30 cm (12 in) in height. Both plants grow well in shade and make particularly good house plants as they can withstand dry air and draughts.

Light and situation: shady.
Temperature: warm in summer; 10–12°C (50–54°F) in winter.
Moisture: water generously in the growing period and spray frequently; water more sparingly in autumn and winter.
Soil: a garden soil with some extra humus.
Propagation: by division.

(above) *Cyrtomium falcatum* 'Rochfordianum'

(below) *Davallia canariensis*

Davallia

This genus of deciduous fern from temperate regions with finely dissected fronds has two species found in home cultivation. *D. canariensis*, the hare's foot fern, takes its name from the brown, hairy roots which spill over the edge of the pot. The fronds are deeply divided and leathery in texture, reaching 30–45 cm (12–18 in). *D. mariesii*, the ball fern, has curious rhizomes which sometimes grow into ball shapes. The light green, feathery fronds are deeply divided and grow to 20–30 cm (8–12 in).

Light and situation: a shady position.
Temperature: warm in summer; 14°C (57°F) in winter.
Moisture: water generously in summer; more sparingly in winter.
Soil: a peat-based compost.
Propagation: by division or from cuttings of the rhizomes in early spring.

Didymochlaena truncatula

This pantropical species of fern, well-suited to room cultivation, has glossy, somewhat leathery, ovate leaflets growing in opposing pairs which change colour from yellowy-green to dark green as they mature. It will reach 45 cm (18 in) in height.

Light and situation: a shady position.
Temperature: warm in summer; 14–16°C (57–60°F) in winter.
Moisture: water generously in summer and spray twice a day with tepid water; water more sparingly in winter.
Soil: a mixture of loam and leaf mould.
Propagation: from spores.

Nephrolepis

This genus of ferns with once or often divided fronds rising at intervals from the rhizomes are best grown in hanging baskets or as a feature at the top of a pillar. *N. exalta*, the sword fern, is a tall-growing plant with dark green fronds, pinnate or often divided

(above) *Didymochlaena truncatula*

Pellaea rotundifolia

This fern as its species name suggests has rounded segments which grow on alternate sides of the rust-coloured, wiry stems of the fronds. It reaches 20 cm (8 in) in height and is bushy. Other species are available.

(above) *Nephrolepis exaltata var.* 'Bostoniensis'

according to strain which will reach a length of 1 m (3 ft). 'Elegantissima' has many bright green, sturdy fronds. *N.e. var.* 'Bostoniensis', the Boston fern, has a cascading habit with tapering fronds up to 1 m (3 ft) in length.

Light and situation: a draught-free, light position shaded from direct sunlight for most species.

Temperature: warm in summer; 14–16°C (57–60°F) in winter.
Moisture: water well in the growing period; more sparingly in winter.
Soil: two parts loam to one part sharp sand.
Propagation: by removing young plants produced at intervals on the rhizomes.

Nephrolepis exaltata

(left) *Pellaea rotundifolia*   (below) *Platycerium bifurcatum*

Light and situation: a good light.
Temperature: warm in summer; 12–15°C (54–59°F) in winter.
Moisture: water normally in summer; sparingly in winter but do not allow the root ball to dry out.
Soil: a peat compost.
Propagation: by division of the rhizomes or from spores in spring.

Phyllitis
Hart's tongue fern

This genus of ferns with simple, strap-like, undivided fronds comes from a wide range of countries. *P. scolopendrium* has numerous cultivars with bright green fronds 45 cm (18 in) long. 'Undulata' has wavy-edged fronds marked as it were with a knife edge. 'Crispum' has a crinkled leaf edge. *P. brasiliensis* has deep green, leathery, tapering fronds 15–30 cm (6–12 in) long. *P. hemionitis* has short fronds resembling those of *P. scolopendrium* with a blunted tip and a heart-shaped base.

Light and situation: a shady position.
Temperature: warm in summer; 14–16°C (57–60°F) in winter.
Moisture: water generously in summer and maintain a humid atmosphere; water more sparingly in winter.
Soil: a proprietary peat compost.
Propagation: by division or from spores in spring.

Platycerium
Stag's horn fern

This genus of unusual ferns from the East Indies consists of epiphytic plants growing

on the branches and in the forks of forest trees. They have two different types of leaves: the layered, broad leaves which are often shield-shaped and are sterile; and the spore-bearing leaves which grow from these in a cascade and are shaped like antlers, narrow at the base and broadening and branching toward the top. In some species they grow to 1 m (3 ft). These ferns are usually grown attached to a log or branch, the roots wrapped in a peaty compost and secured to the branch by soft wire. When the plant attaches itself, the wires may be removed. It may also be grown in pots. *P. bifurcatum* is the species most commonly grown as a house plant and has fertile fronds 60 cm–1 m (2–3 ft) long, branching two or three times. *P. grande* has triangular, fertile fronds, each divided at the top.

Light and situation: a good light without direct sunlight.
Temperature: warm in summer; 16–18°C (60–64°F) in winter.
Moisture: water generously in the growing period; sparingly in winter but do not allow the plant to dry out. Use tepid water.
Soil: a mixture of equal parts proprietary peat compost and sphagnum moss.
Propagation: by detaching the small plantlets that form on the roots.

Phyllitis scolopendrium

Polypodium diversifolium

(below) *Polypodium aureum*

(above) *Polystichum angulare*

Polypodium
Polypody

This genus of low-growing ferns from the tropics has tall, wiry stems rising at intervals from the rhizomes and leathery, mid green fronds, entire or divided. *P. aureum*, hare's foot fern, has deeply incised, handsome fronds up to 1.2 m (4 ft) long and pointed, strap-like segments. The rhizomes are covered with orangy-brown, furry scales. *P.a.* 'Glaucum' has blue-grey fronds.

Light and situation: a shady position.
Temperature: warm in summer; 14–16°C (57–60°F) in winter.
Moisture: water well in summer; more sparingly in winter.
Soil: a loam-based compost.
Propagation: by division of the rhizomes or from spores in spring.

Light and situation: a shady position.
Temperature: warm in summer; in winter 10–12°C (50–54°F) for green species; 16–18°C (60–64°F) for variegated forms.
Moisture: maintain a humid atmosphere. Water generously in the growing period; less in winter. Use tepid, softened water.
Soil: a proprietary peat compost.
Propagation: by division or from spores in spring.

Selaginella
Creeping moss

This genus of flowerless plants akin to ferns comes from tropical and subtropical regions and with its upright, creeping or trailing forms is a good accompaniment to other plants in a bottle garden. The foliage consists of a dense mass of branching stems covered with fine, scale-like leaves. *S. apoda*, a creeping plant, has moss-like foliage on stems 2.5–10 cm (1–4 in) high. *S. martensii* is a trailing species with 15–30 cm (6–12 in) flattened stems covered with small oval leaves. *S. braunii* is an erect plant with 30–45 cm (12–18 in) pale brown stems clad in small, triangular leaves.

Light and situation: shady.
Temperature: warm in summer; 14–16°C (57–60°F) in the winter months.

Moisture: water well in summer and keep moist; water slightly more sparingly in winter. Use softened water.
Soil: a peat-based compost.
Propagation: by division or from cuttings in spring.

(below) *Selaginella apoda*

Polystichum

Only a few species of this genus of terrestrial ferns are suitable for room cultivation. *P. tsus-simense* from China and Japan has delicately arching flat fronds composed of opposing stems each bearing pairs of small leaflets. *P. setiferum* has a number of cultivars with dense, much divided fronds reminiscent of conifer foliage.

Care: as for *Pteris*.

Pteris
Brake

This genus of small ferns from tropical and subtropical regions is remarkable for the beauty of its lacy fronds cut into highly irregular, dentate segments. *P. cretica* with its many cultivars is the best known species. *P. multifida* is smaller and *P. m.* 'Cristata' has fine, grass-like segments. *P. tremula* is a large, decorative plant with upright fronds 1.2 m (4ft) tall, divided many times into light, feathery foliage. The stalks are bright reddish-brown.

(left) *Polystichum setiferum* 'Proliferum densum'

(below) *Pteris cretica* 'Whimsettii'

Flowering plants

The term flowering plants covers an enormous range but is here taken to mean those plants which, given the right conditions, flower for more than one season, together with plants which are predominantly grown for their flowers. Some of the bromeliads, for instance, do produce flowers but are really plants best grown for their foliage. Many cacti and succulents flower but are grouped together elsewhere, as are flowering bulbs. Most flowering plants need more light than do foliage plants to develop their buds. Some, such as geraniums, are happy in normal conditions on a sunny window sill; others such as begonias need more care and a special environment. Some of the most exotic plants, the orchids, need special care and attention and are best left to the experienced grower.

Flowering plants tend to be good room features for only part of the year, requiring a resting period once the flowers have died down and, although annuals are discarded after one season, most may be kept to flower again the following year.

Abutilon
Flowering maple

These evergreen shrubs from the tropics are known as flowering maple because of their leaf shape. The various hybrids with bell-shaped orange, yellow or purple flowers can reach 2 m (6 ft) but will grow to 1.2 m (4 ft) in pots. *A. megapotamicum* is a fine spreading shrub whose pendant flowers with their yellow petals and red calyces 4 cm (1½ in) long appear first in early summer and go on blooming until autumn. *A. striatum* has orange flowers marked with crimson veins.

Light and situation: a good light without direct sunlight; place outside in summer if possible.
Temperature: warm; in autumn and winter keep at 15°C (59°F).
Moisture: water well in summer, twice a day if necessary; sparingly in winter.
Soil: a loam-based compost.
Propagation: from tip cuttings in summer.

(above)*Abutilon striatum* 'Thompsonii'

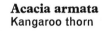

(below)*Acacia armata*

Acacia armata
Kangaroo thorn

This fern-like tree from Australia has delicately curving branches with dark green, spiny 'leaves' (strictly phyllodes) studded in spring with small, ball-like, yellow flowers rather like those of *Mimosa*. *A. drummondi* carries spikes of yellow flowers. Both may reach 3 m (10 ft).

Light and situation: a good light without direct sunlight; place outside in summer.
Temperature: moderate; in winter 4–6°C (40–43°F).
Moisture: water sparingly, especially in winter.
Soil: a loam-based compost.
Propagation: from seed in spring or from stem cuttings with a heel in summer.

Acalypha
Chenille plant, red-hot cat's tail

Acalypha hispida, known as the chenille plant or red hot cat's tail, has long tail-like flowers which look like strips of red chenille and appear in summer. *A. wilkesiana* hybrids are grown for their fine decorative foliage.

Light and situation: a good light without direct sunlight.
Temperature: warm; not below 16–18°C (60–64°F) in winter.
Moisture: keep moist during the flowering period.
Soil: a loam-based compost.
Propagation: from stem cuttings in spring or summer.
Special points: remove side-shoots on young plants; prune in the second year to achieve a good shape.

Achimenes

This Central American genus develops a mass of brilliant, trumpet-shaped flowers in shades of pink, red, purple or yellow and occasionally in white. *A. grandiflora* grows to

Acalypha hispida

Allamanda cathartica

about 60 cm (2 ft) and has pinkish purple flowers up to 5 cm (2 in) wide. *A. longiflora* has trailing stems and long but less broad-petaled, tubular flowers in many colours ranging from purple-blue to lavender or pale pink. It is ideal for hanging baskets. The plants can be bought in flower in summer.

Light and situation: a good light without direct sunlight.
Temperature: warm; in winter 13°C (55°F).
Moisture; maintain a humid atmosphere in summer and water freely.

Achimenes hybrid

Overwintering: after the shoots have died, the stems should be cut off at soil level and the tuberous root removed and kept in sand in a dry place at 10°C (50°F). The tubers are started into growth again in spring using a peat and leaf mould plus sand and loam compost with six or eight tubers to a 15 cm (6 in) pot. Water sparingly at first but later more freely.
Soil: a loam-based compost.
Propagation: by separating the tubers when repotting.

Aeschynanthus

The various trailing species of this evergreen epiphyte are, like *Columnea* to which it is related, ideal for hanging baskets. Unlike *Columnea*, however, it requires warmth and a high degree of humidity especially during the summer flowering period. *A. speciosus* has large, vase-shaped, orange or scarlet flowers with a yellow neck and a fine crown of pale stamens. *A. pulcher* has smaller flowers in brilliant red and yellow.

Light and situation: a half shady position.
Temperature: warm; 18–21°C (64–70°F) in winter.

Moisture: maintain a humid atmosphere and water freely in summer; slightly less in winter.
Soil: a proprietary peat compost.
Propagation: from stem or tip cuttings in spring or when flowering is over.

Allamanda
Golden trumpet

The *Allamanda* is a genus of shrubs and vigorous climbing plants from South America with clusters of yellow flowers and finely pointed, oleander-like leaves which grow in whorls round the stem. Because of their size—*A. cathartica* can reach 6 m (19 ft)—these plants are best grown in a conservatory or a shaded sun porch. If grown in pots, however, their stems should be trained on wires or canes and the plant potted on annually in early spring.

A. c. 'Grandiflora' has lemon yellow flowers 8 cm (3 in) in diameter. *A. c.* 'Hendersonii' has more golden and even larger flowers. Those of *A. neriifolia*, a semi-climbing shrub which reaches 1 m (3 ft), are delicately striped inside with pale brown.

Light and situation: a good light without direct sunlight.
Temperature: warm; in winter, 13°C (55°F).
Moisture: plenty in summer but little in winter.
Soil: a loam-based compost.
Propagation: from stem cuttings in spring or summer.

Aeschynanthus pulcher

Anthurium scherzeranum

Anthurium
Flame plant, flamingo flower, flamingo plant

The *Anthurium*, a colourful member of the Arum family, was introduced to Europe from Central America. Hybrids of *A. scherzeranum* grow to about 45 cm (18in) with large, dark green leaves on long stems and red, pink or white, lily-like 'flowers' consisting of a leaf-like spathe with a curled spadix or central spike. The shape and colour of the spathe and spadix give the plant its name. *A. andreanum* hybrids are larger plants with glossy, heart-shaped leaves and a shiny, brilliant red or orange spathe topped by a yellow spadix. These plants grow well hydroponically.

Light and situation: a good light without direct sunlight. Temperature: warm; not below 15°C (59°F) in winter. Moisture: water well with softened water; maintain a humid atmosphere. Soil: a mixture of peat compost and sphagnum moss. Propagation: by division or from seeds in spring.

Antigonon leptopus
Coral vine

This perennial climber with arrow-shaped leaves and clusters of rose-pink flowers is best suited to the conservatory where it can be grown in a border or in tubs. The long stems should be trained on wire or threads.

Light and situation: a good light without direct sunlight. Temperature: warm. Moisture: maintain a humid atmosphere, and water freely in summer and winter. Soil: a loam-based compost. Propagation: from seeds in spring or stem cuttings in summer.

Antigonon leptopus

Ardisia crispa
Coral berry, spear flower

Ardisia crispa is a small, delicate, evergreen tree from South America growing to about 60 cm (2 ft) as a house plant. It produces clusters of sweetly scented, white flowers in summer followed by a profusion of dark red berries which last for six months or more.

Light and situation: a light and sunny position. Temperature: warm in summer; not above 12–15°C (54–59°F) in winter. Higher temperatures cause the berries to drop. Moisture: spray frequently with lukewarm water. Soil: a loam-based compost. Propagation: from cuttings

Ardisia crispa

of complete lateral shoots from spring to autumn or from seed in spring. Special points: the leaves sometimes develop nodules along their edges. These are harmless natural growths and should not be removed.

Begonia

The *Begonia*, one of the most widely used of house plants, is a genus from tropical and subtropical regions most species of which are grown for their foliage and some of which are grown for their brightly coloured flowers. These vary in size and shape with the species or hybrid from the double, rose-like blooms of the tuberous-rooted types to others far smaller, single and button-like, among them the *Begonia semperflorens*. In between are the trailing types and a large number of hybrids with medium-sized flowers. Flowering begonias can be divided into three groups according to root system and care—the tuberous-rooted begonias, the fibrous-rooted types and among these the shrubby begonias which in their turn require a slightly different treatment. Tuberous-rooted begonias, *Begonia × tuberhybrida*, include the splendid large-flowered Grandiflora group like 'Wedding Day', 'Corona', 'Guardsman' and 'Harlequin' with flowers 8–15 cm (3–6 in) in diameter in a wide range of colours. 'Guardsman' is

Begonia × 'Fireglow'

Begonia × *tuberhybrida* 'Guardsman'

deep orange; 'Harlequin' has dramatic white petals edged with a fine rim of deep red. Another group, known as Pendula, are suitable for hanging baskets with firm leaves and leaf stems about 20–25 cm (8–10 in) high and soft, semi-translucent, trailing flower stems with blooms in many colours 5–8 cm (2–3 in) across. A third group, known as Multiflora, have masses of small single flowers. Many of the species have red-tinged, succulent stems.

Fibrous-rooted flowering begonias bloom either in winter (like the Gloire de Lorraine and Hiemalis groups) or throughout the year like *B. semperflorens*. Gloire de Lorraine begonias, a type of mixed origin which has acquired almost specific status, have single pink flowers 1–2 cm ($\frac{1}{2}$–$\frac{3}{4}$ in) across and small round leaves. Those of the Hiemalis group have somewhat larger flowers which range in colour from white through pink to orange. Hybrids of the Eliator type are some of the most striking, among them *B.* × 'Fireglow' and *B.* × 'Schwabenland' whose large single brilliant red flowers with yellow centres contrast splendidly with their shiny, bright green leaves. These have very small tubers as well as fibrous roots but should be treated as fibrous-rooted begonias although they are extremely difficult to overwinter. *B. semperflorens* has masses of small, single flowers ranging in colour from white through

pink to red and glossy leaves. In addition there are the shrubby begonias like *B. maculata* with its elongated leaves flecked with white, red flower stems and reddish flowers. These are more erect and woody and slightly more fragile, requiring more shade, an even temperature and a richer soil. *B. fuchsoides* reaches 1 m (3 ft) and has fuschsia-like red flowers usually opening in winter and spring. *B. metallica* reaches 80 cm (32 in) and has leaves with a fine silver gloss and clusters of medium-sized red or white flowers.

Tuberous-rooted begonias (Grandiflora, Pendula and Multiflora groups).
Light and situation: a good light without direct sunlight.
Temperature: warm.
Moisture: water well in the growing and flowering periods but avoid excess water in the pot; after flowering dry out.
Overwintering: when the leaves have dropped twist the tuber off the stems and store in a cool, frost-free place or in dry sand. Repot in spring with the hollow side uppermost in a 8 cm (3 in) pot. Keep the soil just moist until growth has begun in earnest.
Soil: equal parts leafmould and sharp sand.
Propagation: cut the tubers into sections each with at least one shoot after growth has started.

Fibrous-rooted begonias (Gloire de Lorraine, Hiemalis, Eliator, *B. semperflorens*).

Light and situation: a good light without direct sunlight.
Temperature: when first bought the plant should be placed in a cool place, 12–15°C (54–59°F), for two or three days. Then transfer to a temperature of 18–20°C (64–68°F).
Moisture: water well using softened water. Maintain a high degree of humidity.
Soil: plant in shallow bowls in a rich, humus-based mixture.
Propagation: from leaf or stem cuttings in spring or summer. *B. semperflorens* cultivars are raised annually from seed by growers.
Special points: do not allow seed formation in Gloire de Lorraine begonias. Discard all types after flowering.

Shrubby begonias
Light and situation: a draught-free, slightly shady position away from direct sunlight. Do not turn the pot.
Temperature: a steady temperature of 18–20°C (64–68°F). *B. metallica* winters at 12–15°C (54–59°F).
Moisture: During the growing and flowering periods water well but avoid leaving excess water in the pot or allowing the root ball to dry out. Spray to maintain a humid atmosphere but do not allow water to fall on the flowers.
Soil: rich, humus-based.
Propagation: from leaf or stem cuttings in spring or summer.

Begonia (Pendula) 'Riga'

(left) *Billbergia × windii*   *Bougainvillea glabra*

Billbergia

This genus is among the simplest of the Bromeliads to grow and flowers easily in the home. *B. nutans*, unlike most Bromeliads, has simple, dark green, grass-like leaves but when in flower displays elegant rose-pink bracts from which hang clusters of bell-like, green and purple flowers. The plant spreads quickly and can easily be divided into clumps and repotted in summer. *B. × windii* has grey-green leaves and small bluish-green flowers on arching stems surrounded by elegantly shaped bright pink bracts. *B. pyramidalis*, a showy species, has a rosette of broad, bright green leaves from which rises a spike of crimson flowers with scarlet bracts.

Light and situation: a good light without direct sunlight. Temperature: warm but tolerant of colder spells in winter. Moisture: maintain a humid atmosphere and water freely in summer; more sparingly in winter. Soil: a mixture of loam-based compost and sphagnum moss. Propagation: by division or by removing offsets in the summer months.

Bougainvillea

This beautiful climbing shrub, named after the 18th-century French admiral de Bougainville, is covered in late spring and early summer with a mass of the scarlet, orange or purple, blossom-like bracts which surround its insignificant flowers. Because of their size—bougainvilleas can reach 3–4 m (9–13 ft) in the wild—they are best suited to the conservatory border but several types, notably *B. × buttiana* and *B. glabra*, can be grown in pots where they will reach 1–1.2 m (3–4 ft). *B. × buttiana* 'Mrs Butt' has rose crimson 'flowers'. *B. glabra* has double, pink 'flowers' and bright green leaves. Both will grow to 3 m (10 ft) in a border.

Light and situation: a good light without direct sunlight. Temperature: warm in summer but well ventilated on hot days; cool in winter and spring, 6–8°C (43–46°F). Moisture: water freely in summer; sparingly in winter. Soil: a loam-based compost.

Special points: in cool rainy weather the bracts will fade but later improve.

Bouvardia

Bouvardia × domestica is an evergreen shrub which produces pendulous groups of sweet-smelling, red, pink or white flowers at the end of its slender branches between summer and autumn. Best grown in a greenhouse or conservatory, it reaches a height of 60 cm (2 ft) and can be brought indoors in summer when in full flower. Pruning the plants in late spring or early summer produces abundant flowering. They may be pruned back hard when flowering stops.

Light and situation: place in a good light but shade from the hottest sun. Temperature: moderate 13°C (55°F) winter and summer. Moisture: water well in summer; sparingly in winter. Soil: a loam-based compost. Propagation: from stem cuttings with a heel in spring.

Bouvardia × domestica 'Pink Giant'

(above) *Browallia speciosa*

Brassia

The slender flower stem of this easily grown orchid rises to 50 cm (20 in) and in the case of *B. maculata* carries closely placed, yellow flowers, triangular and spiky in shape and flecked with brown. Both *B. maculata* and *B. verrucosa* flower in early summer.

Light and situation: a half shady position.
Temperature: warm: 18–20°C (64–68°).
Moisture: water well in the growing period; very sparingly in winter. Use lime-free water.
Soil: a mixture of two parts osmunda fibre to one part sphagnum moss.

Browallia

This tropical relation of the nightshade is called after the Finnish Lutheran bishop and botanist Johan Browallius. Many of its species are herbaceous annuals.
B. speciosa has masses of longlasting, star-shaped, violet-blue flowers with white centres set among a mass of soft, green foliage. *B.s.* 'Major' has deep blue flowers with a white edge; 'Silver Bells' has pure white flowers. Plants can be grown from seed to flower in summer if the seeds are planted in spring at 16°C (60°F) and the seedlings later placed three to a pot. For winter flowering sow in late summer.

Light and situation: a good light without direct sunlight.
Temperature: moderate.
Moisture: water freely.
Soil: a loam-based compost.
Propagation: from seed in spring or summer.

Brunfelsia

This evergreen shrub was named by Linnaeus after the 15th-century German Otto Brunfels whom he called the 'Father of Botany'. It comes from Central and South America and is happiest in a conservatory, although it can do well in a normal living room. *B. calycina* has softly shaped, fragrant, violet-mauve flowers, 5 cm (2 in) in diameter, which bloom from late spring to late summer.

Light and situation: a half-shady situation, well ventilated in summer with slightly more light in winter.
Temperature: moderate, a steady 13–16°C (55–60°F). This plant is very sensitive to changes in temperature.
Moisture: maintain a some-what humid atmosphere and water well in summer; water sparingly in winter.
Soil: a proprietary peat compost.
Propagation: from stem cuttings in summer.

(left) *Brassia brachiata*

(below) *Brunfelsia calycina*

Calceolaria

Slipper flower, slipper wort, pocket book plant

Calceolaria, known as the slipper or pocket-book plant because of the ballooning lower lip of its brightly coloured flowers, comes from the forests of the Andes. *C. × herbeohybrida* produces masses of yellow, orange or red flowers spotted with darker reds or purple above large, soft, hairy leaves, and grows to a height of about 30 cm (1 ft). An annual, it is usually bought in flower in early summer and will last for a long time if kept in a cool, shady place. Many hybrids are available. 'Grandiflora' has yellow flowers marked with shades of red. 'Multiflora Nana', a similar dwarf plant, is particularly suited to pot culture.

Light and situation: a position out of the sun, eg in a north-facing window.
Temperature: moderate, 10–12°C (50–54°F).
Moisture: water and ventilate well.
Soil: a loam-based compost.
Propagation: from seed or, in the case of shrubby species, from cuttings of non-flowering sideshoots in late summer.

(below) *Calceolaria × herbeohybrida*

Callistemon

Bottlebrush

Callistemon is a genus of evergreen shrub from Australia with fine feather-shaped, deep green leaves and in summer crimson or vermilion flower spikes consisting almost entirely of stamens which give the plant its common name. The species *Callistemon citrinus* is commonly grown outside where it reaches 3 m (10 ft) but makes a good

Callistemon citrinus

house plant if placed in a tub or pot where it will reach 1 m (3 ft). *C. speciosus*, a showy species growing to 2 m (6 ft), carries a 13 cm (5 in) rich scarlet flower spike.

Light and situation: a light and airy place in summer.
Temperature: warm in summer; cool in winter, 6–8°C (43–46°F).
Moisture: moderate.

Camellia

Camellia japonica, a relation of *C. sinensis*, the tea plant, is an evergreen shrub from Japan with glossy, dark green leaves and splendid white, pink or red, rose-like flowers usually appearing in spring though winter-flowering types are available. *C.j.* 'Alba Simplex' is a single white form and 'Adolphe Audusson' bears large, semi-double, blood-red blooms. Bought as a 2-year-old pot plant roughly 60 cm (2 ft) in height, it will grow over several years to reach 3 m (10 ft). Key to the survival and flowering of these plants is the maintenance of a cool, steady temperature and consistent treatment.

Light and situation: a semi-shady position; in summer outside if possible, eg on a draught-free balcony.
Temperature: cool, 10–12°C (50–54°F), until the buds open and then not above 16°C (60°F) until flowering is finished. In summer after flowering keep at 6–10°C (43–50°F).
Moisture: use lukewarm, softened water; water moderately in winter and spring but less in summer and autumn. Maintain a moderately humid atmosphere in winter.
Soil: a loam-based, lime-free compost.

Campanula

Bellflower

The *Campanula* is a genus of mainly hardy flowering plants from North Italy which produces a wealth of blue or white flowers in summer. ' Some species, however, do well as house plants. *C. fragilis* and *C. isophylla* are trailing plants with star-shaped flowers ideal for hanging baskets. *C. pyramidalis* has wide, bell-shaped flowers and is a biennial reaching 1.5 m (5 ft) high and for this reason best suited to a greenhouse or conservatory where it can be grown in pots and brought indoors when in flower.

Light and situation: a good light without direct sunlight. *C. fragilis* and *C. isophylla* can be placed on a sheltered balcony in summer. All are very susceptible to frost.
Temperature: in late autumn

Camellia japonica 'L'Avenir'

and spring 6–8°C (43–46°F); warm from mid spring.
Moisture: water moderately in spring and summer; less in winter, taking care that the root ball does not dry out.
Soil: a loam-based compost.

Canna

This genus of showy plants from tropical Asia and America grows to 1–2 m (3–6 ft) with broad, arching, ovate leaves often suffused with red or bronze and terminal clusters of brilliant orchid-like flowers. The dwarf hybrids *C.* × *hybrida* are

more usually grown for room cultivation and reach 50–60 cm (20–24 in). *C.* × *h.* 'Lucifer' has deep vermilion flowers edged with yellow; 'J. B. van der Schoot' has deep yellow flowers flecked with bright red.

Light and situation: a good light without direct sunlight.
Temperature: warm in summer.
Moisture: water sparingly in spring and more freely in full growth. Dry off in the autumn and store in a warm place.
Soil: a loam-based compost.
Propagation: by division of the rootstock when repotting.

Campanula isophylla 'Alba'

Canna hybrid

Capsicum
Christmas pepper, ornamental chilli

This genus of small, shrubby annuals from tropical America are grown for their brightly coloured fruits which ripen from late summer to winter. The genus includes cayenne and paprika as well as red and green peppers. *C. annuun*, the species most commonly grown as a house plant, produces ornamental red and green chilli peppers. Hybrids vary in the shape and colour of their fruits. 'Christmas Greeting' is 45 cm (18 in) tall with small, pepper-shaped fruits in green, violet and red.

Light and situation: a good light without direct sunlight.
Temperature: cool.

(below) *Catharanthus roseus*

Moisture: water moderately.
Soil: a loam-based compost.
Propagation: from seeds sown in spring.

Catharanthus roseus
Madagascar periwinkle

The Madagascar periwinkle, an erect, evergreen perennial usually cultivated as an annual is best suited to the conservatory. It has small, ovate, dark green, glossy leaves and terminal clusters of flat, five-lobed flowers, deep pink in colour with a dark central eye which are produced throughout summer and autumn.

Light and situation: a well ventilated position in a good light without direct sunlight.
Temperature: warm.
Moisture: water freely from spring to autumn; more sparingly in winter.
Soil: a proprietary peat mix.
Propagation: from seed in spring or from stem cuttings in summer.

Capsicum annuum

Celosia argentea

Celosia argentea, a flowering plant from tropical Asia, is usually sold in flower as an annual pot plant. It grows up to 60 cm (2 ft) in height and has light green, slightly dentate, wavy leaves and encrusted plumes or dense flat heads of fine silky flowers in summer and autumn. *C. a.* 'Cristata' has dense flat heads of bright red, orange or yellow flowers and small oval leaves. It grows to 30 cm (1 ft) in height. *C. a.* 'Pyramidalis' has piled plumes of flowers, red or yellow according to strain.

Light and situation: a well ventilated position in a good light but shaded from the hottest sun.
Temperature: warm.
Moisture: keep moist.
Soil: a loam-based compost.
Propagation: from seeds in the spring months.

Chorizema
Flame pea

The *Chorizema* belongs to the pea family and is known as the flame pea because of its red and yellow flowers. *Chorizema cordatum* is a climbing shrub with delicate branches, spiny leaves and clusters of flowers with orange, red and purple markings which appear in late spring and summer. It is best suited to the conservatory where it makes a

Chorizema cordatum

Celosia argentea 'Pyramidalis'

loose bush if pruned in early summer or will cover a trellis 1.2 m (4ft) square if left unpruned. Another species, *Chorizema ilicifolium*, a low, spreading shrub, makes a good house plant when regularly pruned.

Light and situation: a good light without direct sunlight.

Temperature: warm; ventilate well on warm days.
Moisture: water well in summer but allow to dry out a little between waterings.
Propagation: from cuttings taken in late spring.

Chrysanthemum

The *Chrysanthemum*, which came originally from China and Japan, provides some of the best-known flowering house plants though many species are also hardy. Those grown indoors are hybrids and cultivars of *C. indicum* and *C. morifolium*. They reach 45–60 cm (18–24 in) and present an enormous variety of flower colours and forms. If the plant is to be kept after flowering for another year cut back to 5 cm (2 in) above the soil in late autumn.

Light and situation: away from direct sunlight.
Temperature: cool and well ventilated.
Moisture: water well.
Propagation: by young stem cuttings from the new shoots of pruned plants in spring.

(right) *Chrysanthemum* hybrid

Cineraria cruenta

These plants with their densely coloured red, pink, purple or white, daisy-like flowers are easy to grow from seed and often sold as flowering plants in winter and spring. Like flowering chrysanthemums they are disposable. They come in a

number of sizes ranging
from 35 to 75 cm (15 to 30 in)
depending on the hybrid.

Light and situation: shade
from direct sunlight but stand
outside in summer if possible.
Temperature: cool.
Moisture: take care to water
and ventilate well.

Cineraria cruenta hybrid

Clerodendrum thomsonae
Bleeding heart vine, glory
bower

Clerodendrum thomsonae, one
of three or four species of
this pantropical genus of
shrubs and climbing plants
grows to 4 m (13 ft). The
glossy, dark green leaves are
heart-shaped and the dark red
flowers appear in spring
surrounded by white calices
which are the plant's chief
attraction. *C. splendens*,
another climber, also grows
to 4 m (13 ft) and has scarlet
flowers in summer. *C.
ugandense* reaches 3 m (10 ft)
and has glossy, oval, deep
green, dentate leaves and
clusters of bright, mauvy-
blue, trumpet-shaped flowers
appearing mainly in spring
but often throughout much of
the rest of the year as well.
C. speciosissimum, a
particularly showy evergreen
species has large, heart-
shaped leaves and loose
clusters of scarlet blooms
up to 25 cm (10 in) across
with long stamens. All species
require warmth to thrive.

Light and situation: a good
light without direct sunlight.
Temperature: warm in
summer; 10–12°C (50–54°F) in
winter.
Moisture: water generously in
summer and maintain a
humid atmosphere; more
sparingly in winter.
Soil: a loam-based compost.
Propagation: from seed in
spring or from stem cuttings
in summer.
Special points: the plant loses
most of its foliage in winter
and should be cut back in
spring.

Clivia miniata
Kafir lily

A long-lived flowering plant
growing to 45 cm (18 in) high,
the *Clivia miniata* still looks
pleasing when not in flower
and has become a favourite
for restaurants and hotels
because it is undemanding to
keep. It has plumes of strap-
like, evergreen leaves and
clusters of open trumpet-
shaped, orange-red flowers in
spring and summer. Clivias
are usually bought in flower
and the plant and the flowers
multiply each year. They are
best kept in the same place
for successive years and
perhaps happiest in an east-
facing window. Repotting is
done in early autumn when

necessary, yearly in the case
of young plants but with older
plants only after much
longer intervals.

Light and situation: in a good
light but shaded from the
hottest sun.
Temperature: cool; not above
12–15°C (54–59°F) in winter.
Moisture: water freely in
summer, allowing the surface

soil to dry out between
waterings; sparingly in winter
Soil: a loam and sand mixture
Propagation: remove the
small plants formed at the
base of the main plant after
flowering has finished.

Clerodendrum thomsonae

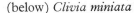

(below) *Clivia miniata*

Coelogyne

Coelogyne, a genus of evergreen tree orchid from East Asia, is one of the easiest orchids to grow as a house plant. With its pairs of dark green, strap-like leaves and delicate, pendulous flower stems it does best in an orchid basket. The flowers, which appear in late winter and spring, are complex in shape and range in colour from white and yellow to pink and tan. The chief species, *C. cristata*, has single white flowers with a yellow tongue up to 10 cm (4 in) across and growing in groups of three or

(above) *Coelogyne intermedia*

four. Mature plants may carry dozens of blooms at once.

Light and situation: a position shaded from the hottest sun, eg in an east-facing window.
Temperature: cool; in winter 14–15°C (57–59°F).
Moisture: water regularly in summer; reduce watering to a minimum in winter.
Soil: a sphagnum moss and osmunda fibre mixture.
Propagation: by division in spring.

(below) *Coleus thyrsoideus*

Coleus

Coleus, best known as a foliage plant (eg *C. blumei*), also has a number of species grown for their flowers. *Coleus fredericii*, an annual, reaches 1 m (3–4 ft) and has clusters of deep blue flowers in winter. *C. thyrsoideus* has taller flower spikes in a paler shade of blue. *C. pumilus*, a trailing species, does well in hanging baskets and produces multi-coloured leaves and blue flowers.

Light and situation: a good light without direct sunlight.
Temperature: warm.
Moisture: water freely in winter and spring; sparingly in summer.
Soil: a loam-based compost.
Propagation: from seed or stem tip cuttings in spring or late summer.

Columnea

This genus of climbing and trailing shrub-like epiphytes from Central and South Africa takes its name from Fabio Colonna, a 16th-century Italian botanist. The trailing types are ideal for hanging baskets, notably *C. gloriosa* and *C. microphylla* with their neatly paired, evergreen leaves and scarlet and yellow tubular flowers which appear in winter and spring.

Light and situation: a good light without direct sunlight.
Temperature: warm, in winter 15–18°C (59–64°F).
Moisture: a humid atmosphere and regular watering with lukewarm, softened water.
Soil: a loam and sphagnum moss or peat mix.
Propagation: from stem cuttings in summer.

(below) *Columnea microphylla* 'Grandiflora'

Convallaria
Lily-of-the-valley

This genus of small hardy plants from the temperate regions is not strictly a house plant but may be forced for flowering in spring in the house if specially prepared crowns are bought in winter. The basal leaves are spear-shaped and the fragrant, white, bell-shaped flowers grow on either side of slender stems 15 cm (6 in) high. Pot the crowns in damp moss with the tops just showing and keep moist and warm. When the crowns put out shoots remove the top layer of moss and place in a cool, light position. In a normally heated room the plants will flower in a few days. The plants are now also available in 'lillipots' at Christmas and Easter and should be watered when received, left in the dark for up to ten days and then brought into the light at a temperature of 12°C (54°F).

Crossandra

Crossandra infundibuliformis is the only species of this originally Indian genus grown as a house plant. A shrubby plant reaching 30 cm-1 m (1–3 ft), it was at first considered too difficult for room cultivation but this is not true of the cultivar 'Mona Wallhed' with its broad, ovate leaves and crinoline-shaped

Convallaria majalis

clusters of soft, orangy-yellow flowers. To maintain a good shape pinch out the young plants.

Light and situation: a good light but without direct sunlight.
Temperature: warm: not below 18°C (64°F).
Moisture: water freely in the growing period; moderately after flowering. Use lukewarm softened water and maintain a humid atmosphere but do not allow drops of water to fall on the flowers as this will stain them.
Soil: a loam-based compost.
Propagation: from basal stem cuttings in spring with a warm soil temperature.

Crossandra infundibuliformis

Cyclamen persicum

These cool-loving, evergreen plants from the Eastern Mediterranean, usually sold in flower in autumn and winter, are often better suited to bedrooms and halls than to the living room which may be too warm and dry. The original species is pink but cultivars (listed as *C. p. giganteum*) range in colour from white to deep crimson. Most types have silver, symmetrical markings on their compact, heart-shaped leaves. *C.p. giganteum* 'Rex' and 'Shell Pink' both have beautiful silver markings on their leaves while 'Rosalie' has pale, warm pink and 'White Swan' brilliant white flowers. When bought the plants should be put in a cool, shady place in the house and the soil kept just moist by plunging the pots into a bowl of damp peat. If the corms are above the surface the pots may be watered in the usual way but if they are buried then it is better to pour off the water in the pot saucer after half an hour to avoid over-watering. Densely leaved plants may need watering twice a day. Often these plants are thrown away after flowering but if carefully looked after may go on to flower for several

years. When the leaves yellow and there are no buds watering should be gradually stopped and the pot laid on its side in a dark, cool place until early summer. It should then be placed outside if possible in a cool, shady spot taking care that it is not subject to frost and watered until leaves begin to appear. The plant is then repotted with half the crown above the surface and kept in a shady place until the buds are seen. As the leaves appear place in a slightly lighter spot.

Light and situation: a shady position.
Temperature: cool; in winter 8–10°C (46–50°F)
Moisture: water well during the growing period; sparingly later and not at all while dormant.
Soil: a loamy mixture.
Special points: dead flowers and leaves should be carefully pulled off.

Cyclamen persicum hybrid

Cymbidium

Most species of *Cymbidium* are terrestrial orchids best suited to the unheated greenhouse but the newer cultivars and hybrids are some of the easiest orchids to grow in the home provided they are given plenty of light and air and kept cool. Their splendid flowers, which appear from autumn to spring in a wide range of colours, grow six or eight to a stem and are excellent for cutting. 'Vieux Rose' has deep rose pink striped flowers; 'Rosanna Pinkie' white flowers with pink and crimson markings to the central cup.

Light and situation: very light but shaded from the hottest sun; a position well ventilated, away from other plants.
Temperature: cool; 7–12°C (45–54°F) in winter.
Moisture: water freely in summer; less after flowering in autumn and winter. Use softened water at room temperature.
Soil: loam, peat and sand, or peat and sphagnum moss.
Propagation: by division after flowering.

(below) *Cymbidium* hybrid

Dipladenia

These twining, evergreen shrubs are happy in a living room in summer and are usually discarded after flowering but may be over-wintered. The flower spikes, 15–20 cm (6–8 in) long, appear from summer to late autumn. The flowers are rose-pink and trumpet-shaped, often lasting a week or more and providing a pleasing contrast with the glossy, dark green leaves. *D. sanderi* 'Rosea' has large, pink flowers with a yellow throat; *D. boliviensis* clusters of three or four white flowers with a yellow throat. Originally found in the tropical rain forests of South America, dipladenias are bushy when young but

Dipladenia boliviensis

later become climbers and should be trained on canes. Certain species will reach 4.5 m (15 ft). The main problem in keeping these plants indoors is the high degree of humidity they require in the growing period and the size to which they eventually grow.

Light and situation: a half shady position.
Temperature: warm; if over-wintered, 12–15°C (54–59°F) in winter.
Moisture: water well in summer; sparingly in winter.
Soil: a loam-based compost.
Propagation: from 8 cm (3 in) stem sections in spring each with a pair of leaves planted with a warm soil temperature.

Dendrobium

This genus of orchids from East Asia includes some of those easier to grow in the home. *D. nobile*, the best-known species for room cultivation, carries a wealth of 5–8 cm (2–3 in) blooms in spring varying in colour according to strain. *D. chrysanthum* has deep yellow flowers borne in late summer and early autumn. *D. densiflorus* has pendent racemes of 50–100 bright yellow blooms which appear in spring and early summer. *D. wardianum* has blooms with white sepals and petals with purple tips which appear in spring.

Light and situation: a good light without direct sunlight near a south-facing window.
Temperature: warm in the growing period, 24°C (75°F); 8–10° (46–50°F) in the resting period.
Moisture: water well in the growing period and maintain a humid atmosphere; water more sparingly in the resting period.
Soil: sphagnum moss and chopped osmunda fibre.

Dendrobium xanthecentrum

Drejerella
Shrimp plant

Drejerella (or *Beloperone gutatta*) is known as the shrimp plant because its delicate white flowers emerge from beneath a cluster of overlapping, petal-like bracts ranging in colour from reddish-brown to violet and yellow and resembling a shrimp's body. The flowers are long-lasting and appear during much of the year. The plant should be cut back in early summer to maintain its shape

Light and situation: a good light.
Temperature: cool in winter, 12–15°C (54–59°F).
Moisture: water freely in summer; less in winter.
Soil: a loam-based compost.
Propagation: from young stem cuttings in spring or summer in an indoor propagator.

Episcia

This genus of trailing, evergreen plants from South America are grown for their decorative foliage and small, brightly coloured flowers. *E. cupreata* is grown chiefly for its foliage which is soft, furry and wrinkled, mid green with a red and silver central band and small bright red flowers. It has many cultivars with silver markings. *E. reptans*, a smaller species, has coppery green, soft, furry, wrinkled leaves with silvery veins and small, scarlet, trumpet-shaped flowers. *E. dianthiflora* has plain green, ovate, incised leaves with delicate white flowers whose petals end in fine white hairs.

Care: as for *Fittonia*
peat based compost

Erica
Heath

These shrubby, evergreen flowering heathers, originally from Africa, are sold covered in rose-coloured flowers in autumn and winter. *Erica gracilis*, a small shrub which can reach 45 cm (18 in), produces clusters of deep pink, bell-like flowers in autumn and winter. *E.×hyemalis* with its pinkish-white, tubular flowers grows to 60 cm (2 ft).

Light and situation: a well-lit position, sunny in summer and with plenty of fresh air.

(above) *Drejerella* hybrids   (below) *Erica × hyemalis*

Temperature: cool in winter, 6–8°C (43–46°F).
Moisture: water generously in summer; less in winter. Use softened water.
Soil: a lime-free, peat compost.
Propagation: from cuttings of young sideshoots in late summer.

(below) *Episcia dianthiflora*

Euphorbia

(above) *Euphorbia fulgens*

Euphorbia, a very varied genus including succulent, herbaceous and shrubby species, includes several well-known house plants. All, however, are poisonous to touch. *E. fulgens* is a bright, evergreen shrub growing to about 1 m (3 ft) as a house plant with masses of orange flowers which can be made to bloom at almost any time of the year but usually appear in autumn and winter. *Euphorbia milii splendens*, a very decorative woody plant with stems covered in long, sharp thorns and small, bright, apple-green leaves, has brilliant scarlet or yellow flowers which appear from late winter to early summer and reaches 1 m (3 ft) in height. It does well in a sunny place and is tolerant of dry air but does not, like other succulent euphorbias, need a cool place in winter. *E. pulcherrima*, a winter-flowering spurge, commonly known as poinsettia, was used a great deal in late 19th-century jardinieres. The terminal frills of coloured bracts in scarlet, pink or white are its main attraction, giving the impression of a delicate but broad-leaved, star-shaped flower. These are 'short day' plants: too much or too long a period of light will stop the formation of the coloured bracts and they will revert to green foliage plants. After flowering cut back to 10 cm (4 in) leaving a few shoots.

E. fulgens
Light and situation: a good light without direct sunlight. Temperature: warm in summer; cool in winter. Moisture: water freely in summer; less in autumn and keep almost dry during spring. Soil: a sand and loam mixture. Propagation: from cuttings of cut back plants in spring. Special points: the spurge juice is very poisonous; lesions in the stem will normally dry up but if the juice gets on to skin it should be washed off immediately with cold water. Use gloves.

E. milii splendens
Light and situation: a good light. Place outside in summer if possible. Temperature: warm. Moisture: water moderately; in winter, just enough to prevent the root ball drying out. Soil: a sand and loam mix. Propagation: from seed or cuttings in spring. It is best to take tip cuttings from old branches. Special points: the plant is poisonous. Use gloves.

E. pulcherrima
Light and situation: short day plants; a good light without direct sunlight. Temperature: warm; in winter 18–20°C (64–68°F). Moisture: water freely in summer and autumn using only tepid water; water very sparingly after flowering in spring. Propagation: from shoot tips in summer. Special points: the plant is poisonous. Use gloves.

(above) *Euphorbia pulcherrima*   (below) *Exacum affine*

Exacum affine
Persian violet

This small, bushy annual from Socotra with its shiny, bright green leaves and sweet-smelling, purple-blue flowers with yellow centres grows to 15 cm (6 in) in height and often flowers from summer until late autumn. Plants are bought in June. *E.a.* 'Midget' is the commonest form.

Light and situation: a good light without direct sunlight. Temperature: moderate to cool. Moisture: keep the soil moist with softened water. Soil: a loam-based compost.

(right) *Gardenia jasminoides*

Fuchsia

This genus of flowering shrubs from Central and South America make good plants for the conservatory or short term pot plants for the house. The flowers are pendent and consist of a many petalled, double bell shape usually in contrasting colours with protruding stamens. There are numerous species and many hybrids with a range of flower shapes and colours from red, white and pink to purple and mauve.

Light and situation: a well ventilated, half-shady position.
Temperature: warm in summer; 10–12°C (50–54°F) in winter.
Moisture: keep constantly moist and maintain a humid atmosphere in summer; water more sparingly in winter.
Soil: a loam-based compost.
Propagation: from stem cuttings in spring or late summer.

Gardenia

Many species of this flowering shrub with its glossy, dark green leaves and magnificently scented, rose-like, white flowers are difficult to grow except in a greenhouse but the winter-flowering *G. jasminoides* and its smaller hybrid *G. j.* 'Veitchii' make suitable house plants. Like the *Camellia*, they need careful attention, in particular to prevent damage from cold in the winter months but with it

can last for several years and grow to between 30 cm and 2 m (1–6 ft). *G. j.* 'Fortuniana' has waxy double white flowers 10 cm (4 in) across.

Light and situation: a good light without direct sunlight and good ventilation.
Temperature: warm, 16–18°C (60–64°F), and a constant soil temperature of 18–20°C (64–68°F).
Moisture: water moderately with softened, tepid water.

Fuchsia 'Dr. Foster'

Maintain a humid atmosphere by spraying.
Soil: a rich, lime-free compost.
Propagation: from shoot tips in spring. Place under a plastic bag to retain moisture and give some bottom heat.
Special points: when repotting be careful not to damage the roots and to plant at the same level as before. This plant is particularly suscep-tible to red spider.

Gloriosa
Glory lily

This genus of tender, tuberous-rooted, perennial climbers from Tropical Africa needs the protection of a greenhouse except in the warmest regions. The mid green leaves are elongated and spear-shaped ending in fine tendrils. *G. rothschildiana* grows to 2 m (6 ft) with yellow-edged crimson flowers appearing singly or in groups from early to late summer. *G. superba* has smaller flowers with petals that change in colour as they mature from green through yellow to red. Twigs or wires are needed to give the plant support.

Light and situation: a good light without direct sunlight.
Temperature: warm in spring and summer.
Moisture: water normally in summer.
Planting and overwintering: tubers are planted in late spring and should be started into growth at 16–19°C (60–66°F) and kept in a humid atmosphere. After flowering, when the stems die back, the tubers are dried out and stored at a temperature of 10–13°C (50–55°F) ready for replanting the following spring.
Soil: a loam-based compost.
Propagation: by division of the tubers (somewhat difficult); from seed or from offsets.

Gloriosa rothschildiana

(above) *Hoya carnosa*

Heliotropium
Heliotrope

This perennial, usually treated as a half-hardy annual, has one of the most beautiful scents in the flower world. The large flower trusses range in colour from deepest violet (*H. arborescens*, the common heliotrope) and pale mauve to white (hybrids of the former) and appear in summer and early autumn. These plants can be used in window boxes and containers outside but also make a pretty pot plant in the house. As a bushy plant they can grow to 30 cm (1 ft) or may be trained as a single stem 1·2 m (4 ft) tall.

Light and situation: a good light.
Temperature: warm in summer; cool in winter.
Moisture: water moderately keeping the root ball moist.
Soil: a loam-based or soilless compost.
Propagation: by stem cuttings in autumn or early spring.

Hibiscus
Rose mallow

The *Hibiscus*, a member of the mallow family from China and a relation of the *Abutilon*, is a flowering shrub which if kept well as a pot plant may grow into a small tree 2 m (6 ft) in height. Its dramatic, broad, trumpet-shaped flowers

Heliotropium hybrid

with their protruding stamens vary in colour with species and type from brilliant orange through pink and crimson to deep scarlet. Each flower lasts for a day only but new buds appear constantly in the flowering period which usually lasts from summer to autumn. Cultivars of *H. rosa-sinensis*, the best developed species for growth as a house plant, include 'Apricot', 'Cooperi' with its variegated leaves and cream and dark red flowers and 'The President', which has deep crimson pink blooms with yellow stamens.
H. mutabilis produces pale pink blooms which deepen to clear red in a day.

Light and situation: a good light but without direct sunlight.
Temperature: warm in summer; moderate in winter 12–15°C (54–59°F).
Moisture: water generously, twice a day if necessary, in summer; less in autumn and winter, spraying occasionally.
Soil: a loam-based compost.
Propagation: from tip cuttings in early summer with a soil temperature of 24–26°C (75–79°F).

Hibiscus rosa-sinensis
hybrid

Hoya

The *Hoya* is a genus of vigorous, evergreen climbers from the Far East with clusters of star-shaped, waxy white flowers and fleshy, dark green leaves which do well in a conservatory and as house plants are usually sold trained round wires or canes. Two species are grown in the home: *Hoya carnosa* with its hybrids 'Variegata' and 'Compacta', the former with dark green leaves edged with rosy pink, the latter with leaves twisted into unusual shapes round the stem; and *Hoya bella*, a dwarf species with more pendulous stems ideal for a hanging basket in a plant window. Its flowers have purplish-red centres.

Light and situation: a good light without direct sunlight, well ventilated but free from draughts.
Temperature: warm in summer; in winter 10–12°C (50–54°F). Prior to flowering again the plant should be kept for two weeks at 15–18°C (59–64°F). This can best be achieved by placing it out of direct sunlight behind a curtain on a window sill (without a radiator below).
Moisture: maintain a humid atmosphere. Water moderately in summer; sparingly in winter. *H. bella*: spray before the plant shoots and then not until after it has flowered.
Soil: a loam-based mixture.
Propagation: from stem cuttings in summer or by layering.

Hydrangea

This familiar and popular flowering shrub comes from Asia Minor but is also found in North and South America, growing to 4 m (12 ft) in its wild state. Cultivated strains of *H. macrophylla*, usually hardy, are bought in flower in spring and can be grown in the home where in a pot they will reach 1 m (3 ft). The shrub has broad, oval, dentate leaves and large heads of flat florets ranging in colour according to strain from white and pale pink to deep pink, carmine red or blue (the last only if aluminium sulphate is used). The plants should be repotted each year when young; older plants less often. Dead flowers should be removed with one or two pairs of leaves.

Light and situation: a shady, well ventilated position in spring; in summer place outside on a shaded balcony if possible or by an open window.
Temperature: cool; in winter 4–8°C (40–46°F).
Moisture: water well, twice a day if necessary, using softened water and making sure the root ball remains moist.
Soil: a loam-based, life-free mixture.

Impatiens
Touch-me-not, busy lizzie, balsam

Impatiens is a genus of freely-branching evergreen shrubs with thick, fleshy, almost translucent stems and a mass

Impatiens New Guinea hybrid

of semi-phosphorescent flowers in orange, vermilion, scarlet or mauve. *I. wallerana holstii*, known as busy lizzie because of its vigorous growth, has red stems and scarlet flowers with flat petals 2·5–5 cm (1–2 in) in diameter and green or brown-tinged, pointed oval leaves. The flowers appear throughout the year and the species reaches 30–60 cm (1–2 ft) in height. *I. balsamina* is a low-growing, half-hardy annual with pink flowers in summer.

Light and situation: a good light without direct sunlight; a half-shady position in autumn and spring.
Temperature: warm in winter

20°C (68°F) in a good light. A darker position requires a temperature of only 15°C (59°F).
Moisture: keep the root ball moist. Do not spray on the flowers as this will stain them.
Soil: a loam-based compost.
Propagation: from cuttings or from seed.

Ipomoea
Morning glory

Ipomoea, known as morning glory because its splendid soft, trumpet-shaped flowers last only one day, is a genus of vigorous climbing annuals from the tropics which are easily trained on canes and wires. *I. purpurea* has purple stems and purple blooms 8 cm (3 in) across appearing in summer. Its cultivar 'Scarlet O'Hara' has deep crimson flowers. *Ipomoea rubro-caerulea* (syn. *I tricolor*) bears a large number of pale mauvish-blue flowers up to 13 cm (5 in) across.

Light and situation: a good light without direct sunlight.
Temperature: warm.
Moisture: keep barely moist.
Soil: a loam-based mixture.
Propagation: from seed in spring.

Ipomoea rubro-caerulea

Hydrangea macrophylla hybrid

Ixora coccinea 'Peter Rapsley'

Ixora coccinea
Flame of the woods

Ixora coccinea, an evergreen shrub from tropical India, is a greenhouse plant that flourishes in a densely planted flower window. It grows to 1 m (3 ft) in height and has bright green, shiny, leathery leaves and large clusters of scarlet flowers on red stems. The flowers appear in summer and vary in colour with the strain, and include orange and salmon pink types.

Light and situation: place in a tropical plant window, in a slightly shaded position in spring and summer.
Temperature: not below 16–18°C (60–64°F) in winter with a soil temperature of 18–20°C (64–68°F).
Moisture: water well in spring and summer; less in autumn and winter. Maintain a humid atmosphere.
Soil: a loam-based mixture.

Jacobinia

Three species of this flowering shrub from tropical America are suitable as house plants. *J. carnea* has soft, furry leaves and plume-like pink and orange flowers which appear from among terminal heads of green, leaf-like bracts in summer. *J. pauciflora* bears similiar flowers with yellow tips in winter and spring. *Jacobinia pohliana* reaches 1·2 m (4 ft) and has large

terminal clusters of pink or carmine flowers.

J. carnea, J. pohliana
Light and situation: a half shady plant window with plenty of space.
Temperature: warm; in winter 18–20°C (64–68°F).
Moisture: a humid atmosphere.
Soil: a loam-based compost.
Propagation: from cuttings in spring at a soil temperature of 20–22°C (68–72°F).

J. pauciflora
Light and situation: a good light. Place outside in a sunny

Jacobinia pohliana

position in summer if possible.
Temperature: moderate: in autumn and winter 8–10°C (46–50°F).
Moisture: water very freely during the growing period using tepid, softened water; maintain a humid atmosphere in spring, spraying the plant from time to time.
Soil and Propagation: as for *J. carnea*.

Jasminum
Jasmine

Jasminum is a genus of flowering, often climbing shrubs from China, the tropics and sub-tropics which represents a borderline case between garden and house plants. Most species have white or yellow tubular flowers opening out into a star shape and pinnate groups of pointed, oval, dark green leaflets along the slender arching stems. The plant should be trained on supports. *J. mesnyi* (*J. primulinum*), the primrose jasmine, has semi-double, pale yellow flowers 5 cm (2 in) across in spring and early summer. *J. polyanthum* grows to 3 m (10 ft) and has clusters of white and pink flowers appearing in winter and spring.

Light and situation: a good light without direct sunlight.
Temperature: warm in summer; cool in winter.
Moisture: water well in summer; less in winter.

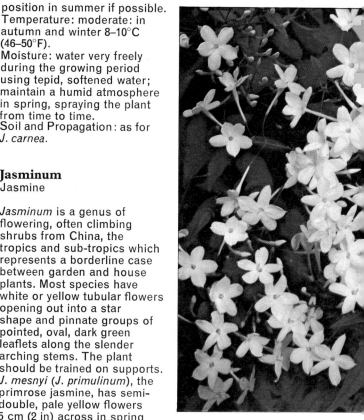

Jasminum polyanthum

Soil: a loam-based compost.
Propagation: from stem cuttings in spring or autumn.

Kohleria

This genus of evergreen plants from Central and South America includes many species which may be grown in pots or in hanging baskets. The flowers are tubular, somewhat like foxgloves, and turned back at the rim into speckled lobes. They appear along the main stem growing from the leaf axils in summer and autumn. *K. amabilis* reaches 60 cm (2 ft) and has dark green leaves with purple-black markings and rose and purple flowers. *K. eriantha* has more finely pointed, deep green leaves edged with red hairs on reddish stems and has brilliant scarlet flowers marked with yellow spots on the lower lips.

Light and situation: a good light without direct sunlight.
Temperature: keep warm when started into growth at 21°C (70°F); when in flower reduce the temperature to 18°C (64°F).
Moisture: water moderately in spring and freely in summer.

Gradually dry off after the leaves have withered. Overwintering: store pots of rhizomes on their sides in a dry place at 12°C (54°F). Soil: a loam-based compost. Propagation: by division of the rhizomes in spring or from stem cuttings in summer.

Kohleria hybrid

Lycaste

Lycaste, a genus of orchid from Guatemala with dramatic proportions, includes several species which are relatively easy to grow in the home. *L. virginalis* has white, waxy, blooms touched with pink up to 15 cm (6 in) across. In addition there are many hybrids, among them the Auburn group with flowers in shades of pink and red.

Light and situation: a shady, well ventilated position. Temperature: cool. Moisture: water freely. Soil: a mixture of loam, osmunda fibre, leaf mould and sphagnum moss. Propagation: by division in spring.

Miltonia
Pansy orchid

This genus of orchids which resembles *Odontoglossum* and *Oncidium* comes from South America. The flowers are flat, somewhat pansy-like, with pointed upper petals and a rounded double lower lip. The blooms appear along arching flower stems 30–45 cm (12–18 in) long and the strap-shaped leaves grow from the base of the plant. Several species are cultivated. *M. candida* bears flowers in autumn up to six to a stem with yellowy-green petals, reddish-brown markings and a white lower lip tinged with

pink. The flowers appear in autumn three or six to a 30 cm (12 in) stem. *M. regnelli* has white or pale pink flowers 5–8 cm (2–3 in) across with a purple lower lip and yellow crest appearing in summer and autumn. A striking species, *M. spectabilis*, produces one flower 8–10 cm (3–4 in) across to each flower stem, with white petals tinged with pink and a large pinkish-purple lower lip with a white rim.

Lycaste 'Auburn' hybrid

The flowers appear in autumn. *M. clowesii* has chestnut brown blooms with yellow tips, dark purplish banding and a white and violet lip. The flowers appear in autumn. There are also many hybrids between species.

Care: as for *Odontoglossum*.

Miltonia hybrids

Myrtus
Myrtle

Myrtus communis, called bride's myrtle because of its traditional use in bridal bouquets, is an evergreen fragrant-leaved hardy shrub. Its pretty, cream-coloured flowers topped by a rich star of stamens appear in profusion in early summer contrasting boldly with the plant's deep green, finely shaped, oval leaves.

Light and situation: a good light and a well ventilated position.
Temperature: warm in summer; cool in winter, 4–6°C (40–43°F).
Moisture: water moderately using softened water.
Soil: a rich, lime-free, humus-based mixture.
Propagation: from cuttings of the flowering stems in summer.

Myrtus communis

Those suitable for room cultivation include *C. ornithorhynchum*, which in winter produces groups of sweetly scented, pale pink flowers with a yellow crest, and the spectacular *O. varicosum* which has pendulous stems up to 1 m (3 ft) in length each carrying 80–90 blooms. The flowers present an unusual mixture of yellowy-greens, bright yellows and reddish browns and appear in autumn. They are good for cutting.

Light and situation: a shady position.
Temperature: according to species (see instructions when buying the plant).
Moisture: maintain a humid atmosphere; water sparingly.
Soil: two parts osmunda fibre to one sphagnum moss.

white crisped petals touched with pink, crimson and yellow. The flowers appear at all times of the year but most freely in spring.

Light and situation: shady.
Temperature: cool.
Moisture: keep moist.
Soil: two parts osmunda fibre to one part sphagnum moss.

Oncidium

The *Oncidium*, one of the largest genera of orchids comes like *Odontoglossum*, to which it is related, from Central and South America. Most species are epiphytic.

Oxalis
Wood sorrel

Oxalis is a low-growing genus from tropical South America with clover-like leaves and a profusion of small five-petalled flowers appearing from spring to autumn. *Oxalis boweiana* has mauvish-pink flowers; *O. rubra* rose red. *Oxalis deppei*, which is often given as a New Year's gift in Continental Europe because its leaves which grow in groups of four are considered lucky, has pale crimson flowers with yellow centres. If planted as a

Oncidium hybrid

Odontoglossum

Odontoglossum is a genus of remarkably beautiful, epiphytic orchids from the tropical rain forests of Central and South America with fine complex flowers sometimes 16·5 cm (6½ in) across and long, pendulous or erect flower stems. They are delicate plants some of which may be grown in pots or orchid baskets in the home. The Mexican species and their

(above) *Odontoglossum crispum*

hybrids are some of those best suited to be grown as house plants. These include *O. grande* and its hybrids whose 30 cm (12 in) flower spikes carry a cluster of butterfly-like blooms up to 18 cm (7 in) across. *Odontoglossum crispum*, the lace orchid, has arching flower stems 60 cm (2 ft) long each bearing several 10 cm (4 in) blooms with brilliant

172

Oxalis rubra

Light and situation: a good light without direct sunlight. Temperature: moderate; in winter 15°C (59°F). Moisture: water generously in the growing period, using softened, tepid water; less in winter, spraying occasionally. Soil: a loam-based compost. Propagation: from stem cuttings in spring or summer, preferably taken from non-flowering young shoots from cut-back plants.

Paphiopedilum
Lady's slipper, slipper orchid, Venus slipper

The *Paphiopedilum*, called the slipper orchid because of its generous, slipper-shaped lower lip, is a genus of tropical, mainly terrestrial orchids from East Asia and the Pacific. The tall flower stems of *P. insigne* appear in autumn and winter, each usually bearing only one bloom 8–10 cm (3–4 in) across, a yellow-green orchid with purplish-brown markings. It has many cultivars, some of the best known of which are *P.i.* 'Aureum', 'Chantinii', 'Harefield Hall' and 'Sanderae'. *P. glaucophyllum*, a native of Java, bears several flowers each 10 cm (4 in) across throughout the year on stems 40 cm (16 in) high.

Light and situation: a good light. Temperature: moderate; in winter 12–15°C (54–59°F). Moisture: water well in summer; sparingly in winter. Use lime-free water and maintain a humid atmosphere. Soil: a mixture of osmunda fibre, sphagnum moss and loam. Propagation: by division in spring.

Paphiopedilum glaucophyllum

bulb four or six to a pot it should be kept in a cool place at 6–8°C (43–46°F) and watered sparingly until shoots appear.

Light and situation: a sunny position. Temperature: cool, 12–14°C (54–57°F). Moisture: water sparingly. Soil: a loam-based mixture. Propagation: by removing offset bulbs or from seed in autumn.

Pachystachys lutea
Lollipop plant

This plant resembles the *Drejerella* in the structure of its flowers and the treatment it requires. Its delicate, creamy-white flowers emerge from terminal groups of long-lasting, bright yellow bracts like dense ears of corn and appear in spring, summer and autumn.

(below) *Pachystachys lutea*

Passiflora
Passion flower

The *Passiflora*, or passion flower vine, is a genus of powerful climbing plants, many of them from tropical South America, which must be trained on wires or canes to be grown in the home. The large flowers 5–10 cm (2–4 in) across according to species have a complex arrangement of petals and filaments giving a halo or crown of thorns effect at the centre of which the stamens and ovaries rise on a stem. *P. quadrangularis*, a very large and particularly exotic species, has white petals flushed with pink and deep purple and a crown of long filaments striped purple, white and blue. The flowers appear in summer.

Light and situation: a good light with direct sunlight in a well ventilated position, eg round a window.
Temperature: moderate in summer; cool in winter, 6–8°C (43–46°F).
Moisture: water well in summer, twice a day if necessary; sparingly in winter.
Soil: a rich humus-based soil with some loam.
Propagation: remove runners and pot singly.
Special points: before repotting in spring, cut back the old stems leaving six or eight buds.

(above) *Passiflora quadrangularis*

(above) *Passiflora caerulea*

Pelargonium
Geranium

This genus of flowering plants from Southern Africa consists of over 200 species but the forms now grown as house plants belong to four main groups of cultivars only one of which, the scented-leaved geraniums, includes some original species. *Pelargonium grandiflorum* hybrids have large, light green almost circular leaves with dentate edges and very large flowers which appear in summer in clusters and range in colour from white through pink and red to deep violet. The flowers are always streaked or veined with contrasting shades or colours. The second and third groups, *P. zonale* and *P. peltatum* hybrids, are ideal for window boxes. *P. zonale*

hybrids have a dark ring on their velvety leaves and are erect plants with single or double flowers usually in spherical umbels in every shade of red and pink. The flowers appear from late spring to early autumn. *P. peltatum* hybrids, the hanging geraniums, have smooth, jointed, trailing stems over 45 cm (18 in) long and shiny, ivy-shaped leaves. The single or double flowers appear at the same time as those of *P. zonale* but come in a range of paler colours. The last group, the scented-leaved geraniums, are less easily available and have small, relatively insignificant flowers and beautiful foliage. *P. capitatum* and *P. radens* and *P. graveolens*, the most commonly grown of the group, have rose-scented foliage; *P. crispum* and *P. odoratissimum*, lemon-scented.

P. grandiflorum
Light and situation: a well ventilated position in a good light.
Temperature: warm in summer; not above 10–15°C (50–59°F) in winter.
Moisture: water generously in the growing period; sparingly in winter.
Soil: a rich, slightly alkaline compost.
Propagation: from cuttings in spring or autumn. Use potting compost and place cuttings in good light but away from sun.

Pelargonium zonale 'Dr Muir'

P. zonale and P. peltatum
Light and situation: place outside in summer and ensure a good light and fresh air in winter. *P. zonale* needs a sunny position; *P. peltatum* requires semi-shade.
Care otherwise as for *P. grandiflorum*.

Pentas lanceolata

Scented-leaved geraniums
Light and situation: a sunny
position in summer.
Care otherwise as for *P.
grandiflorum*.

Pentas lanceolata
Egyptian star cluster

Pentas lanceolata is a shrubby,
winter-flowering plant with
light, hairy leaves and clusters
of trumpet-like flowers in
white, pale pink or carmine.
Pinch out the growing shoots
when the plant is young to
give it a good shape.

Light and situation: a good
light without direct sunlight.
Temperature: warm; 14–16°C
(57–60°F) in winter.
Moisture: water moderately
well until flowering finishes;
then more sparingly.
Soil: a loam-based compost.
Propagation: from stem
cuttings of unflowering shoots
in spring.

Plumbago
Leadwort

One species of *Plumbago*, a
genus of tropical and
subtropical semi-shrubs, is
cultivated as a house plant.
Plumbago auriculata (also
known as *P. capensis*) is a
climbing shrub with terminal
clusters, 23–30 cm (9–12 in)
across, of very pale blue
flowers, trumpet-shaped and
ending in five simple petals

2·5 cm (1 in) in diameter. It is
best grown with the support
of canes or wires.

Light and situation: a slightly
shady position in summer if
possible.
Temperature: cool to
moderate—not below 6–8°C
(43–46°F); keep cool in spring
to hold back flowering.
Moisture: water freely in
summer; keep just moist in
winter.
Soil: a loam-based compost.
Propagation: from cuttings of
unripe shoots with a heel
taken in late autumn or spring
and planted at a soil
temperature of 20–25°C
(68–77°F).

Primula
Primrose

The *Primula* is a genus of
spring-flowering plants from
the temperate regions which
includes mainly hardy species
with some few suitable for
cultivation in the home. The
simple, funnel-shaped flowers
with widely flexed petals and
soft, slightly dentate leaves
vary in their arrangement
from species to species. *P.
vulgaris*, the common
primrose, a hardy plant, now
has hybrids which can be
cultivated as house plants if
placed in very cool positions.
The flowers which grow singly
on short stems from the leaf
rosette at the base of the
plant appear in winter and
spring and vary in colour
from white and yellow to red
and dark blue. *Primula ×
polyantha*, a *P. vulgaris*
hybrid and another hardy
plant which has found its
way into the home, blooms
in early spring, carrying its
flowers in a range of rich
colours well above the leaves.
P. × kewensis has clusters of
bright lemon yellow flowers
borne on long stems in spring.
The mid green leaves and
stems are covered with a
whitish deposit or farina. The
flowers of *P. malacoides* are
borne at different levels on
stems which rise from
rosettes of leaves. They are
smaller and appear in a range
of colours in late winter and
spring. *P. obconica* from
China is covered with downy
hairs and has long stemmed
leaves and flower umbels on
upright stems up to 9 cm
(3½ in) across with slightly
incised petals in a variety of
pastel shades. The plant
usually flowers in the spring.

P. sinensis resembles *P.
obconica* in size and shape
but has flowers with slightly
dentate petals which grow in
clusters appearing from early
spring to late summer. The
plant is covered in fine hairs.

*P. × kewensis, P. malacoides,
P. vulgaris*
Light and situation: a good
light without direct sunlight
and a well ventilated position.
Temperature: cool; not above
10–12°C (50–54°F).
Moisture: water sufficiently to
prevent the root ball drying
out. Maintain a slightly humid
atmosphere.
Soil: a loam-based mixture.
Propagation: from seeds
when ripe or in spring.
Special points: *P. vulgaris*

Plumbago auriculata

must be placed outside in
summer if it is to flower a
second year.

P. obconica and *P. sinensis*
Light and situation: a good
light without direct sunlight.
Temperature: cool; not above
12–14°C (54–57°F) in winter.
Moisture: water to prevent
the root ball drying out.
Soil: a loam-based mixture.
Propagation: from seeds when
ripe or in spring.
Special points: these plants
may produce a skin allergy.

Primula malacoides

Punica granatum
Pomegranate

Punica granatum, a slow-growing shrub from Southern Europe, may reach a height of 2.5–3 m (8–10 ft) over several years in a conservatory border or a tub. The flowers are brilliant scarlet and bell-shaped appearing in summer and autumn. The firm, narrow, glossy leaves are bright green. The dwarf hybrid 'Nana' has more tubular flowers and will make a particularly good pot plant.

Light and situation: in summer a sunny draught-free position outside if possible or a well ventilated but draught-free place indoors.
Temperature: warm in summer; cool in winter, 4–6°C (40–43°F).
Moisture: water freely during summer; in winter very sparingly taking care that the root ball does not dry out. In spring watering should be gradually increased.
Soil: a loam-based compost.
Propagation: from seed in spring or from cuttings of sideshoots with a heel taken in summer.

Rechsteineria
Cardinal flower

This sturdy genus of tuberous-rooted perennials from South America has large, soft, velvety leaves and cowslip-like heads of bright tubular flowers. *R. cardinalis* has brilliant scarlet flowers appearing in summer and grows to 45 cm (18 in). *R. leucotricha* has silvery grey leaves covered in fine white hairs and coral pink flowers which appear in late summer and autumn.

Light and situation: a draught-free position with a good light but without direct sunlight.
Temperature: cool and constant.
Moisture: keep moist and maintain a humid atmosphere. Use lukewarm water.
Overwintering: when the leaves have withered gradually dry off the plant and store in a frost-free place until spring.
Soil: a loam-based compost.
Propagation: by division of the tubers; from basal cuttings taken in spring each with a piece of tuber attached; or from seed.

(below) *Punica granatum* 'Nana' (right) *Rechsteineria leucotricha*

Rhododendron

This popular genus of shrubs was first brought to Europe from Asia in the early 19th century and is now usually sold in flower in winter and spring. The shrubs vary enormously in size, the larger strains reaching 3 m (10 ft) in a conservatory border or 1.2 m (4 ft) in a pot or tub. The flowers are broad and trumpet-shaped in a splendid range of colours from white through mauve to deep red, single or double-flowered according to species and type, with dark green, elliptical leaves. *R. simsii*, and *R. indicum*, commonly known as azaleas, make ideal house plants growing up to 60 cm (2 ft) in height with terminal clusters of brightly coloured flowers borne from Christmas to early summer. If bought in bud and destined for a warm living rocm the plant should first be kept for one or two days in a shaded position at a temperature of 10–12°C (50–54°F).

Light and situation: a well ventilated position, shaded from direct sunlight.

Temperature: ideally cool, 10–12°C (50–54°F).
Moisture: water moderately taking care that the root ball does not dry out. Maintain a humid atmosphere.
Soil: a lime free, humus-based mixture.
Propagation: from seed, by layering or from stem cuttings with a heel taken in summer or early autumn.
Special points: remove dead flowers with their stems.

Rosa chinensis var. minima
Miniature rose

Rosa chinensis var. minima, the miniature rose, grows to a height of 20–25 cm (8–10 in) and has small, pale pink, double or single flowers appearing in summer. The hybrids of *Rosa chinensis* and *Rosa noisettiana* provide most of the existing extremely varied stock of dwarf roses in home cultivation ranging in colour from white and yellow through pink to deep red. In addition, however, there are the Dutch miniature roses which grow to 20–30 cm (8–12 in) and bear a profusion of blooms.

Rhododendron simsii hybrid

Light and situation: a well-lit and well ventilated, sunny position shaded from the hottest sun.
Temperature: moderate; cool in winter, 6–8°C (43–46°F).
Moisture: maintain a slightly humid atmosphere. Water moderately in the growing period; less after flowering.
Soil: a loam-based mixture.
Propagation: from seed, which will produce flowering plants in six months.

Saintpaulia ionantha
African violet

Saintpaulia ionantha is a compact, low-growing rosette-shaped perennial from East Africa with deep green, rounded leaves and clusters of simple four-petalled purple flowers which appear during most of the year. Hybrids have been developed with white, pink and mauve single or double blooms.

Light and situation: a draught-free shaded position in summer; more light in winter without direct sunlight.
Temperature: cool in summer, eg near a north-east-facing window; in winter a constant temperature of 16–18°C (60–64°F).
Moisture: to prevent leaves and heart of the plant from becoming wet, always water from below with tepid, softened water, keeping the plant moist; water more sparingly in winter.
Soil: a peat-based compost.
Propagation: leaf cuttings (spring) rooted in sand or water will produce flowering plants in six months.
Special points: Use pans rather than pots. Prolonged sunlight will make the plants fade. Water stains the leaves.

Saxifraga
Saxifrage

Only one species of this genus of flowering plants from the mountains of the temperate regions is regularly cultivated as a house plant. *S. stolonifera* is a trailing plant from China and Japan whose thin stems up to 45 cm (18 in) long produce young plantlets at their tips, giving the plant its name mother of thousands. The small, white and yellow flowers appear in summer. The hybrid 'Tricolor' has variegated leaves.

(above) *Rosa chinensis var. minima* 'Pink Carol'

Light and situation: a well ventilated but draught-free and very well-lit position, shaded from the hottest sun and away from other plants.
Temperature: cool; in winter 8–12°C (46–54°F). The hybrid 'Tricolor' will flourish in a warm living room.
Moisture: keep constantly moist from spring to autumn; water more sparingly later.

Saintpaulia ionantha hybrid

'Tricolor' requires more water than other strains.
Soil: a loam-based compost.
Propagation: separate the plantlets from the parent plant in summer and repot in groups of three.

Sinningia hybrid

Sinningia
Gloxinia

This genus of tuberous-rooted perennials from South America has velvety leaves and magnificent, trumpet-shaped flowers. *S. regina* has violet foxglove-like blooms appearing in summer. *S. speciosa*, the best developed species, is a rosette-forming plant with a central cluster of large, purple, mauve or red flowers some with white edges according to strain. The blooms have a wide frill of petal lobes and a deep, bowl-shaped heart. *S.s.* 'Defiance' is bright red; 'Emperor Frederick' red edged with white; 'Mont Blanc' is pure white; 'Prince Albert' violet-blue and 'Reine Wilhemine' is a deep rich pink. The blooms appear in summer and autumn.

Light and situation: a well-lit position shaded from the hottest sun.
Temperature: cool in summer; in winter 16°C (60°F).
Moisture: keep moist but avoid spraying the flowers as this will stain them; after flowering water less.
Soil: a propinctary peat compost.
Overwintering: to keep the plants for a second year gradually dry out after the leaves have withered, over-winter in a warm, dry place and lift the tubers in early spring leaving only one or two shoots attached. Remove old roots and repot just below the surface of the soil. Water a little and start into growth at 18–20°C (64–68°F).

Smithiantha

This genus of tuberous-rooted perennials from the tropical mountain forests of Mexico is called after Matilda Smith, an artist at Kew Gardens. The species have in general been replaced in cultivation by the more impressive hybrids. The plant has somewhat succulent stems, hairy, dentate leaves and colourful, foxglove-like flowers growing on erect stems 60–90 cm (2–3 ft) high. *S. cinnabarina*, temple bells, has velvety, heart-shaped, dark green leaves flushed with red, and vermilion flowers with a red spotted yellow throat. The flowers appear in summer. *S. zebrina* is taller with hairy leaves and long scarlet and yellow pendulous flowers which appear in summer. It also has a rich variety of cultivars with flowers ranging in colour from golden orange through scarlet to rose pink and white. For room cultivation new plants should be grown from rhizomes.

Light and situation: in a tropical plant window shaded from direct sunlight.
Temperature: moderate.
Moisture: keep moist while in flower.
Overwintering: after flowering allow to dry out and overwinter at 10–12°C (50–54°). Lift the tubers at the end of winter and plant 3–4 to a pot 2 cm (¾ in) below the soil. Keep at a soil temperature of 22°C (72°F) until the flowers appear. Water moderately and spray overhead with lukewarm water.
Soil: a humusy mixture.

Solanum capsicastrum

Solanum
Nightshade, Jerusalem cherry

Solanum, a very varied genus from the tropical and sub-tropical regions, includes many well-known fruits and vegetables and a number of species grown for their ornamental fruits. *S. capicastrum*, the winter cherry, and *S. pseudocapsicum*, the Jerusalem cherry, a similar but tougher species, both have small tomato-like flowers in summer and bright fruits maturing from green through yellow to brilliant scarlet.

Light and situation: a sunny situation.
Temperature: increasingly warm from spring onwards.
Moisture: water freely in summer; less thereafter.
Soil: a loam-based compost.

Smithiantha hybrid

Spathiphyllum
White flag

Spathiphyllum is a genus of plants from the arum lily family with dark green leaves on long stems and flowers consisting of a finely pointed, leaf-like spathe and a straight central spadix. *S. floribundum* reaches 30–40 cm (12–16 in) and bears white flowers in summer. *S. wallisii* is a slightly smaller species with a yellow spadix and an oval white spathe. The hybrid 'Mauna Loa' produces flowers throughout the year.

Light and situation: a shady position.
Temperature: room temperature: not below 16–18°C (60–64°F).
Moisture: keep the soil moist in summer and spray occasionally during bud formation; water sparingly in winter. Provide a humid atmosphere.
Soil: a loam-based compost.
Propagation: by division when repotting in spring or from seed.
Special points: this plant is sensitive to dry air in the winter resting period.

Stephanotis floribunda

Stephanotis floribunda
Madagascar jasmine

This fragrant flowering shrub from Madagascar with firm, glossy, dark green leaves and white, star-shaped flowers growing in radiating clusters from the leaf axils will reach a height of 3 m (10 ft) on a conservatory wall

Spathiphyllum wallisii

or can easily be trained on canes or bent wire as a pot plant in the home. The flowers appear throughout summer and early autumn.

Light and situation: a well ventilated but draught-free position with plenty of space in good indirect light.
Temperature: warm in summer; in winter 12–14°C (54–57°F).
Moisture: water freely in spring and summer using softened tepid water and spraying frequently at first; gradually decrease watering

from autumn on but do not allow the root ball to dry out.
Soil: a loam-based compost.
Propagation: from cuttings of non-flowering sideshoots in early summer.
Special points: do not move or turn the plants as this will cause the flower buds and leaves to drop.

Strelitzia reginae
Bird-of-paradise flower

This evergreen perennial with extraordinary flowers like a bird's head comes from South Africa and will reach 1–1.5 m (3–5 ft) as a pot plant. The leaves 45 cm (18 in) long are a blunt oval and carried in fan-shaped groups. The flowers are produced on stems 1 m (3 ft) high and take the form of a long, red-tinged, beak-shaped bract from which blue and orange blooms emerge one after the other like a crest of flames.

Light and situation: a very well-lit position but shaded from the hottest sun. Place outside in summer if possible.
Temperature: warm in summer; 10°C (50°F) in winter.
Moisture: water freely in spring and summer; keep dry in winter.
Soil: a loam-based compost.
Propagation: from seed or by division. In either case the plants will take several years to flower.

Strelitzia reginae

(left) *Streptocarpus* hybrid

balcony pot plant trained up wires or canes and may reach 3 m (10 ft) in one season. Its flowers, which are profusely borne in summer from the leaf axils, have yellowy-orange lobes, a dark brown centre and purple tube.

Light and situation: place in a sunny position on a balcony in early summer.

Temperature: warm in summer; cool in winter, 8–10°C (46–50°F).
Moisture: water well in summer.
Soil: a rich compost with some lime.
Propagation: from seed in spring planted in groups of two or three. Pot on once and then place outside when all danger of frost is past.

Tillandsia cyanea

Streptocarpus
Cape primrose

Streptocarpus, a low-growing herbaceous biennial from South Africa, has soft green leaves resembling those of the *Primula* and clusters of fine, trumpet-shaped flowers in a wide range of colours from white through pink to red and deep blue which grow on a flower stem 25 cm (10 in) tall. *S. × hybridus* 'Constant Nymph' has lavender blue flowers which appear throughout most of the year. *S. × h.* 'Weismoor' has crimson pink flowers with a magenta and white throat. This plant is autumn- or spring-flowering.

Light and situation: a well-lit and well ventilated position away from direct sunlight.
Temperature: warm; in winter 18–20°C (64–68°F). *Too warm !*
Moisture: water freely in summer and maintain a humid atmosphere; more sparingly in winter depending on the temperature. Use tepid, softened water.
Soil: a loam-based or peat compost.
Propagation: from seed or, in the case of tufted species, by division in spring, or from leaf cuttings divided along the central vein and rooted in damp sand in summer.

Thunbergia

Thunbergia is a genus from the tropics consisting largely of perennial climbers whose long, funnel-like flowers have widely flexed petals and occur in a wide range of colours. Many of them are too large to be grown in the home but *T. alata* (black-eyed Susan), an annual, is often used as a

Tillandsia

Tillandsia is a genus of evergreen perennials, members of the Bromeliad family, from Central and South America where it grows in a wide range of habitat. *T. cyanea* a showy epiphyte, has fine grass-like vertically ribbed arching leaves and a central feather-like sheaf of green-tinged pink bracts from which the violet-blue funnel-shaped flowers emerge in summer.

Light and situation: a good light in a tropical plant window.
Temperature: warm.
Moisture: water well and maintain high humidity.
Soil: equal parts sand, peat and osmunda fibre.
Propagation: remove well-developed offsets from the parent plant in summer.

Thunbergia alata

Hessayon says 55°.

Vriesia splendens

Vriesia

This genus of dramatic Bromeliads from South America, most of whose species are cultivated for their rosettes of decorative foliage, has some species which are grown in particular for their flowers. *V. psittacina* has a rosette of shiny bright yellowy-green leaves from which rises a flower stem 25–30 cm (10–12 in) in height producing a single feather-shaped flower. This is composed of closely packed bracts, red at the centre and yellow toward their tips, from which the small green flowers protrude. *V. splendens* has leaves with dark green and purple transverse bands in a widely branching rosette. From it rises a 45 cm (18 in) stem bearing a blade-shaped sheaf of red overlapping bracts lightly touched with yellow towards the tip which gives the species its common name, flaming sword. These species are only suitable for a heated plant window but new hybrids are being produced which are better suited to room cultivation.

Light and situation: in a heated flower window shaded from direct sunlight.
Temperature: warm; a soil and air temperature of at least 18–20°C (64–68°F).
Moisture: pour water into the central cup and keep the compost moist. Use only softened lukewarm water. After flowering pour off most of the water from the leaf cup. Maintain a high degree of humidity.
Soil: a mixture of peat, sand and sphagnum moss.
Propagation: take rooted offsets from the parent plant in spring and summer.

Zantedeschia
Arum, calla or trumpet lily

Zantedeschia, the arum lily, comes from Southern Africa. The flower takes the form of a short, yellow spadix which is surrounded by the well-known trumpet-shaped, curving spathe which varies in colour with the species. The leaves are usually large, soft and deep green, heart-shaped or arrow-shaped. *Z. aethiopica*, the white arum lily, has a pure white spathe and mid to dark green leaves 60–90 cm (2–3 ft) in length. The flower stems, which appear in spring and summer, may reach 1.5 m (5 ft). *Z. elliottiana*, the golden calla, has dark green, heart-shaped leaves 30 cm (1 ft) long with transparent

(right) *Zantedeschia elliottiana*

spots. The spathe is bell-shaped at the base and pale green opening to a deep rich yellow and appears in summer. *Z. rehmanni* has narrow, spear-shaped leaves with transparent streaks and a deep bell-shaped spathe shading from pale green through yellow to rose pink, purple or cream. The flowers appear in spring and summer.

Light and situation: a position with a good light shaded from the hottest sun and outside in spring and summer if possible.

Temperature: warm in summer; cool in winter, 8–12°C (46–54°F).
Moisture: water freely in the growing period; keep dry after flowering; gradually increase water again from spring onwards.
Soil: a proprietary peat compost.
Propagation: by removing offsets or by division of the rhizomes when repotting.

(below) *Zantedeschia rehmanii*

Bulbs and Corms

The silky skins of bulbs are the outer layers of a dormant, underground bud beneath whose surface the food the plant will require for growth is stored in concentric layers of plump, starch-filled leaves. Its structure, like that of the corm, the swollen base of a plant stem, allows the plant to survive cold winters when the soil water is frozen or the droughts characteristic of semi-arid regions. Bulbs play their most dramatic role in spring, breaking into flower in the short, dark days when few other plants bring colour to the house. These are the hardy bulbs from the temperate regions which can be forced to flower indoors earlier than they would outside and include hyacinths, single and double early tulips, narcissi, daffodils, the large-flowered crocus, *Scilla*, dwarf iris and *Chionodoxa*. Once they have been forced they will not flower indoors again and should be allowed to ripen naturally and then planted outside. By contrast tender bulbs like *Freesia*, *Nerine* and *Vallotta* will bloom indoors for several years though they cannot be forced and are best cultivated in a conservatory. The same is true of the exotic *Hippeastrum* and *Lilium* which will bloom throughout much of the year. An additional section (pp 70–71) is devoted to the process of forcing bulbs and gives details of planting, watering and temperature. Plants with rhizomatous or tuberous root systems, which are sometimes included with bulbs, will be found in the other sections of the Dictionary.

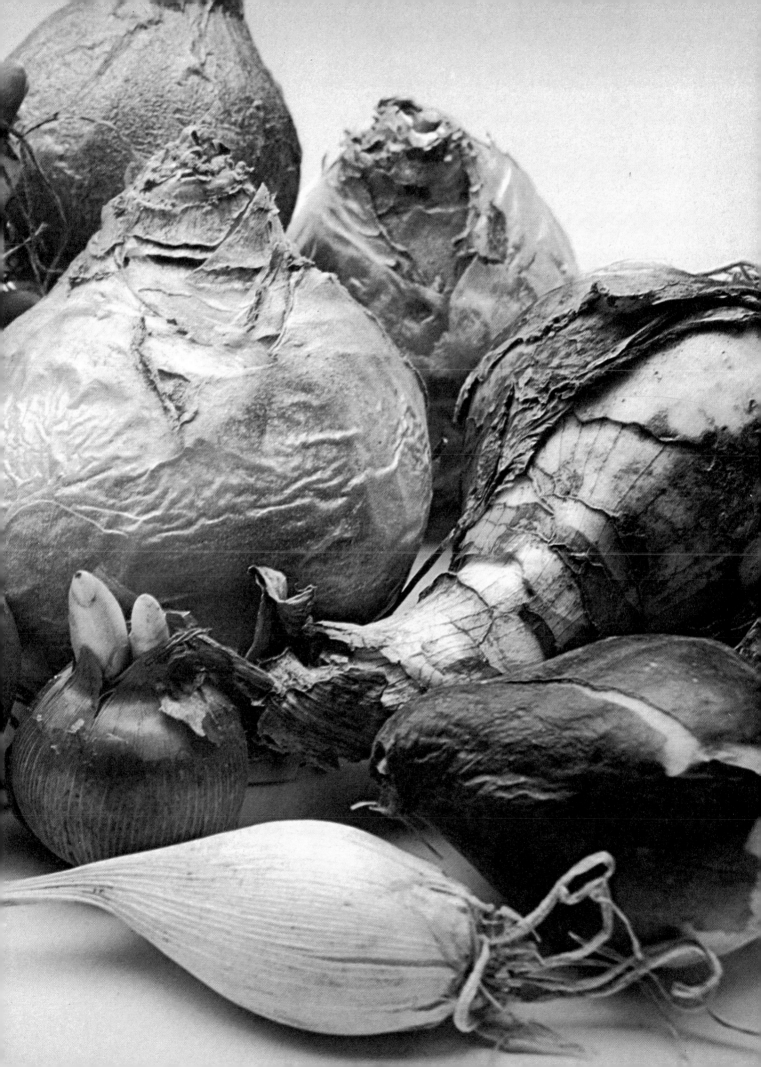

Chionodoxa

This genus of small flowering plants from Asia Minor has strap-shaped leaves and a terminal inflorescence of blue, trumpet-shaped flowers opening into a six-pointed star which appear from early spring onwards. *C. luciliae* is 15 cm (6 in) tall and has groups of up to ten, bright blue flowers with white centres. *C. luciliae* 'Alba' has fewer, larger white flowers. *C. l.* 'Gigantea' is violet-blue with large flowers 4 cm (1½ in) across. *C. sardensis* has deep blue flowers with a very small white eye at the centre.

Cultivation: plant bulbs 8 cm (3 in) deep in groups in early autumn. Place in a light situation and water well.

Crocus

The crocus, a genus of hardy plants grown from corms originates in the Mediterranean region and Asia Minor and includes autumn-, winter- and spring-flowering species. Several species and cultivars make good container plants some of which can be forced into flower in early spring inside. The flowers are cup-shaped, almost stemless and grow to a height of 15 cm (6 in) preceded by fine grassy leaves. They range in colour from white through golden yellow and bronze to pink, pale blue, mauve and dark purple. *C. vernus*, the parent of the large Dutch crocus, has with its many hybrids become the most popular to grow. Flowers appear in spring. *C. chrysanthus* and its hybrids, *C. longiflorus* and *C. zonatus* are also fine spring-flowering plants.

Crocus vernus hybrid

(above) *Chionodoxa sardensis*   (below) *Freesia × hybrida*

Cultivation: plant the corms in autumn 5–8 cm (2–3 in) deep, 1–2 cm (½–1 in) apart in a shallow bowl. For forcing see the bulb section pp. 70–77.

Freesia

This genus of tender bulbous plants of the Iris family with magnificently scented flowers comes from the temperate regions. The flowers are trumpet-shaped, 5 cm (2 in) long and grow in arching groups along one side of the slender, slightly stiff stems which can reach 45 cm (18 in). *F. refracta* has golden yellow flowers. *F. × hybrida* plants come in a wide range of colours among them yellow, mauve and a deep crimson pink. The plants are best suited to a cool greenhouse or conservatory and require support from a group of twigs. They are also ideal for cutting.

Cultivation: plant the corms in late summer or autumn 5–8 cm (2–3 in) apart in pots or pans and water only a little

until growth begins. From autumn onwards the temperature should be a steady 5°C (41°F). Give more water once the flower buds appear.

Haemanthus

Two species of this unusual flowering plant from Africa are cultivated as house plants. *H. albiflos* is an evergreen with thick, fleshy leaves to which it owes its common name 'Elephants' Ears'. The flowers grow in groups, packed into a globe-like neck of white bracts from which their long, white stamens and yellow anthers protrude, somewhat resembling a thick painter's brush. *H. katharinae* is more typical of the genus. It has thin leaves and a large, starry head of fine, bright pink flowers 23–30 cm (9–12 in) across which appears in summer on a stem 30 cm (1 ft) high. This is really a greenhouse plant but can be grown in a warm, shady living room.

H. albiflos
Light and situation: leave undisturbed in a sunny spot. Temperature: moderate; in winter 12–15°C (54–59°F). Moisture: water moderately depending on the room temperature. Soil: a loam-based compost. Propagation: allow to grow into a group of plants in one pot.

H. katharinae
Light and placing: a slightly shaded position. Temperature: warm. Moisture: water moderately in spring and summer; less in autumn and winter. Soil: a loam-based compost. Propagation: This plant can be raised from seed but will flower only after several years.

Hippeastrum
Amaryllis

Hippeastrum is a genus of lily-like flowering plants from Central and South America whose hybrids range in colour from white through pink to deep red. *Hippeastrum* 'Jenny Lind' has crimson pink flowers; 'Nivalis' delicate white flowers with a yellow centre; and 'Johnsonii' bright crimson red flowers with a single central white stripe on each petal. The flowers appear two or three to a stem in winter and spring and are followed in summer by the leaves. Both grow directly from a single bulb on long stalks 50–70 cm (20–28 in) high.

Cultivation: The cycle of the *Hippeastrum* goes from winter to winter. Plant the bulb up to half its depth and water. Place in a warm position at 25°C (77°F) and water sparingly. When the buds appear increase the watering and place in a good light. To lengthen the flowering period return to a cooler spot once the flowers have begun to appear and prevent seed formation to ensure a vigorous bulb. Do not cut the flower stems until they have completely dried out. After flowering place the plant in a sunny, well ventilated position to ensure that the growing leaves feed the bulb well. Properly cared for bulbs increase 1–2 cm (½–¾ in) each year. Rest the plant in late autumn, gradually decreasing moisture, and eventually cease watering about six weeks before the

184

Prolong flowering period by removing stamens (turn plant on side to avoid damaging flower.

Iris reticulata 'Harmony'

smaller plant with white or light blue flowers.

Cultivation: plant the bulbs in early autumn with the tips just showing. For forcing see the bulb section pp. 70–71.

Iris

Bulbous irises which are found in most countries in the northern hemisphere include one species, the small *Iris reticulata* which blooms in early spring. The plants grow to 15 cm (6 in) tall with narrow, strap-like, pointed leaves and produce delicate flowers ranging from blue to purple with yellow markings.

Cultivation: plant six bulbs to a pot in late summer and place in a cool, light position in a conservatory or near a north window. Water moderately and bring into the living room when in flower.

Lilium
Lily

This genus of mainly hardy plants from East Asia includes some species which are suitable for room cultivation. The bulbs can be planted at any time for summer or winter flowering but it is possible to force them into flower in winter or spring. *L. auratum*, the largest species, has large, open trumpet-shaped, fragrant flowers 20–25 cm (8–10 in) wide

Lilium auratum

cycle begins again. Then place the pots in a moderately heated position at 10–12°C (50–54°F). After six weeks repot in a slightly larger pot and begin the cycle afresh. Propagate from offsets.

Hyacinthus
Hyacinth

Various species of *Hyacinthus* are found in Southern Africa and the mediterranean area but only *H. orientalis*, the

Hyacinthus 'Blue Jacket'

Hippeastrum 'Jenny Lind'

common or Dutch hyacinth, and *H. orientalis var. albulus*, the Roman hyacinth, are grown indoors, flowering in winter and spring. The plants grow to 30 cm (1 ft) with narrow, glossy, strap-like leaves ending in a point and a dense inflorescence of bell-shaped flowerets occurring in the case of *H. orientalis* in a wide range of colours from white through yellow and pink to red, mauve and deep blue. One of the most famous is 'Delft Blue'. *H. orientalis var. albulus* is a

which are white and streaked with gold and borne on 1.2–2m (4–6 ft) stems. Cultivars present a wide range of colours including the well-known orange 'Enchantment', which will grow to 75 cm (30 in). 'Destiny' is golden yellow and grows to 60 cm (2 ft). 'Harmony' is red and yellow and grows to 50–75 cm (20–30 in).

Cultivation: plant the bulbs as soon as possible after buying in a mixture of sand and peat with a little bonemeal. Give good drainage and place a thin layer of sand immediately below the bulb. When shoots appear place in a warm, light, well ventilated position shaded from the hottest sun. Lilies should be kept slightly moist throughout the year.

Muscari
Grape hyacinth

The genus of hardy bulbous plants with an inflorescence consisting of small bell-like flowerets ressembling a miniature hyacinth varies from 15 to 30 cm (6 to 12 in) with the species. *M. botryoides* has deep blue flowers; *M.b.* 'Album' has white flowers. *M. × tubergenianum*, a two-toned type, has dark blue flowers at the top of the inflorescence and light blue flowers at the bottom. Flowers appear in spring or early summer.

Cultivation: plant 5 cm (2 in) deep in autumn in a window box or pot with up to twelve bulbs to a 13 cm (5 in) pot.

Narcissus

This genus of hardy bulbs, ideal for forcing, includes a wide variety of types from tall, brilliant yellow or bicoloured daffodils with their trumpet-shaped heart and wide frill of petals to small narcissi with double, creamy centres or contrasting orange trumpet and white frill. Among daffodils 'Dutch

Narcissus hybrids:
(top row, left to right)
'Home Fires', 'Orion', 'Kilcoran', 'Galway';
(middle row) 'Hawaii', 'Ludlow', 'Tudor Minstrel', 'Debutante';
(bottom row) 'Aleppo', 'Bantam', 'Mary Copela'

Master' is clear yellow; 'Gold court' a deep lemon yellow with a darker yellow trumpet; 'Foresight' has creamy white petals with a mimosa yellow trumpet; 'Cantatrice' is pure white. Among narcissi one of the best known types for indoor growth is the tazetta narcissus 'Paper white' with its pure white short cup and frill with several flowers to a stem.

Cultivation: plant in autumn 8–15 cm (3–6 in) deep according to size leaving 2.5 cm (1 in) between bulbs. For forcing see the bulb section pp. 70–71.
N. 'Paper White' does not require darkness for forcing but will grow on a cool window sill.

Nerine

This semi-hardy or tender bulbous plant from South Africa belongs to the Amaryllis family. The inflorescence consists of a spherical cluster of star-like, funnel-shaped flowers with protruding stamens which are borne on stems 30–45 cm (12–18 in) high in late summer and autumn. Most species have pink or red flowers though hybrids are available in other colours. The narrow, strap-like leaves appear with or after the flowers. *N. bowdenii* is the hardiest species

Nerine bowdenii

with glossy green leaves and pale pink flowers with a darker stripe. Hybrids come in deeper shades. *N. curvifolia* has scarlet and gold flowers with striking protruding filaments. *N. sarniensis* has crimson flowers with an iridescent sheen and grows to 60 cm (2 ft) in height.

Cultivation: plant the bulbs in autumn 8–10 cm (3–4 in) deep one to a 10 cm (4 in) pot. Cover only the lower half with soil and water regularly in winter and spring maintaining a temperature of 10–13°C (50–55°F). Move the pot out of

doors in summer to a slightly shady spot and withhold water after the leaves have dried out. Split the plant only after five years.

Ornithogalum
Star of Bethlehem

This genus, which includes over 100 species and grows wild in Africa, Asia and Europe, has terminal clusters of simple, star-shaped flowers appearing in spring and summer. *O. arabicum* has waxy, white flowers carried on stalks 60 cm (2 ft) tall. The plant is grown outside in all but the coldest areas and the flowers are ideal for cutting. *O. umbellatum* is however the best-known species, growing to 30 cm (1 ft) with narrow, strap-like leaves and white flowers with an external green stripe. *O. thyrsoides*, has white or cream flowers.

Cultivation: plant in autumn with small bulbs 5–7.5 cm

(below) *Ornithogalum umbellatum*

(2–3 in) deep in a container or
in a conservatory. Keep just
moist throughout the winter
at a minimum temperature of
10–13°C (50–55°F). *O. thyrsoides*
is planted in spring.

Puschkinia

Puschkinia scilloides, the best-
known species of this genus
belonging to the Lily family,
has delicate, arching stems
and bears in spring and early
summer blue, bell-shaped
flowers with a darker blue
stripe.

Cultivation: plant the bulbs
5 cm (2 in) deep seven or
eight to a 15 cm (6 in) pot in
autumn. Ideally the pots
should be plunged in a
garden for six to eight weeks
and brought into a cool
conservatory, garden room or
a cool, dark corner of the
house at midwinter. Keep
moist when growth starts;
withhold water gradually after
flowering and repot annually.

Scilla
Squill

This member of the Lily family
produces bell-shaped or
star-like flowers in spring. The
flowers are blue, purple, pink
or white and are borne in
terminal clusters on erect
stalks above the basal strap-

Scilla peruviana

like leaves. *S. peruviana*, a
native of the Mediterranean
area has large spherical
clusters of purplish-blue
flowers growing on 25 cm
(10 in) stalks. The least hardy
scilla, it blooms in early
summer. *S. sibirica*, a small
spring-flowering species, has
deep blue, small, widely flexed
bells on 15 cm (6 in) stems.

Cultivation: plant the bulbs
10 cm (4 in) deep in late
summer or early autumn
with six bulbs of *S. siberica*
to a 13 cm (5 in) pot. *S.
peruviana* is a larger bulb and
should be planted one to a
15 cm (6 in) pot. For forcing
see bulb section pp. 70–71.

Sparaxis
Wand flower

Sparaxis, a tender or semi-
hardy plant from Southern
Africa, produces small funnel-
shaped flowers with widely
flexed lobes opening into a
six-pointed star. The flowers
appear in late spring in a
range of yellows, blues,
purples and reds or white and
are often splashed in a
contrasting colour. The
flowering period will last for
between six and eight weeks.

Cultivation: plant the corms
5 cm (2 in) apart in autumn.
Provide light and warmth
when the plants start to grow
and bring them into the
living room when in flower.

(above) *Sparaxis grandiflora* hybrid

(above) *Tulipa* (Mendel) 'Orange Wonder'

Tulipa
Tulip

This hardy genus of bulbous
plants is found wild in the
northern Mediterranean
region and throughout the
Caucasus and Asia. Single
and double early flowering
forms are forced as indoor
bulbs and include a huge
range of cultivars with almost
limitless colour variation.

Cultivation: the bulbs should
be bought in early autumn,
potted and put outside or in
a cool basement. Plant the
bulbs at a depth of 2½ times
their width and 1–2 cm (½–1 in)
apart. For forcing see the
bulb section pp. 70–71.

Vallota speciosa
Scarborough lily

This species of tender bulbous
plants comes from Southern
Africa and produces terminal
clusters of deep orange-red,
star-shaped flowers on stems
60 cm (2 ft) high surrounded
by gently arching strap-shaped
leaves.

Cultivation: plant the bulbs
15 cm (6 in) deep in summer
before flowering. The tip of
the bulb should show above
the soil. The pot should be
placed in a cool conservatory
or on a sunny window sill.
Water thoroughly while in
bloom and dry out gradually
once the leaves have died.

187

Cacti and Succulents

The bizarre forms of many succulents are the result of adaptation to their natural habitat – the semi-deserts and dry steppes of the tropical and sub-tropical regions. Pebble-like leaves present the smallest transpiring area for a given volume of water; swollen stems contain reservoirs which allow the plant to store water for long periods; and spines are thought to help the plant collect dew as well as discouraging predators. Cacti are a special group of succulents, natives of Central and South America, which are distinguished by the woolly areoles that surround their breathing pores and from which their spines emerge often in dazzling geometrical patterns.

Agave

This genus of succulent plants, now classified by some botanists as a separate family, comes from Central America. The fleshy and often thorny leaves grow in tight rosettes, the largest up to 3 m (10 ft) high. The smaller species suitable for room cultivation include *A. victoria-reginae*, which has white edged, rounded leaves 10–30 cm (4–12 in) long ending in a thorn and developing into a semi-spherical filled rosette up to 50–70 cm (20–28 in) across. The whole plant dies after producing a tall flower

Agave victoria-reginae

stem. *A. filifera* also produces a spherical rosette, this time with pointed leaves whose white markings flake off.

Light and situation: a good light.
Temperature: warm in summer; cool in winter, 4–6°C (40–43°F).
Moisture: water well in summer; very sparingly in winter.
Soil: a mixture of loam, peat and sharp sand.
Propagation: from sideshoots or from seed.

Aloe

This genus of rosette-forming shrubs resembling the agaves comes mainly from Africa. *A. arborescens* is an erect plant with tentacle-like fleshy leaves growing round the stem and edged with sharp thorns. *A. variegata*, the most suitable species for room cultivation, is a stemless plant with dark green leaves, triangular in section, marked with white 'V' shaped bands.

Light and situation: a good light.
Temperature: warm in summer; cool in winter, 4–6°C (40–43°F).
Moisture: water well in summer; sparingly in winter.
Soil: a mixture of loam, peat and sharp sand.
Propagation: from offsets.

Aloe arborescens

Argyroderma
Mesems

Argyroderma, a genus of strangely shaped succulents from South Africa are known as pebble plants because the glaucous green, almost spherical leaves appear to lie like pebbles on the soil. *A. delaetii* has leaves growing in pairs like split stones up to 5 cm (2 in) across and purple or yellow flowers produced in summer.

Argyroderma delaetii

Light and situation: a good light.
Temperature: warm in summer; cool in winter, 8–10°C (46–50°F).
Moisture: water sparingly in summer; keep dry in winter.
Soil: a mixture of loam, peat and sharp sand.
Special points: grow in shallow bowls.

Astrophytum ornatum

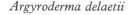

Astrophytum
Bishop's cap cactus

The *Astrophytum*, a genus of handsome cacti with swollen stems divided into several sections, is popular because it is easy to grow. *A. myriostigma* has indented edges to the body of sections and a yellow, thistle-like central flower appearing in summer. *A. ornatum* has white scales on the body sections and 5 cm (2 in) spines growing in groups on the ribs. The yellow flowers appear in summer.

Light and situation: a good light; *A. ornatum* should be shaded from direct sunlight in spring.
Temperature: warm in summer; cool in winter, 5–8°C (41–46°F).
Moisture: water sparingly in summer; not at all from autumn to spring.
Soil: a mixture of loam, peat and sharp sand.
Propagation: from seed.

Cephalocereus
Old man cactus

Cephalocereus, a genus of tall, columnar cacti from Central and South America, has as its best known representative the Old Man Cactus, *Cephalocereus senilis*, which is covered with soft white hairs.

Light and situation: a good light and a draught-free situation.
Temperature: warm in summer; not below 15°C (59°F) in winter.
Moisture: water lightly during the summer; keep dry in winter.
Soil: a mixture of loam, peat and sharp sand.
Propagation: from cuttings or from seed.
Special points: small stones placed around the column will prevent the hair getting dirty.

Cereus
Torch thistle

This genus of columnar cacti from South America derives its name from the Greek for 'torch' and grows into strangely branching shapes. Many species have a waxy bloom in white, green or blue which acts as a protective layer on the epidermis and is very decorative. *C. chalybaeus* has a magnificent blue sheen making it the bluest cactus. *C. peruvianus* is green and jade-like. *C.p.* 'Monstrosus',

Cereus chalybaeus

a multiple branched form, is very popular. *C. repandus* has a grayish green branched stem with several low ribs and many spines.

Light and situation: a well ventilated, sunny position.
Temperature: warm in summer; cool in winter, 6°C (43°F).
Moisture: water occasionally in summer and spray to remove dust. Keep dry in winter.
Soil: a mixture of loam, peat and sharp sand.
Propagation: from cuttings or from seed.

(left) *Cephalocereus senilis*

Ceropegia

This genus of succulent twining plants from tropical Africa and Asia have small, often rudimentary, leaves strung along the stems and make ideal plants for hanging baskets. *C. woodii*, the species most commonly grown as a house plant, has purplish stems and pairs of small, rounded, dark green leaves with silver-grey markings and purple undersides. The small flowers are also purple and lantern shaped. *C. haygarthii* has pale mauve flowers with a hairy knob at the centre of the stem. *C. sandersonii* has pale green flowers.

Light and situation: a good light.
Temperature: warm in summer; cool in winter—but it is possible to keep these plants in a living room.
Moisture: water very sparingly in summer; even less in winter.
Soil: a mixture of loam, peat and sharp sand or soilless cultivation.
Propagation: by division or from stem cuttings in summer which should be left to dry out for a few days.

(below) *Ceropegia woodii*

Chamaecereus
Peanut cactus

Chamaecereus silvestrii is the sole representative of this genus of cacti from South America. It has stems 2.5–8 cm (1–3 in) long and 6–12 mm ($\frac{1}{4}$–$\frac{1}{2}$ in) thick with low ribs and pale spines. The dramatic flowers are vermilion and a broad funnel shape with 5 cm (2 in) long petals and yellow stamens.

Light and situation: a light but not too sunny position.
Temperature: warm in summer; very cool in winter, –2°C (28°F).
Moisture: water regularly in summer; keep dry in winter.
Soil: a mixture of loam, peat and sharp sand.
Propagation: from detached shoots which should be dried off a little before planting.

Coryphanta

Coryphanta, a genus of cacti from the south-western United

(above) *Chamaecereus silvestrii*

States and Mexico, comprises two groups with different requirements. The summer-flowering species, which resemble *Mammillaria*, are best suited to home cultivation. *C. elephantidens*, for example, has a globular green stem with large tubercles and produces pink flowers.

Light and situation: a good light.
Temperature: warm in summer; cool in winter but not below 4°C (40°F).
Moisture: water sparingly in spring and summer; keep dry in winter.
Soil: a mixture of loam, peat and some sharp sand.

Conophytum
Cone plant, living stones

This genus of succulent from Southern Africa has spherical leaves fused together in pairs except for a slit at the top

Conophytum flavum

where the flower appears in winter. They resemble a pile of small stones. *C. flavum* has grey-green leaves with dark blue-green lines and spots. *C. scitulum* has white flowers and grey-green leaves with reddish-brown markings.

Light and situation: a well ventilated position in a good light.
Temperature: warm in summer; cool in winter.
Moisture: water moderately in autumn and winter; spray occasionally in spring and summer.
Soil: a mixture of loam, peat, sharp sand, and marble chips.
Propagation: from seed in early summer.

Crassula

Crassula is an enormous family of leaf succulents from Southern Africa and Europe which includes stone-crops and house leeks. One of the most beautiful and often seen tender species cultivated as a house plant is *Crassula arborescens* which is like a plump miniature tree and is known as jade tree. Its 'bark' is dark grey and the succulent leaves have a silvery sheen. It has white, star-shaped flowers which turn pink, borne in terminal panicles in summer. *Crassula falcata* has paired, scythe-shaped succulent leaves and

Crassula argentea

occasional panicles of bright red flowers. *C. argentea* has bright green, shiny leaves and terminal clusters of pink flowers in summer.

Light and situation: a good light but shaded from the hottest sun.
Temperature: warm in summer; cool in winter, 6–10°C (43–50°F).
Moisture: water moderately when in growth.
Soil: a mixture of loam, peat and sharp sand.
Propagation: from cuttings of shoot tips or leaves.

Echeveria gibbiflora 'Crispa'

(left) *Echinocactus grusonii*

Echeveria

Echeveria is a large genus of succulent plants belonging to the Crassula family and coming mainly from Central America. Most produce rosettes of fleshy leaves, grey with a bluish tinge, from which rise long stems of orange and red flowers. Some species are almost stemless like *E. agavoides*, which, as its name implies, is agave-like and has rosettes of succulent pointed leaves, and *E. setosa* which has rosettes with a web of white hairs and yellow-tipped red flowers. *E. gibbiflora* produces blue-green rosettes of leaves which in mature plants grow on trunks 45 cm (18 in) high. *E. harmsii* is similar with leaves a little more pointed.

Light and situation: a good light.
Temperature: warm in summer; cool in winter, 6–10°C (43–50°F). Winter-flowering species require warmer temperatures.
Moisture: water sparingly in summer; even less in winter.
Soil: a mixture of loam, peat and sharp sand.
Propagation: by removing side rosettes; from leaf cuttings; or from seed.

Echinocactus

This genus of dramatic cacti from Mexico is spherical or cylindrical in shape and divided into many ribs each surmounted with long spines. *E. grusonii*, golden ball, is an

almost completely round, pale green globe and its many ribs are edged with golden yellow spines. It may reach 15 cm (6 in) in diameter.

Light and situation: a position in a good light shaded from direct sunlight in spring. Temperature: warm in summer; not below 10°C (50°F) in winter.
Moisture: keep moist in summer; dry in winter.
Soil: a mixture of two parts loam to one part sharp sand.

Echinocereus

This low-growing genus of cacti comes from the southern USA and Mexico. The column-shaped stems are branched and either smooth green or covered in fine ridges with hairs or spines. They produce large flowers.

Echinocereus pectinatus

E. knippelianus and *E. puchellus* have few or no spines. *E. delaetii* has fine spines or hair. *E. pectinatus* is covered in short spines and produces purple flowers 8 cm (3 in) across.

Light and situation: a well ventilated position in a good light, outside in summer for smooth green species if possible.
Temperature: warm in summer; cool in winter.
Moisture: keep moist in summer; dry in winter.
Soil: a mixture of loam and sharp sand.
Propagation: from stem cuttings in spring and summer or from seed sown in early spring in gritty compost at 21°C (70°F).

Echinopsis
Sea urchin cactus

Echinopsis, a genus of small, globular cacti from South America produces large, beautiful flowers in a range of colours from white through yellow to pink and scarlet. *E. calachlora* has bright green globes with short spines and dish-shaped, white flowers 15 cm (6 in) long and 10 cm (4 in) across. *E. eyriesii* has a deep green, sharply ribbed body 15 cm (6 in) across and prominent white areoles with small dark spines. The white flowers are 23 cm (9 in) long and 5–8 cm (2–3 in) across. *E. kermesina* grows to 15 cm (6 in) in diameter and has variegated spines and deep red flowers 18 cm (7 in) long and 9 cm (3½ in) across.

(left) *Echinocactus grusonii*

Epiphyllum hybrid

Light and situation: a good light.
Temperature: warm in summer; cool in winter.
Moisture: water well in summer; keep dry in winter.
Soil: a rich, humusy mixture with some sand.
Propagation: from offsets or from seed.

Epiphyllum

This genus of epiphytic cacti from Central and South America is among the easiest to grow and the most beautiful, producing dramatic, often delicately scented, white flowers. The plant grows to 30 cm–1.5 m (1–5 ft) and the stems are flattened in section, giving the appearance of strap-like, dentate leaves. Hybrids are the most commonly grown and these range in the colour of their flowers from red and purple through pink to yellow and white. Bi-coloured strains are also available.

Light and situation: a well ventilated position in semi-shade, out of doors in summer if possible.
Temperature: warm in summer; cool in winter, 8–10°C (46–50°F).
Moisture: water freely in the growing period; sparingly in winter.
Soil: a rich compost.
Propagation: from cuttings which have been left to dry off for a few days.

Echinopsis eyriesii

(above) *Faucaria tigrina*   (below) *Ferocactus acanthodes*

Espostoa

This genus of columnar cacti from South America resembles *Cephalocereus* with its ridged body covered in fine white hairs. The main species *E. lanata* reaches 1 m (3 ft).

Care: as for *Cephalocereus*.

Euphorbia

Euphorbia pseudocactus, a succulent species of spurge, has a cactus form with jointed spiny green shoots growing in a candelabra shape. Other

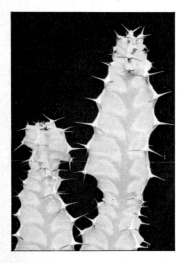

(above) *Espostoa melanostelle*

succulent spurges include *E. caput medusa*, which has several snake-like branches growing from the short stem. *E. obesa* is similar in appearance to *Astrophytum asterias*, from which it is distinguished by the spurge juice and flowers.

Light and situation: a good light and well ventilated position in summer.
Temperature: warm in summer; cool in winter.
Moisture: water moderately in summer; sparingly in winter.
Soil: a mixture of loam, peat and sharp sand.
Propagation: from cuttings and from seed.
Special points: the spurge juice is poisonous. If it gets on to the skin wash repeatedly in cold water.

Faucaria

This genus of almost stemless succulent perennials from Southern Africa is characterized by the opposite growing leaves which form an open rosette and are edged with hooked, back-

Euphorbia pseudocactus

wards-facing spines like teeth. *F. tigrina* produces yellow flowers in autumn.

Light and situation: a good light and a position outside in summer if possible.
Temperature: warm in summer; keep dry once the leaves begin to shrivel.
Moisture: water lightly from spring to autumn; moderately in autumn; keep dry in winter.
Soil: a mixture of loam, peat and sharp sand.
Propagation: by division or from seed.

Ferocactus

Species of these spherical and cylindrical cacti from Central America may grow to 3m (10 ft) in the wild but generally remain much smaller

in room cultivation. *F. latispinus*, a large spherical species, is sharply divided into segments with long red and white curving spines. *F. acanthodes* has a perfectly circular, blue-green stem and up to ten pink or red radial spines growing from the woolly areoles with four central spines which can grow to 10 cm (4 in) in length. It bears orange or yellow flowers in summer.

Light and situation: a very well-lit position; outside in summer if possible.
Temperature: warm in summer; cool in winter, 8–10°C (46–50°F).
Moisture: water normally in summer; keep dry in winter.
Soil: a mixture of loam, peat and sharp sand.
Propagation: from seed.

(above) *Gasteria liliputana* (below) *Glottiphyllum oligocarpum*

Graptopetalum

Graptopetalum, a genus of succulent shrubs from Central America includes *G. paraguayense* which has flat clusters of diamond-shaped fleshy leaves on branches up to 5 mm (¼ in) thick and *G. filiferum* which has pointed leaves growing in a tight, stemless rosette and small white flowers tinged with red at the end of the petals.

Care: as for *Echeveria*.

Gymnocalycium

Gymnocalycium is a genus of small, globular cacti from South America. It includes the species *G. denudatum*, which has long, fine white

Graptopetalum filiferum

spines and white flowers up to 5 cm (2 in) long and *G. mihanovichii* whose pink-flowered cultivar 'Friedricii' is shaped like a clear red lantern and has to be grafted on to a green stock to grow as it lacks chlorophyll.

Light and situation: a very light to half-shady position depending on the species.
Temperature: warm in summer; cool in winter, 6–10°C (43–50°F).
Moisture: water sparingly in summer; keep dry in winter.
Soil: a mixture of loam, peat and sharp sand.
Propagation: from seed.

Gymnocalycium mihanovichii 'Friedricii'

Gasteria

This large, succulent genus belongs to the lily family and comes from Southern Africa. The leaves of the plants are thick and fleshy, sometimes decoratively blotched with white and often growing in rosettes or in a fan shape. The flowers are red and appear in spring and summer. *G. liliputana* has tiny leaves 5–8 cm (2–3 in) high; *G. candicans* has rosettes of leaves 25–30 cm (10–12 in) long.

Care: as for *Haworthia*

Glottiphyllum

This genus of succulents from Southern Africa resembles *Argyroderma* except that the pairs of thick, fleshy leaves look like tongues rather than stones.

Light and situation: a good light with some sun (too much turns the foliage mauve).
Temperature: warm in summer; cool in winter.
Moisture: water sparingly in summer; keep dry in winter. Do not feed.
Soil: two parts sand to one part loam with some peat.

(above) *Kalanchoë blossfeldiana* hybrid

Haworthia fasciata

Haworthia

Haworthia is a succulent member of the lily family from Southern Africa. Of the many species, all are small plants with thick, fleshy leaves forming rosettes. In some the rosettes are flat; in others tall and narrow. They all produce small, pinkish white flowers in spring and summer. *H. fasciata* has a wide open rosette with triangular, pointed leaves; *H. margaritifera* is slightly more closed with decorative white markings. *H. reinwardtii* has dark upright leaves flushed with purple and covered with white nodules round a short trunk. *H. cymbiformis* has short erect grey-green leaves. *H. planifolia* is a larger plant with semi-translucent leaves.

Light and situation: a good light without strong sunlight in a closed room.
Temperature: warm in summer; cool in winter 10–12°C (50–54°F).
Moisture: keep well-watered in spring and summer; dry in winter except for the translucent-leaved species.
Soil: a mixture of loam, peat and sharp sand.
Propagation: from offsets or from seed.

Kalanchoë

Kalanchoë is an enormously varied genus of evergreen succulents many of whose species come from Southern Africa. *K. blossfeldiana* is the best known, a plant 25 cm (10 in) high with dark green, glossy leaves and compound, orange-red flowers in winter. There are now many other strains, some smaller, some flowering at different times with yellow and orange blooms. *K. tomentosa* is a shrub with silvery, furry leaves with rust-coloured, hairy edges.

Light and situation: a half shady position in summer and a full light in winter.
Temperature: warm in summer; moderate in winter, not below 15°C (59°F).
Moisture: water normally in summer; less in winter.
Propagation: from seed or from cuttings.

Kalanchoë (Bryophyllum)

The original succulent genus *Bryophyllum*, most of whose species come from the island of Madagascar, is now part of the genus *Kalanchoë* but the two groups of plants remain distinct for the amateur.
Unlike *Kalanchoë* these plants are usually grown for their attractive foliage and are marked by their habit of producing plantlets in the axils or at the edges of the leaves. *K. daigremontiana* grows to 75 cm (30 in) and has pointed, bright green leaves 8–15 cm (3–6 in) long, paler beneath and patterned with purple. These produce plantlets like frills in the indentations at their edges. *K. tubiflora* grows to 1 m (3 ft) and has tubular leaves 8 cm (3 in) long and 6 mm ($\frac{1}{4}$ in) thick which grow at right-angles to the stem. Plantlets grow at the end of the leaves.

(above) *Kalanchoë daigremontiana*

Light and situation: a well ventilated position in a good light but screened from direct sunlight.
Temperature: warm in summer; cool in winter, 10–12°C (50–54°F). Dry air is tolerated.
Moisture: water normally in summer; keep almost dry in winter.
Soil: a mixture of loam, peat and sharp sand.
Propagation: from rooted plantlets in spring several to a pot. Prick out in late summer.

Lithops
Pebble plants, living stones, stone face

This remarkable succulent from Southern Africa resembling *Argyroderma* is called living stones because the enormously thick, rounded leaves, 2·5 cm (1 in) high, resemble in colour and marking the pebbles that surround them. The leaves grow in pairs just separated by a central cleft from which the white or yellow flowers grow in summer.
Care: as for *Argyroderma*.

Lobivia

This genus of almost spherically stemmed, small cacti from South America have large spines and stiff hairs. They freely produce

Lithops aucampi

brilliant red and yellow flowers which open in the day and close at night. *L. allegraiana* has pink or red trumpet-shaped flowers on 15 cm (6 in) long, green ribbed stems. *L. hertrichiana* has scarlet flowers and pale to dark yellow spines. *L. jajoiana* has deep mauvish-red flowers borne on ribbed stems covered with radial spines with one large, central spine.
Light and situation: a well ventilated position in a good light.
Temperature: warm in summer; cool in winter, 4–6°C (40–43°F).
Moisture: keep moist in summer dry in winter.
Soil: a humusy mixture with some sand.
Propagation: from seed.

(below) *Lobivia hertrichiana*

Mammillaria

This large genus of mainly spherical cacti with tubercles arranged in spiral rings comes from Central America. *M. bocasana* has groups of spherical stems 15 cm (6 in) high covered in white spines and hairs, each areole having a long yellow and red central spine. *M. elongata* a freely branching plant, 15 cm (6 in) high, has columnar stems with attractive yellow spines and white or yellow flowers. *M. geminispina* has globular stems covered in long white spines *M. hahniana* has flat-topped, globular stems up to 10 cm (4 in) in diameter and carries small crimson flowers in summer. *M. zeilmanniana* has bright green stems, globular when young, and grows to 10 cm (4 in) in height. The tips of the aeroles are surrounded by a profusion of silvery, radial spines with four larger, central spines, the largest being hooked. A ring of mauve flowers with pale yellow centres form around the top of the stems in summer.

Light and situation: a good light; turn the plants occasionally to achieve a good shape.
Temperature: warm in summer; cool in winter, 6–8°C (43–46°F).
Moisture: water sparingly in

summer; keep dry in winter.
Soil: a rich, loamy mixture with sand and mineral elements.
Propagation: from offsets.

Neoporteria

This genus of small, spherical cacti from South America are chiefly remarkable for their beautiful spines ranging from white through yellow to brown and black. They produce pink flowers and grow more cylindrical with age.

Care: as for *Mammillaria*.

Neoporteria subgibbosa

Mammillaria geminispina

Notocactus

Notocactus is a large genus of globular cacti from South America carrying fine long radiating spines on the areoles of their ribbed bodies. *N. leninghausii* grows to 10 cm (4 in) in diameter and as a column reaches 1 m (3 ft) in height. It has yellow spines and pale yellow flowers up to 5 cm (2 in) in diameter. *N. apricus* has red spines on its ribs and large yellow flowers. *N. coccineus* is green and glossy with yellow or red spines and large yellow flowers. *N. haselbergii* is globular, 10 cm (4 in) in diameter, and has fine white spines and red flowers which are borne on the crown of its head.

Light and situation: a good light and a position out of doors in summer if possible. Shade from strong sunlight in spring.
Temperature: warm in summer; moderate in winter, 10°C (50°F).
Moisture: keep moist in summer and syringe on hot days; keep dry in winter.
Soil: a mixture of loam, peat and sharp sand.
Propagation: from seed.

Notocactus leninghausii

Opuntia
Prickly pear

Opuntia, to many people the archetypal cactus, grows wild over the entire American continent. The best-known types with flattened sections making weird shapes are those grown as hedging in their native habitat and these are generally the best for indoor cultivation. All have tufts and barbed bristles, called glochids, which stick to clothing and skin and can be painful. Some plants produce large, clear coloured flowers in summer. *O. basilaris* has many glochids and will produce a few reddish-purple flowers. *O. rufida* has spiny tufts but no thorns and bright yellow flowers. *O. bergeriana* readily produces orange-red flowers and *O. microdasys* has yellow flowers.

Light and situation: a good light.
Temperature: warm in summer: cool in winter, 6–8°C (43–46°F).
Moisture: water normally in summer; keep dry in winter.
Soil: a mixture of loam, peat and sharp sand.
Propagation: from seed or from cuttings of sections which should be allowed to dry out for fourteen days.

(above) *Opuntia rufida*   (below) *Oroya peruviana*

Oroya

This genus of small globular cacti comes from the Andes. The main species, *O. peruviana* grows to 8 cm (3 in) high and up to 15 cm (6 in) across. Its dark green body has vertical ribs divided into hexagonal tubercles. The spines range from transparent yellow through brown to black. The flowers are pink and yellow.

Care: as for *Mammillaria*

Pachyphytum

This genus of succulent, thick-leaved foliage plants comes from Mexico. *P. hookeri* is shrub-like, growing to 60 cm (2 ft). *P. oviferum* has thick, egg-shaped leaves and produces red flowers in early summer.

Care: as for *Echeveria*

(right) *Pachyphytum oviferum*

Parodia

Parodia mairanana

Parodia, a genus of fine globular cacti from South America, has tubercles arranged in a spiral and fine, red-tinged spines. The largest species, *P. maxima*, reaches 30 cm (12 in) in height and all species flower readily, producing daisy-like blooms in groups on the top of the plant ranging in colour from yellow through pink to scarlet.

Care: as for *Mammillaria*

Pereskia aculeata
Barbados gooseberry

A non-succulent, shrubby cactus with erect stems and spiny branches, *P. aculeata* comes from Florida, Mexico and the West Indies. This unusual, primitive type of cactus which bears leaves is a semi-evergreen shrub with thorns on the underside of each leaf which enable the plant to climb. It should be trained on wires or canes. The flowers are saucer-shaped and open in autumn.

Light and situation: a good light.
Temperature: warm in summer; not below 10°C (50°F) in winter.
Moisture: water well in summer and autumn; sparingly once the leaves have shrivelled.

Pereskia aculeata

Soil: a mixture of loam, leaf mould and sharp sand.
Propagation: from cuttings or from seed.

Rebutia

This genus of small cacti from South America will flower when only a year old and in an amazing variety of colours. The species are all clump-forming and most are globular. *R. chrysacantha* has yellow spines and red flowers; *R. miniscula var. grandiflora* has particularly large flowers.

Care: as for *Mammillaria*.

Rebutia chrysacantha

Cuttings: Put almost all one "leaf"
into John Innes No1 + sharp sand.
Do not overfeed (R. Smith)

Rhipsalidopsis
Easter cactus

This genus of epiphytic cacti from Brazil, known as 'link leaf' cacti because of their flat leaf-like, branching stems, produce a profusion of flowers in early summer and are ideal for hanging baskets. *R. gaertneri* (syn. *Schlumbergera gaertneri*) has scarlet tubular flowers. *R. rosea* has reddish pink flowers opening into a wide star shape.
Light and situation: semi-shade in summer; a good light in winter.

Temperature: warm in summer; 10–12°C (50–54°F) in winter.
Moisture: water well in summer and autumn; sparingly in winter and spring but do not allow to dry out.
Soil: a mixture of leaf mould, loam and sharp sand.
Propagation: from cuttings.

Pull young ones from branches facing inwards. Do not trim.

Rhipsalis

This genus of branched epiphytic cacti comes from the forests of tropical America. *R. cereuscula* is an erect plant with clusters of branches ending in short angular twigs covered with small bristles. It bears pink or white flowers at the end of the stems and these are followed by white berries. *R. cassutha*, a hanging cactus, bears cream flowers.

Light and situation: semi-shady position.
Temperature: warm.
Moisture: keep moist.
Soil: a mixture of loam, peat and sharp sand.
Propagation: from stem cuttings or from seed.

Rhipsalis cereuscula

Rhipsalidopsis gaertneri

Sansevieria
Bowstring hemp

Sansevieria, a genus of leafy succulents from tropical Africa, has a maximum of six stemless, fleshy leaves which grow from the soil and may reach 1·5 m (4½ ft) in height. The leaves are dark green with grey transverse bands and grow to a fine point. *S. trifasciata* 'Laurentii' has golden bands edging the green leaves; *S. t.* 'Hahnii' grows in a low rosette and looks like a Bromeliad. A 'Golden Hahnii' also exists.

Light and situation: a good light.
Temperature: warm in summer; not below 15°C (59°F) in winter.
Moisture: water normally in

(right) *Sansevieria trifasciata* 'Laurentii'

summer; keep dry in winter.
Soil: a proprietary peat compost.
Propagation: from seed in spring or from offset tubers when repotting.

Schlumbergera

Schlumbergera, a genus of epiphytic succulents from Brazil, has as its best known species *S. truncata* and its many hybrids. The branches are made of abutted, leaf-like, flattened stem sections each 4–5 cm (1½–2 in) long and the flowers, which last for three or four days, appear singly in winter at the end of the branches—a complex, trumpet shape with protruding stamens. *S × buckleyii* has mauvish pink flowers; 'Frankenstolz' has deep red flowers; 'Noris' has pink flowers; and 'Winter Tales' white flowers with a deep crimson blush.

Care: As for *Rhipsalidopsis*.

Sedum
Stone crop

This genus of succulent plants grows in the temperate regions of the world but it is the Mexican species which

are grown as houseplants. These have fleshy, often circular leaves. *S. bellum*, a semi-trailer, has stems 15 cm (6 in) long carrying the blue-green, spatula shaped leaves and creamy-white flowers. It is coated with a mealy farina. *S. morganianum* has trailing shoots 45 cm (18 in) long and succulent grey-green leaves. *S. rubrotinctum* has miniature rosettes of tiny, pebble-like leaves on freely branching stems. The leaves are pale yellow or grey-green and are tinged with red. *S. sieboldii* has round, flat, scarlet-edged leaves growing in threes and blotched with yellow circles.

Sedum sieboldii 'Variegata'

Selenicereus grandiflorus

Selenicereus grandiflorus, a semi-epiphytic shrub from the Argentine, has large, highly scented flowers lasting only one night, borne on thick, ribbed stems. The plant flowers best against a wall and will need support on canes. Crossings with *Epiphyllum* are also available.

Light and situation: a good light without direct sunlight.
Temperature: warm in summer; 10–12°C (50–54°F) in winter.
Moisture: water moderately in summer; sparingly in winter.
Soil: a mixture of leaf mould, loam and some sharp sand.
Propagation: from cuttings.

Schlumbergera truncata

Sempervivum
Houseleek

Sempervivum, a genus of largely hardy succulents found in the temperate regions, is a a vigorous, low-growing plant whose fleshy, almost triangular leaves grow in closely formed rosettes. *S. tectorum* has dark purplish tips to its pointed, grey-green leaves. *S. arachnoideum*, a miniature species, has red leaves covered in cobweb-like threads.

Care: most are hardy and grow indoors at very cool temperatures, 2–7°C (35–47°F).

Trichocereus

This genus of largely columnar cacti from South America, classified by some botanists with *Echinopsis*, has stems with neatly vertical ribs and prominent, showy spines. It produces beautiful flowers in yellow, orange, pink, red or white with sweetly scented nocturnal blooms. *T. candicans* has deep green, vertically ribbed stems up to 15 cm (6 in) in diameter and 80 cm (32 in) in height. The areoles have large yellow spines. The flowers are white, sweetly scented and are produced at night in summer. *T. spachianus* grows to about 1·2 m (4 ft) and is light green.

Light and situation: a good light and a position outside in summer if possible.
Temperature: warm in summer; cool in winter.
Moisture: water freely in summer; keep dry in winter.
Soil: a mixture of loam, peat and sharp sand.
Propagation: from seed or from cuttings.

Light and situation: a good light.
Temperature: warm in summer; 8–10°C (46–50°F) in winter.
Moisture: water normally in summer; keep almost dry in winter.
Soil: a mixture of loam, peat and some sharp sand.
Propagation: from stem cuttings or from seed.

(above) *Sempervivum tectorum*

(above) *Trichocereus candicans*

(right) *Selenicereus grandiflorus*

Miniature gardens

Groups of small-scale plants in bowls, sinks, dishes, even in a teacup are fun to arrange and visually very effective. They carry that fascination of things in miniature: a whole landscape is contained within a tiny space, complete with trees, bushes, flowers, perhaps even a little imitation lake made out of a mirror, or a delicate pottery bridge or Chinese pagoda.

Traditionally miniature gardens were used to create Japanese-style landscapes, with miniature shrubs and succulents or they were used to group together cacti. These arrangements can be seen to good advantage and need very little water and no cosseting. Nowadays miniature gardens are used for a wide range of different displays. In the winter months you might wish to show off the little plants of 10–13 cm (4–5 in) that were propagated from seeds or cuttings in the summer and will be set out individually in pots the following spring.

Your choice of plants will depend on where your container is to be placed, whether it's a warm or cool place, in bright light or shade. Your plants must all have the same light and water requirements. A cactus will never be happy growing in the same dish as a shrub.

For people with little spare time or spare space the creation and care of a miniature garden can be a most satisfying pleasure. Deciding what kind of a delicate scene you wish to create is like doing plant embroidery. The design will demand a lot of planning, but the upkeep of your garden will be simple and straightforward.

The most attractive container to use is the most inconvenient and difficult to obtain: one of those old stone sinks you sometimes see in farmhouses. But any kind of bowl or dish is suitable. The container should be fairly shallow, in proportion to the plants it will hold, and a soil depth of 7.5 cm (3 in) is sufficient. The container is unlikely to have drainage holes, so you must make a drainage layer of gravel mixed with a handful of charcoal. This layer should be about 2.5 cm (1 in) deep. Place a layer of peat on top of it to act as a moisture absorbant, and add a top layer of well-balanced potting compost.

Since the water evaporates rapidly in such a shallow container overwatering can be a problem. To preserve moisture, cover the top soil with a layer of gravel. This gravel will also give an attractive finish to the display. Once your garden is fully established regular spraying of the leaves is as important as regular watering.

The layout of your garden will depend mainly on where you plan to put it, and whether it will be seen from one side, from all sides or from above. It is sometimes a good idea to contour the soil, so that you build up a scene around tiny hills and valleys. Trailing plants can be used very effectively to soften the edges, and a tall, slender palm or columnar cactus will work well as the centre piece. Take care that any

A nursery of seedling *Echinocactus*, *Astrophytum*, *Cereus* and *Mammillaria* makes a pleasing miniature landscape in a wooden trough (above).

The mottled, brain-shaped forms of *Lithops* (far left) are effectively camouflaged by pebbles. They flower with yellow or white blooms.

The flowering succulent *Gasteria* (left) comes in sizes small enough to please the miniature garden enthusiast.

Large rocks, in reality modest pieces of stone, dwarf *Mammillaria* and *Opuntia* (right).

little rocks you use do not conceal the plants, and be sparing with those tiny garden ornaments which tend to create a cluttered look if they are used too enthusiastically.

Working in such a small area does mean that you must think carefully beforehand about what kind of visual effect you are seeking. Build up your display slowly and with consideration; a mass of shapes and colours which look fine in a window box will look confused in one small shallow dish.

For a spring show, miniature bulb gardens are deservedly popular. The mauves and yellows of crocuses make a beautiful complement to the shining white of snowdrops, while grape hyacinth and *Chionodoxa* give a brilliant blue display.

Viola hederacea with its white and purple flowers, together with the trailing stems and pink flowers of the *Anagallis tenella* and the white flowers of *Lobelia linnaeoides* are miniature flowering plants which all look charming together. Trailing plants, such as *Selaginella krausiana* with its vivid green, fern-like foliage will soften the outline of the group. Plants with small patterned leaves make good mixed groups for example *Fittonia*, *Saxifraga* and *Tradescantia*.

Once your garden is complete, trim and prune it to keep it in good condition. Mist the soil frequently with a spray, and water sparingly. Only use fertilizer if the plants are lacking in colour. If they are overfed they will try to over-reach themselves and that will be the end of your neat, small display.

Opuntia, *Euphorbia*, *Trichocereus*, and *Mammillaria* make up a classic, miniature garden. Decorative gravel helps to retain moisture while Japanese figures, mirror lakes and tiny pagodas are time-honoured accessories.

Peperomia hederaefolia, ivy, *Tradescantia*, *Helxine soleirolii* and avocado make a decorative garden (below).

An unusual silhouette composed of *Aloë*, *Kalanchoë*, *Echinocereus*, *Opuntia* and *Ferocactus* grouped in a see-through container (far right).

Terrariums and bottle gardens

Terrarium gardening began nearly 150 years ago when an English doctor, Nathaniel Ward, experimented by placing a moth chrysalis and some ordinary garden soil in a closed glass container, so that he could watch it emerging. In a very short time all the seeds and spores in the soil burst into life. Dr Ward assumed that they would soon die off in this 'airless' atmosphere, but much to his surprise they flourished, and went on flourishing unattended for the next four years.

Dr Ward experimented with other plants and other containers, and came to the conclusion that tropical foliage plants and ferns did especially well when grown under glass. His glass containers became known as Wardian cases and were a popular feature in late 19th-century homes. They are the great great grandparents of our modern terrariums.

The principle of a terrarium is quite simple. Water in the compost is taken up by the plant and given off into the surrounding atmosphere by the leaves. This water condenses on the glass and then runs back into the soil. The plants have a balanced atmosphere taking in oxygen at night, and giving off carbon dioxide during daylight hours. Plants growing in the well balanced microclimate of a completely sealed-off terrarium will need very little attention; in fact Dr Ward claimed that one of his cases remained undisturbed and healthy for fifteen years. Plants in a terrarium which has an opening need watering from time to time, but far less than if they were freestanding in a room.

Terrariums are particularly suited for tropical and subtropical plants which need a warm and humid atmosphere. They also serve to counterbalance the dryness of so many of our modern centrally heated homes. Apart from these purely practical advantages they are very attractive to look at and fascinating to experiment with, if you want to create a miniature ecosystem in your own home.

Today the elegant Wardian cases are rarely seen outside museums and, according to modern definition, a terrarium is any transparent plant container with a sealed covering or small opening. Bell-jars and large sweet jars with glass stoppers are excellent for a single plant such as a fern or a *Selaginella*, both of which are inclined to droop in a dry room. Covered cheese dishes and fish tanks with a sheet of glass for a lid are ideal for plant groups. You can make a terrarium quite simply by putting a glass dome over a container, making sure that the glass fits quite tightly just inside the rim of the container. Or you can buy a ready-made terrarium. These come in glass and plastic and range in size from 5 cm (2 in) cubes to those big enough to support a small indoor garden. Simple designs have a fitted lid and adjustable air vents, more complex designs have air heating equipment and artificial lighting, and these work as complete miniature conservatories.

When planting a terrarium first make sure that your container is thoroughly clean. If you are going to use a jar with a lid, remove the cardboard that lines it. If the container is large and easy to reach into such as a fish tank, it is possible to stand your plants inside in their pots on a tray of damp sand or gravel. But if it's small or awkward your plants will need to be planted. Small sized plants are best; they are easy to put in and therefore less likely to be damaged. It is best to use small rooted cuttings or seedlings. Some easy plants to grow are palms, begonias, *Dracaena*, and ivies. Baby's tears, *Fittonia* and ferns make good ground cover.

A terrarium originally meant a collection of wild plants grown in an enclosed plant container. And it is still possible to make a miniature reproduction of the outside world in your own house. The choice of plants depends on the kind of countryside that is nearest to you or that interests you most.

Your terrarium could contain a miniature desert complete with cactus varieties growing in sand. These flourish under glass, although they should never be sealed off completely as the build up of condensation is harmful to them.

The most popular terrarium displays use a collection of wild woodland plants. When you are on holiday or walking through a wood, look out for such things as partridge berries, violet plants, plantain, and all the little ferns like spleenwort and polypody. Seedlings of spruce, pines, and other woodland conifers make ideal larger plants. For ground cover sections of moss can be used as well as small rocks and pieces of bark with lichens growing on them. You can learn to appreciate the extraordinary quiet beauty of these woodland treasures once you have them isolated in your terrarium. The best time to collect wild plants is in the autumn just before the leaves fall, but do obtain permission from the owner of the area first. Also with the pressures on the plant kingdom today, it is best to collect seed where possible or go to a nursery specializing in wild plants.

As with miniature gardening, when choosing your plants you need to have an overall design in mind.

The plants you decide to put together must be able to thrive in the same conditions. Your assortment must also work visually. A wide range of different leaf shapes and plant heights always makes an interesting display, but it does mean that you must be careful about positioning them.

Whatever plant you are going to use, a terrarium should provide perfect drainage. To ensure drainage the terrarium must have a layer of drainage material, either a mixture of gravel and some charcoal or charcoal alone. The layer should be 2.5 cm (1 in) deep in a small container, and double that in a larger one holding several plants. Next comes a layer of moist potting compost which is put in to twice the depth of the drainage material. It is a good idea to build up the compost in some places to provide a more scenic effect. If the plants are crowded together they will look unattractive; your terrarium should receive plenty of light although direct sunlight will shorten the life of the plants and could cause their leaves to scorch. The compost should always be moist; in a closed terrarium there should be a slight condensation on the inside of the glass. If this increases, remove the lid until the glass becomes dry again. If, on the other hand, there is no condensation, you can begin the cycle again by misting the leaves with a fine spray.

Modern versions (above and left) of the nineteenth-century Wardian case (below) are very popular today, as they maintain a permanent display with the minimum of care.

A glass and cast iron terrarium turned plant window filled with light-loving geraniums.

Whatever the size and shape of your chosen plants, there is a glass container to fit them, from a humble pickle jar to an exquisite, bell-shaped dome or large carboy.

Glass is the ideal setting for a miniature moss garden.

With ingenuity, a terrarium can be made out of more or less anything. One solution is a glass aquarium tank (below), here shown without lid. The simple lines of the tank do not detract from the display of *Cryptanthus*, croton, African violet, *Dracaena* and *Peperomia* within.

Plants in bottles have the same protected, humid and warm life as plants growing in any enclosed or partly enclosed glass container. They differ in the fascination they exert. To see a large, flourishing fern in a bottle is as perplexing and exciting as seeing a fully rigged sailing ship in a bottle. It all seems like magic and you long to discover the secrets of the art.

You should start with small plants and let them grow to size once they are inside their container. In order to get the plants into the bottle you must have a collection of specially adapted elongated tools which you can buy or make yourself. These will enable you to prepare the compost, plant the plant, prune and dig up. Your general kit should include a funnel for putting in the compost and a small fork and spade, a tamper for firming the soil around the plants, a piece of sponge to clean the inside surface of the glass and a razor blade to do all your pruning and trimming work. Finally, you need something for lifting the plants out and lowering them

in. For this you can use a piece of strong flexible wire with a loop at one end or a pair of long tweezers. If you feel daunted by the prospect of all this construction work, then it is possible to buy the necessary tools at a garden centre.

There are a number of suitable bottles to choose from: chemical acid carboys are perhaps the most attractive and popular. Wine or cider flagons of the 4.5 and 2.2 litre (gallon and half gallon) sizes are also good. And decorative perfume bottles are effective for displaying the small single plant.

A rule which applies to all container growing is that the glass must be clear and thoroughly cleaned before planting. Wash your container carefully in lukewarm water and, if there are stubborn stains that refuse to disappear, these can usually be removed by putting uncooked rice into the bottle and swirling it about in the water.

To plant your plants you will need a layer of small pebbles for drainage, lumps of charcoal 1.25 cm (½ in) in size, peat

Begin by cleaning the inside of the bottle thoroughly, using a damp sponge held in an improvized wire loop.

Using a funnel and cardboard tube pour in a layer of gravel, followed by crushed charcoal. Then add the soil mixture.

Make indents in the soil. Protect larger plants with a cylinder of rolled paper and lower them into place.

Use bamboo 'tweezers' to insert smaller plants. They are also invaluable for moving plants into their final position.

Tamp down the soil around the plants with a cotton reel wedged firmly to the end of a piece of bamboo cane.

Use a syringe to water the plants and clean the soil from the glass. The syringe can be used dry to 'dust' the leaves.

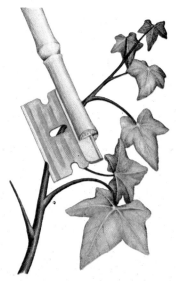

A razor blade attached to a piece of bamboo can be used to cut away dead growth which might cause mildew.

When you want to rearrange or remove plants, use the wire loop to lift them, since this will support the leaf spread.

and a potting compost, which can be either loam or peat-based depending on the plants you are planning to grow. The soil should be sterilized to ensure that it does not contain insect pests or weed seeds, and the plants must be healthy and free of pests; once they are in place it will be very difficult to rid them of any pests and diseases.

The correct level of humidity has been reached when there is just the slightest film of moisture on the inside of the glass. Too much water will cause so much vapour that the plants will be obscured from view. A sealed bottle which has been adjusted to the correct balance of humidity should not require any re-watering. A bottle with an opening will need to have the compost moistened very occasionally.

A well-planned and planted bottle garden should need scarcely any attention for years and years. Plants that grow too vigorously can be pruned back. Remove dead leaves promptly and keep a watchful eye for pests and diseases.

An almost otherworldly effect is created when the miniature landscape of the bottle garden is observed closely (above). The plants included in this display are the speckle-leaved croton, *Pilea cadierei*, *Pilea* 'Moon Valley,' *Begonia rex* and *Fittonia argyroneura*.

Aphelandra thrives in a humid atmosphere and is an ideal choice for the protective globe of the bottle garden. Here (left) it is teamed with *Chlorophytum* and *Hedera*, both resilient plants which nonetheless enjoy the luxury of the protected humid environment of a glass container.

Bromeliads flourish under glass in conditions that are a recreation of their native habitat. They look particularly elegant when enclosed in a glass dome such as the one shown (below).

Plant windows

A window is a natural display case for plants. The one danger is that you may lose your view of the outside world, and be left looking into a jungle of greenery. All the sunlight will benefit the plants, but not the room that lies behind them.

The last century with its fondness for elaborate clutter developed all sorts of plant window designs, which were in fact miniature greenhouses attached to the window outside. These made full use of the glass and steel frameworks so popular at that time in the construction of large conservatories and were often such extremely elaborate designs that few people nowadays would even consider trying to imitate them. Since these constructions drew little benefit from the warmth indoors, they needed to have their own form of heating, as well as their own ventilation system.

Today's plant windows are less complicated and the simplest kind of plant window is made by arranging a collection of plants in decorative pots along a window sill, covered with glass or plastic for protection. The window should receive good light, but direct sunlight is not advisable as this will scorch the leaves of most plants. It is a good idea to fit a canopy over a window which faces due south and then on very bright days the plants can be shielded from the fierce rays beating through the glass.

You can extend the basic use of the window sill by firmly fixing an ornamental plant trough to it. This trough should be deep enough to hold a minimum of 18–20 cm (7–8 in) of moist peat. It should be no wider from front to back than your arms can comfortably reach to rearrange plants or clean the window. A more complex way to create a plant window is to replace the entire sill with a shallow, concrete trough, fitted with drainage and soil-heating cables in its base. For its construction you will probably need the advice of an architect or building expert. Once in place cover the trough floor with a layer of gravel or shingle, moistened to provide humidity. Above this place a layer of peat at least 18–20 cm (7–8 in) in depth. The trough can be planted with plants out of their pots: slow-growers, such as cacti, *Fittonia* and African violet are a good choice. But almost any plants can be used.

Plate glass shelves fitted across an actual window show plants to great advantage. First make certain that your window frame will support the weight of shelves and ensure that the shelves are well supported, otherwise the glass may

A welcoming glow in the night from a spacious, brightly lit glass entrance porch, alive with greenery. The two storeys easily accommodate more statuesque plants than those usually available to the indoor gardener.

shatter. They work best in a square window rather than a curved bay one. Without blocking too much light from the room, they allow everything about the plants to be seen clearly: their shapes, their foliage and flowers.

The most elaborate sort of plant window popular today is based on building a conservatory inside the room. An old fashioned bay window can be fitted with well supported glass shelves, and then divided from the rest of the room with a well fitted glass door. In more modern houses a single large plate glass window can be equipped with a well-drained trough and sealed off from the room with glass doors. With this method the temperature and humidity level inside the plant window should be kept considerably higher than in the room behind it. What you have in fact created is a large terrarium, ideal for growing rare tropical varieties of plants. Cacti, however, will not thrive in this elaborate closed window since the humidity is too great for them. Another danger with this system is that the combination of heat, moisture and light could cause your plants to become a wild mass of vegetation, which might not be quite the effect you wanted. So they will need a lot of pruning and care.

A mass of geraniums curtain this charming 18th century window (above).

Dieffenbachia, *Clerodendrum* and *Nephrolepis* (left) growing in a spotlit trough relieve the austerity of large glass windows and plain white walls.

The boundary between inside and outside is blurred by a plant-crowded glass doorway. (below left). *Ficus elastica*, *Dracaena*, ivy, *Pittosporum* and *Philodendron* are the plants used to achieve this indoor jungle effect.

Not so much a plant window, more a plant wall (below). *Fatsia japonica* and *Cyperus alternifolius* line the glass and wood of this elegant, inverted boat-shaped room.

Bonsai

It was the Chinese who first saw the beauty of naturally stunted and dwarfed trees growing in windblown and rocky places. They transplanted them into decorative containers and brought them into their homes. The Japanese perfected the art of cultivating these trees and it is from them that we have the name bonsai, which means quite simply a plant in a tray or shallow container.

The bonsai technique of cultivation has a long history of records dating from the 14th century, and it is believed to have been first discovered over a thousand years ago. True bonsai is an art. These little trees, sometimes fifty to a hundred years old or even more, are exact reproductions of full scale trees. They are selected and trained over the years so that, although they have been kept in the confines of a garden or a pot, they look as though they have weathered tempestuous storms and winds. Bonsai are judged not just on the beauty of their overall effect, but for each facet of composition: the harmony between the pot and the tree, the texture of the trunk, the way the roots are patterned and the leaves and branches are set.

Bonsai trees are cultivated in a variety of ways, from seeds, cuttings, layering and grafting. Sometimes a naturally dwarfed tree is dug up with extreme care from the wild, and afterwards its natural environment is maintained artificially. A large variety of trees can be used and they are then categorized under three general headings: the type of tree, the style it has been trained to grow in and the height it reaches. Of the evergreen trees the most popular are pine, juniper, spruce, cedar and yew. Small-leaved deciduous varieties are most suitable and these include maple, elm, hornbeam, beech, and birch. Among the flowering trees there are winter jasmine, magnolia and garden camellia. Flowering trees which bear quite small-sized fruits such as the cherry and the crab apple can also be used to great effect.

Bonsai trees are grown in various styles, classified by the angle at which they stand. The formal upright tree is vertical, with a triangular outline; the informal upright bends slightly, as if it were windblown; the cascade curves downwards and the semi-cascade is almost horizontal. These last two styles are particularly suitable for pines and junipers, and give you a sense of the strong winds that sweep the high, exposed places where the trees grow naturally. Another style is created by training the roots of the tree to grow over a rock, and yet another by grouping a number of bonsai together, or by setting them within a small landscape, among rocks and gravel. An uneven number of trees are always grown in a group, since the Japanese see odd numbers as a symbol of longevity. Four trees are never grown together because the Japanese word for four is very similar to the word meaning death.

As far as the size is concerned, there is no fixed standard of measurement, nor does a particular tree need to grow to a certain height. A tree the height of a cigarette is considered small; a tree smaller than this is called miniature; a 90 cm (3 ft) tree is large, while 45 cm (18 in) is about average height. Size depends less on species and more on training and the type of environment in which the tree is grown.

Bonsai styles imitate naturally occurring forms as shown in the artfully informal 'pose' of this weathered and dignified Chinese juniper tree, over a hundred years old (above).

On the bonsai scale, the tiny, berries of the *Pyracantha* (left) look very much like fruit.

Acer palmatum, the Japanese maple (top right), is traditionally trained into the double trunk formation.

Flowering trees are particularly attractive, but only those with small enough blooms, such as *Crataegus oxycantha* 'Flore Pleno Rosea' (right) are suitable.

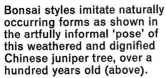

The roots of an *Acer* (maple) trained to grow clinging to a rock (above). Not all trees are suitable for this style.

A complete miniature landscape can be created by grouping spruces and elms in a natural setting (right.)

Bonsai trees are grown and sold at specialist nurseries and garden centres. They are usually in good condition, but when choosing one it is wise to make sure that it is standing firmly in its container, that the soil is moist but not too wet, and that the leaves of the tree are bright and healthy.

The tree will probably be in its own bonsai container. The best of these are manufactured in Japan. They come in muted, delicate colours and have a simply-proportioned beauty of their own. The pots must be frost proof, glazed on the outside, but not on the inside. Drainage holes are an important feature, because in such a constricted space the roots must have aeration and must never be allowed to become water-logged. The depth of the container can vary from 2.5 cm (1 in) to 45 cm (18 in) or more. As a rough guide the depth measurement of the pot should be one half that of the upper part of the tree. But this will also depend on the type of display you have chosen.

Bonsai, unlike tropical forest plants, cannot live permanently indoors. They are as hardy as their full-sized relatives: they flower, fruit, change colour, if they are deciduous, and loose their leaves in autumn in exactly the same way as full-grown trees. They need as much open air as they can get and should, if possible, live out of doors and only be brought inside the house for not much more than a week at a time. When they are indoors they must stand in a light, cool place, such as an airy window sill, away from any source of heat. Spray the whole tree once or twice every day; rainwater is best for this, or tap water that has stood for some hours.

Bonsai pots are ornaments in themselves. They come in traditional forms and colours and most of them are shallow in order to restrict root spread. Tall pots are used for cascade styles. At least one hole is necessary for drainage and the insertion of training wire.

Bonsai styles are based on the relationship between the angle of the trunk and its pot. The dramatic windswept style imitates a tree which has grown up exposed to the elements. Traditionally, this style is complemented by a suitably gnarled pot.

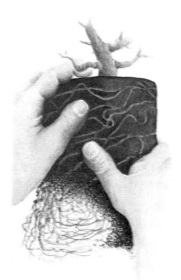

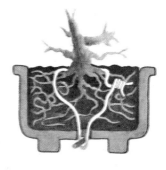

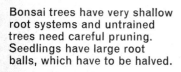

Bonsai trees have very shallow root systems and untrained trees need careful pruning. Seedlings have large root balls, which have to be halved.

Holding the root ball near the trunk base, break away the lower part of the soil. Prune the roots back in relation to the size of the tree and pot.

The trunk base must be anchored to secure the tree. Loop wire through two-holed pots, or wrap around a piece of cane for a one-holed pot.

There are two methods of training the trees into shape: pruning and wiring. The latter is a difficult and harsh technique, which involves binding wire around various parts of the tree in order to bend it to a particular shape.

Pruning, however, can be done without any violence to the plant, and should be done constantly, a little at a time. This removes old wood, shapes the tree and encourages budding. The effect of balance and proportion seen in a beautiful tree is achieved by cutting off branches where you do not want them and encouraging those where you do. Twigs should be shortened in order to keep the overall balance of the tree. This should be done at the end of the winter, when the main branches must also be pruned. Flowering trees should be cut back only after they have flowered.

It is also possible to grow a bonsai tree from cuttings, seeds or seedlings. However, all these methods are extremely slow and painstaking, and without very skilful attention you will end up with a dwarf shrub growing in a pot or a mass of twigs weighed down by large flowers. If you feel that you don't have the patience either to nurture a miniature tree from a seedling, or carefully collect a wild specimen, it is possible to reach a compromise by adapting other plants to bonsai growing methods. Any plant of small stature and attractive appearance can be used. A small ficus is perfect for imitation bonsai, and a small begonia with its gnarled growth makes an excellent subject. Mistletoe, gardenia, geranium, English ivy and miniature holly are all well suited and can be trained into interesting shapes and beautifully balanced forms.

Pruning depends on the final design you want to achieve. Branches which are too long or too ungainly can be shortened, cutting them back as far as a suitable bud sprout. If you want a branch to take a new direction, cut it off just beyond a well grown shoot.

Unnecessary branches, or those which confuse the overall design, can be eliminated. Traditional branches to remove are those that are too low, those that directly oppose another, those that cross over the trunk. Hollow out stumps with a sharp knife.

Classical semi-cascade style achieved by selective pruning.

A wire-trained tree in the informal upright style (below).

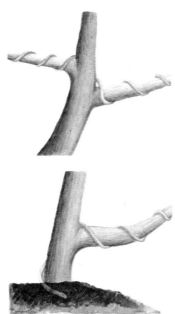

The desired shape may take years to achieve. Copper wire will hold the growing limbs in the required position until they can stand on their own. Wrap the wire round the branch at an angle of 45°. If it is too tight it will cut into the tree, if too loose it will slip. Insert the ends into the soil.

Trees in the house

A tree adds a new dimension to an interior. Small and attractive plants have a decorative quality, but a tree actually affects the whole design concept of a room. As a general rule indoor trees are not very demanding and that is why they are so popular in offices and showrooms.

Some indoor trees are true trees, such as *Araucaria*, the Norfolk Island Pine, the many varieties of palm and even the common garden specimens such as oaks and chestnuts which make temporary house guests. The *Ficus elastica*, or rubber plant, can be grown into a tall tree shape, so can the tall *Dracaena*, and the beautiful succulent *Crassula arborescens* with its fat green leaves and grey trunk. What they all have in common is their size and their commanding presence. It is wise not to have too many trees in your room, not because they won't look attractive, but because they are liable to become rather overpowering.

Perhaps the prettiest indoor tree is *Ficus benjamina*, called the weeping fig. It grows reasonably fast and given time it will reach the ceiling. The pale grey trunk is delicately contrasted with the shiny pointed bright green leaves. As long as the leaves are sprayed regularly, this particular ficus is undemanding and likes being indoors all the year round.

Sparmannia will grow to a height of 1·8–2·4 m (6–8 ft). It can be kept in a formal shape with regular pruning and cutting. Pretty gold-centred white flowers usually appear in the spring, and the leaves are soft and furry and pale green. As long as it is kept in a good light it will flourish all the year round. If it gets so large that you have to remove it, take some cuttings; they will root very easily and in a very short while you will have not just one plant but possibly two or three.

Date palms make exotic indoor trees. Two sorts can be recommended: *Phoenix canariensis* which needs to be bought from a garden shop, and *Phoenix dactylifera* which is a fast grower and gets very tall. You can raise the latter from a date stone, although it will take some time for it to reach the height of a self-assured tree and even longer before you might actually harvest a date crop.

Many *Dracaena* resemble small palm trees with their long thin stems and big glossy leaves. They may reach a height of several metres, and thrive in a warm room; but the temperature should not be allowed to drop below 10°C (50°F). *Dracaena marginata* has very narrow leaves and grows to about 2 m (6 ft), *Dracaena reflexa*, sometimes called song of India, grows into a graceful bush of numerous little trunks and branches. It will reach true tree dimensions of 3 metres (10 ft) or more only after 15 years or so of well-tended growth. All the *Dracaena* make wonderful thin-trunked formal 'trees', and most of them are easily maintained.

Crassula arborescens is a smaller 'tree' which grows to a height of 1 m (3 ft). It likes a light cool place which must not get warmer than 10°C (50°F) in the winter. A well lit hallway with no draughts would make an ideal home.

Small oaks and chestnuts make pretty houseplants, but they can only be kept indoors on a temporary basis, and even then they need as much light as possible, and should be planted outside after a year or so. Some fruit-bearing trees can also be brought in, but again they need a bright airy position if they are to survive. A fig in a pot may do well, and a climbing vine planted in a large tub will clamber all round a window.

Dracaena massangeana (above)
responds to indoor warmth.

A long, roomy and generously
lit gallery (far left) is possibly
one of the few settings that is
not overwhelmed by these
large tropical trees, more
often seen outdoors.

An interesting contrast can be
achieved by teaming the spiky
exuberance of *Yucca aloifolia*
with the broad, flat leaves of
Banana (*Musa cavendishii*)
as shown here (left).

Ficus carica (above) makes a
breathtaking display of aerial
greenery filling the glass dome
of what was once a chapel.
Tradition has it that the dome
was built round the tree.

Bromeliads; topiary; water gardens

Many houseplants are strange and exotic looking specimens whose natural home is a steamy jungle swamp, or a brutally hot desert, and perhaps the strangest of them all are the bromeliads. Most of them are epiphytes or air plants, which means that in their natural habitat in South American jungles they live perched in the nooks of the branches of large trees with only the most meagre foothold. Their food and their water comes mostly from what falls into the natural cup which is formed by the stiff rosette of their leaves. The most familiar bromeliad, and the only one with any commercial use is the pineapple, but there are 1,800 other plants belonging to this species, all of which rival each other in oddness. Each rosette blooms only once in its lifetime and the flowers are usually surrounded by incredible colored bracts. The flowering lasts for several months and during this time the plant also sends up little offsets or suckers. A bromeliad can be encouraged to flower by being placed in a plastic bag alongside a ripe apple for a few days; the ethylene gas from the apple initiates flower buds.

Bromeliads are adaptable to most indoor conditions and they need only modest attention. Mistings keep the foliage clean, and the little 'jug' must be kept full of water. This little pool of water will keep cut flowers fresh, and many bromeliad owners like to use them as vases. In fact the *Aechmea* group has earned itself the title 'the living vase plant' for this reason.

Bromeliads can be potted in shallow pots with a fibrous porous compost mixture, which could be an orchid potting mix. There is also an attractive and unusual way of displaying these plants by making a bromeliad 'tree'. Choose a strong, well-shaped tree branch, preferably of *Acacia*, elm, chestnut or apple (at pruning time). It should be attached to a solid base like a box or tub of cement, but also be light enough to move once it is planted. Take each plant in turn from its pot, wrap its roots in damp sphagnum moss, then bind the moss 'ball' to the branch gently but securely with wire, preferably green in colour so that it will not be easily seen. Set the plants in the forks and angles of the branches. The best varieties for growing on a 'tree' are *Tillandsia* and *Cryptanthus*. Spray the moss round the roots regularly so that they never dry out.

The epiphytes *Tillandsia* (above) and *Vriesia imperialis* (below) can be grown on trees as in their jungle homes.

The colourful bracts of *Aechmea splendens* and *A. rhodocyanea* (below) last for several months.

Topiary is the art of training plants to grow in stylized shapes so that they look as if they have been carved into growing sculptured forms. This art was made popular in the formal gardens of Europe and many splendid examples can be seen today in historic parks and gardens. The genuine kind of topiary cannot be practised indoors as all the hedge plants used such as yew, box or privet have to be out in the open air. But it is possible to translate the techniques of pruning and clipping and use them on indoor plants.

There are two styles of indoor topiary. You can train a trailing plant to climb over a wire frame or you can simulate topiary in a very effective manner by growing a number of small plants all over a ready-made wire form which has been stuffed with moss. Constructions for both can be bought commercially in many shapes and sizes or you can set them up yourself at home. It takes a lot of time and patience to achieve a really good imitation of outdoor topiary but a very attractive yet simple display can be made by thoughtfully directing and planning the way a trailing plant grows.

Climbers such as *Stephanotis* and *Passiflora* are often sold tied to wire hoops or coils: as the tendrils grow they should be attached to the wire or cane supports with wire ties. Among the most successful shapes that can be bought or made are globes, obelisks and pyramids on wire stems placed in flower pots. Climbing plants that can be trained and tied to these are *Ficus pumila* (creeping fig), *Cissus antarctica* (kangaroo vine), *Rhoicissus rhomboidea* and various ivies. These must be regularly tied and pruned and trimmed to keep the shape neat and formal.

Simulated hedge topiary is made with cubes or globes of wire mesh over chicken wire stuffed with moist sphagnum moss. The frame is covered with more moss and held in place with rust-proof wire. Rooted cuttings are planted in the moss and pinned down with bent wire. Ivy is commonly used. This takes a while to thicken up and become hedge-like but with time the ivy can be trained into a reasonable semblance of a hedge. Spraying daily with tepid water is essential and feeding is needed every two or three weeks.

Water is a perfect foil for plants and a source of endless fascination. An indoor pool could be part of your planning for a conservatory or garden room. Water is very heavy so weight is a problem and the introduction of any pond or pool will have to be discussed with an architect or builder, especially if you are not on the ground floor. There must be drainage to remove surplus water and a tap nearby for filling.

Pools can be made of concrete, heavy plastic sheeting or prefabricated fibre-glass shapes. The last two are available from water garden stockists and for roofs and balconies the lightest are obviously the best. Plants only thrive in shallow indoor pools when they are well lit, so lighting is obviously a very important feature.

Plants that like their roots in water can stand with their pots submerged; *Cyperus* varieties are ideal for this. Water lilies (*Nymphaea*) can be planted in pots or aquatic baskets in deeper pools. The compost you choose should be as unorganic as possible. Peat and fibrous loam will not do as they turn the water green. The best compost to use is a plain heavy loam with a little bonemeal added. A small pool should be quite shallow, only a bit deeper than a shower tray, and contain potted marginal plants that like only their roots in water such as *Cyperus*, the Egyptian papyrus, *Xanthosoma nigrum* which has a yellow arum-like flower, *Calthas* (kingcup or marsh marigold,) with yellow buttercup flowers, aquatic irises and even rice (*Oryza sativa*). All these plants are obtainable from water garden specialists. The flowering rush (*Butomus umbellatus*) grows to 60 cm (2 ft) with pink umbel flowers and long narrow leaves, the ebra ush (*Scirpus tabernaemontana*) has spiky quills and grows to 1 m (3 ft). In unheated pools you could have a fish population of shubunkins, comets and moors, while heated pools would be right for the many varieties of tropical fish.

If you don't want to go to the full extent of having a pool garden but like the idea of water, you could make a water garden in a wooden or plastic tub; a half barrel is a good size. It can hold water lilies and a few small fish. Water crowfoot (*Ranunculus aquatilis*) and pondweeds act as oxygenators and should be put in weighted baskets at the bottom to keep the water pure. Late spring is the best time for all planting.

The smallest water garden is one in a bowl 15–23 cm (6–9 in) deep, which can be planted with miniature water lilies such as *Nymphaea pygmaea* 'Alba', *N. candida* and *N. pygmaea* 'Helova'. Plant these in spring in 7.5 cm (3 in) of soil covered with small pebbles or gravel. The floating water hyacinth *Eichhornia crassipes*, fairy moss (*Azolla caroliniana*) and frogbit (*Hydrocharis morsus-ranae*) are all small water plants that can be planted in a goldfish bowl.

How to make a herb sculpture

An exciting and unusual project for the urban indoor gardener is a hanging plant column which can be suspended from a suitable point creating an organic and ever-changing mobile. This can be a visually attractive addition to an interior and is easily constructed from readily available materials. Plant columns are particularly suitable for cramped rooms or areas which do not usually house plants, such as window bays or recesses, provided they are well lit. You can adjust the size of the column to suit the location and, with plenty of light and enough space to breathe, it will produce a plentiful crop.

The growth of a plant column depends on the capillary action of a central core of perforated pipe. The pipe is encased in the expanded, water-retaining foam used by florists and flower arrangers known as oasis. Water poured through a gravel-filled funnel at the top of the column drains through the pipe and is absorbed by the oasis which in turn feeds it to the soil. A shallow dish at the bottom of the pipe catches the excess water.

A column can be successfully planted using a wide variety of plants; but as individual conditions vary enormously, do ensure that whatever plants you choose are suitable for the location you have in mind. Relatively hardy plants are the best choice. Columns can either be planted or seeded out, but seeds tend to make a stronger growth.

An exciting visual effect can be created by planting a selection of wild flowers or you can make a particularly diverting sculpture with a column of variegated turfs. The most popular and attractive of columns is a herb column which not only looks good and smells delicious but also provides a fresh daily supply of herbs. Herb columns can be hung anywhere but make particularly useful additions to the kitchen.

Like any house plant, columns need watering and feeding and must be regularly rotated to ensure adequate lighting. They can be hung out of harm's way and are a good investment for those with inquisitive children or exuberant pets. As it slowly swings in the sunlight the column presents a constantly changing aspect and can be a welcome alternative or addition to your usual display of plants.

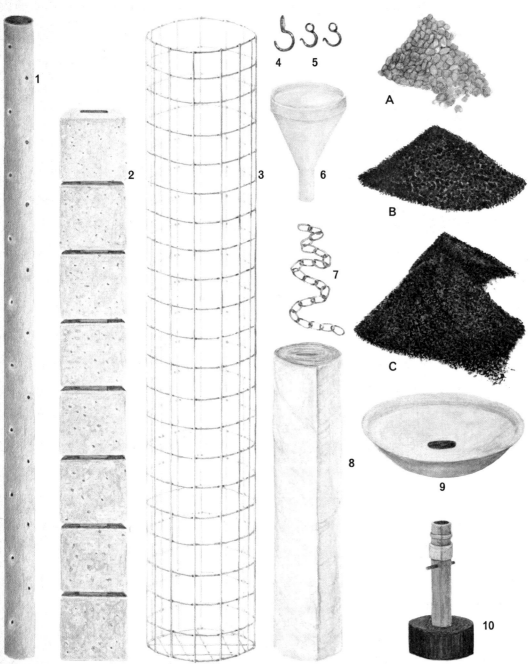

When you have chosen the plants you want to use and selected a suitable location, you will need the following materials to construct a herb column of approximately 1·5 m (5 ft) long. The ultimate overall length depends on the length of chain you use.

1 Perforated plastic water pipe 10 cm (42 in) long and 1·5 cm (½ in) in diameter.
2 Length of oasis (expanded foam which retains moisture) 105 cm × 6·5 cm (42 in × 2½ in).
3 Cylinder of 2·5 cm × 2·5 cm (1 in × 1 in) gauge weld mesh wire, 17·5 cm (7 in) in diameter.
4 A steel hook 5 cm (2 in) in diameter to suspend whole creation.
5 Two steel hooks, 2·5 cm (1 in) in diameter to attach chain to wire cylinder.
6 Plastic funnel with 17·5 cm (7 in) lip.
7 Length of steel chain with 1·5 cm (½ in) links.
8 Roll of polythene sheeting 120 cm (48 in) wide.
9 Shallow glass or plastic dish with 5 cm (2 in) diameter hole.
10 Copper pipe large enough to fit over water pipe; copper pin to affix it.
You will also need some flexible sealing compound.

For the contents of the column you will need:
A Small pebbles for the funnel.
B Compost
C Peat
Mix two parts peat to one part compost.

You will also need mustard and cress seeds to bind the soil, and your plants.

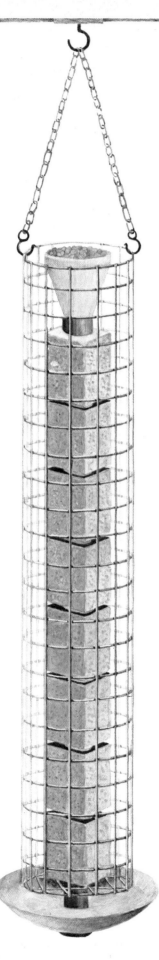

Sink the large hook into a ceiling joist or other weight-bearing structure. Make sure that your anchor point is secure, since the column will be very heavy.

Slot the cubes of oasis over the water pipe and insert the funnel into the top end of the pipe.

To assemble the bottom part of the structure, slide the copper pipe through the hole in the glass dish. This should fit snugly. The lip at the bottom of the pipe will prevent water from escaping, but if necessary you can plug gaps with a flexible sealing compound. Fit the upper end of the copper pipe over the lower end of the water pipe and fix with a copper pin.

Place the wire cylinder over the structure and fill the space between the cylinder and the oasis-clad pipe with the soil compound. Sew mustard and cress seeds liberally to bind the soil. Wrap the column in the polythene sheeting and leave to stand for about a week. Fill the funnel mouth with pebbles to make a filter and pour a little water into it.

When the mustard and cress has sprouted, unwrap the column and sew your chosen seeds. Seeds are preferred to cuttings as they bind the soil together better and the resultant growth lasts longer. Plant bog plants, such as sedge grass in the glass dish to soak up the moisture.

This herb column contains: *Hebe subalpina*, thyme, mint, basil, rosemary, sedge grass and *Carex panicea* for the glass dish.

You can now hang up your column. Use the two small hooks to attach the steel chain to the wire of the cylinder and hang the whole structure from the large hook. Choose an airy, spacious, well-lit position. The whole column can swivel so that each part receives even lighting; the slowly turning column is soon transformed into a beautiful plant mobile.

House plants for children

Children can be very keen and dedicated gardeners once they have overcome their initial impatience. They tend to plant seeds one day and dig them up the next wanting to have a look and see if they are growing yet. But children can be captivated by the mystery and excitement of the plant world, if they are encouraged to experiment with fast growing plants that burst into life quickly and spectacularly. And if they can actually see the roots as well as the shoots growing, they will persevere with their horticultural experiments much more patiently.

The quickest of all the quick growers are a mixture of cress seeds, which you can easily buy at a garden centre. Sprinkled on damp blotting paper or a wet flannel, they burst into life in a few days and are ready to eat by the end of a week. It's fun to plant them on top of a cut potato where they stand up like a shock of hair, or in other unlikely places such as on a melon peel.

Lentils grow just as quickly. Fill a saucer with enough water to moisten them, set them on a window sill, and in less than a week the little green shoots will appear.

Beans are the traditional seeds for demonstrating plant growth to children and it's wonderful to watch them grow. They can be rooted on a damp flannel or in a jam jar with

Plants need not be kept out of children's reach, so choose tough specimens that can stand some neglect. The Kangaroo vine (above) is a perfect playroom plant.

The streamlined shape of the space ship marrow (below) takes its place on a ledge full of other transport models. The alien tendrils are fast-sprouting broad beans.

A potato 'bust' can be created by securing one potato on top of half of another. Cress will sprout as green hair, and a face can be added to taste.

a piece of blotting paper of the same height rolled up inside. Soak a bean overnight. Press it between the blotting paper and side of the jar so that it can be studied easily. Put a little water in the base of the jar to keep the blotting paper damp. Very soon roots followed by shoots will appear on the bean. When this happens, plant it in a pot of compost.

A damp sponge can be converted into an ideal seed tray and planted with seedlings left over from your own plantings. Radish, *Alyssum*, dwarf marigold (*Tagetes*) and lettuce will all obligingly root in these simple conditions; and they will all show a good display of greenery even if they never reach the flowering stage.

An amusing project for children is making a potato 'vine'. A seed potato with plenty of eyes is best for this. Place it in the top of a jam jar with its base just in the water and its eyes at the top. Place the jar and the potato in a dark, cool place and wait for the roots to appear, which should take just a few days. Shoots will sprout from the eyes. Some shoots should be removed, leaving one or two only to grow. Plant the rooting and shooting potato in potting compost and place it by a window. The shoots will grow to 1–2 m (3-6ft) and can be left to trail down or be tied to strings. Sweet potatoes may be treated in the same way; place them in the jar narrow end down and remember that, unlike ordinary potatoes, they do not need a dark place to sprout.

Unroasted peanuts also produce pretty vines. Just plant one or two peanuts in moist compost in a warm place and wait for them to shoot.

Other growing things with which children can experiment are the vegetable scraps destined for the dustbin or compost heap. One which makes a charming little fern-like plant is the common carrot. Cut off the top of a fresh carrot and stand it in a saucer of water in a good light. It will sprout into feathery leaves. The same can be done with parsnip and beetroot tops.

The most popular and effective plant to be grown in this way is the pineapple, which is in fact a member of the bromeliad family. Slice off the top of the fruit, taking a rosette of sharp, serrated leaves and about 5 cm (2 in) of fruit. Scoop out the flesh to prevent rotting, and leave the slice to dry for two or three days. Remove the lower leaves and place the rosette in a damp, sandy compost in a warm light place, about 18°C (64°F). With much patience and regular spraying the slice will develop roots and turn into a proper houseplant like its relations, the *Aechmea* and the *Billbergia*.

Broad beans (left) are the ideal plant for the young and impatient horticulturist. Placed in a jam jar of water, the seeds sprout quickly and in pleasingly varied shapes.

Your child's name in lights, or rather in mustard and cress grown on a wet flannel, blotting paper, a damp piece of linen or cotton wool. This method of cultivation both improves spelling and prevents any ownership squabbles between children.

Kitchen throwouts (left) grow easily in water. Carrot tops produce delicate fronds and beetroot leaves are dramatically coloured.

Lentils are another easy source of attractive plants. They grow very quickly in water and root development can be easily seen.

Very satisfactory plants can be easily grown from the pips of such everyday fruits as melon and grapefruit (above). The plants grow rapidly with plenty of sunshine, water and air in the summer and a constant warm temperature in winter.

A little more time and care is needed to coax a date palm from its stone. This thriving specimen (below), successfully raised in the warm, light conditions of a modern office, is eight years old and still growing.

Self-sown seedlings have a habit of appearing in the most suitable and also sometimes the most unexpected places. One of the healthiest lemon trees I have ever seen grew out of the compost heap at the bottom of my garden, and a conker that dropped into a pot of geraniums is now a 1·5 m (5 ft) high horse chestnut tree. In the house these natural accidents are unlikely to happen unaided, but it is possible to get children to take on the job of birds, squirrels and other chance planters by encouraging them to plant all kinds of different seeds in all kinds of different places and containers. If one avocado stone or one lemon pip is solemnly placed in a pot and then nothing happens for a long time, the disappointment will be enormous. But if a dozen possibilities are set up around the house, some of them are bound to be successful.

Trees and shrubs grown from pips and stones are very easy to grow, although they do need a little cosseting. The stones and pips of most fruits will germinate in damp potting mixture in a dark place. Do not give up too soon; some take a long time to germinate. Each stone or pip you use must of course be fresh and not out of a tin, as canning and cooking kill seeds.

The most popular plant grown in this way is the avocado. It is very easy to grow and makes a good-looking plant. The avocado pear (*Persea gratissima*) is a member of the laurel family, which grows into a large tree in tropical America. Avocado stones root easily in water or in damp compost. If you use water put pins or toothpicks into the sides of the stone and suspend it pointed end upwards across the neck of a jam jar so that its base is in the water. To root in compost push it in gently, so that half of it stands above the surface. Whichever method you use a warm, not too bright place is best. When the stone splits and the pinkish shoot appears, usually within four to eight weeks, move it to a lighter place. When strong roots appear pot it into a sandy potting mixture.

The avocado grows into a tall plant with pointed, leathery leaves and a woody trunk. To avoid it getting tall and thin, pinch out the growing point and make it form side shoots. Like many house plants it likes a well-lit place out of drafts. If rooted in water, you could continue growing it hydroponically. If in soil feed it every three weeks or so. Winter temperature should be 10°C (50°F).

Large seeds of marrows, pumpkins and courgettes are easy to collect and dry on trays or saucers in the sun. These seeds, sown in seed compost and well watered, will produce small plants very fast in a warm place in summer; with feeding they may even produce flowers and subsequently fruit. The trailing varieties can also be made into vines by tying the long shoots to strings.

One of the most exciting plants grown from a pip is the date palm (*Phoenix dactylifera*). For this you use stones from fresh dates. The stones can be germinated in water, or be sown pointed end upwards 2 cm (½ in) deep in potting mixture. Keep them damp, warm, at a temperature of 21°C (70°F), and in a dark place. In four to ten weeks, a blade-like leaf will emerge. When this happens bring the pot out into the light, and keep it moist. With proper care this elegant little palm can turn into an enormous plant in some years.

The pips of the citrus fruits, orange, lemon, grapefruit, lime and tangerine, all germinate well in moist compost. Plant three or four pips together in a pot, about 2 cm (½ in) deep in moist compost, and keep the pot in a warm, dark place until shoots appear. The seedlings should go into individual pots when they are about 10 cm (4 in) tall and, if they do well, they may need potting on each year.

All these citrus plants have small, oval leaves of a shiny, dark green, and those of the tangerine are the most lush. However, they are not very hardy, and do not like frost. They prefer a temperature of 8–10°C (45–50°F) and an airy, sunny position. It is best to put them outside in summer, so that their stems become strong and woody. Water them well and feed every three or four weeks. Prune the plants into shape as they get larger.

The miniature orange tree (*Citrus mitis*), sold as a decorative house plant and often bearing tiny fruits, can be grown from pips in the same way. It flowers and fruits when it is only about 30 cm (1 ft) tall, whereas normal-sized citrus have to reach 1·8–2·0 m (6–7 ft) before they bear flowers and fruit, and this is too tall for the average living room.

Other small trees that can be grown from stones or pips are peach, plum, cherry, almond, nectarine, apricot, apple and pear. Since they come from cooler places than citrus fruits, they do not need heat to germinate. In fact, the hardier ones, such as plum and cherry, germinate best after a winter out of doors.

Plant each stone in an individual pot of compost. The harder stones such as peach, plum and almond should be slightly cracked with nutcrackers before they are sown, but very gently so that the white kernel, which is the seed inside the tough shell, is not damaged. When the plants are at bush height they will bear pink or white flowers in spring. If they thrive, they do not make ideal houseplants for long as they grow into trees and have to be replanted outside. While they are still small enough to be indoors they should be potted up each spring.

Many forest giants are easy to grow from their fruits. The acorn in its cup and the conker (horse chestnut) in its silk-lined prickly casing are the two most likely to be collected by children. Few children anywhere near a horse chestnut tree manage to get through autumn without pockets full of glossy, mahogany coloured conkers. As well as acorns and conkers, pine nuts from a pine cone, beech nuts, hazel nuts and walnuts may be sown in firm potting mixture in a small 10 cm (4 in) pot and put somewhere cool and airy such as a balcony, window sill or porch. Oaks are slow to germinate but make excellent small trees, horse chestnuts are a little quicker, and pine nuts quicker still. Keep the young trees watered and pot them on each year until they have to be found a final growing place for the next two or three hundred years. There is something particularly fascinating to a child about the fact that an oak, which has stood for hundreds of years, started from an acorn such as the one he is planting now.

Mighty forests can begin life in a modest corner of the house (below). Nuts, stones, pips and leaves grow well, and young pineapple, avocado, pomegranate, chestnut, evergreen oak and citrus trees make decorative houseplants.

Some children love to spend long hours creating intricate tiny landscapes and strange miniature worlds. For them it can be very rewarding to learn the simple techniques of gardening in miniature. Dish gardens, terrariums, bottle gardens and water gardens can all be adapted so that they are simple enough for any child to set up.

Cacti, which are by nature so resilient and sturdy, are ideal for miniature dish gardens especially if you can provide off-shoots from your own plants. They need little water during the summer months, and even less in the winter. Put a layer of gravel in a small shallow dish for drainage, and cover it with ready-made cactus compost. The surface can be decorated with a variety of attractive coloured pebbles, although some children might prefer model cowboys and Indians charging across their tiny desert land.

Bottle gardens and terrariums can be set up in the usual way. Good sturdy plants easily obtainable as offshoots or cuttings are ivy, lady fern, African violet and scaly spleenwort. Children also love to collect their own specimens from nature, although for plant preservation reasons this should not be encouraged too much. If the odd beetle or other insect gets included in your child's collection it will probably live quite happily in its new protected world.

Children of all ages enjoy planting their own seeds and a supply of paper cups and potting mixture is ideal for them. Or they could have their own window box garden or collection of pots. If paper cups are being used fill them about three quarters full. As a rule three large seeds such as nasturtiums will fit into one cup and five or six of the smaller varieties such as radish.

The best seeds to plant are those which have quick and dramatic results. Morning glory (*Ipomoea*), edible peas and beans, and gourds are all ideal; they grow fast and extravagantly. Sunflowers make the largest plants. They need a big pot and a stake, but the idea of anything so tall growing so fast from such a small seed is quite astounding. The old fashioned pot marigold (*Calendula*) grows well even in poor soil and without great encouragement. Nasturtiums can climb or trail and their bright scarlet, yellow and orange flowers brighten up summer's end. Candytuft (*Iberis*) is a pretty, quick-growing flower, and cornflower (*Centaurea cyanus*) grows and flowers well in white and pink, as well as the traditional cornfield blue. Poppies, always a favourite with children, flower easily as does *Convolvulus minor* with its bright, jewel-like trumpet flowers in blue, white and pink.

Bulbs are always favourites with children. As well as the usual varieties, onion and garlic cloves can also be easily grown and will produce heads of flowers: the onion flowers are a light purple colour while the garlic are white with a touch of red. Since both have a strong smell, it is better to leave them outside on a window sill rather than indoors.

Plants that are easy to propagate from cuttings are always popular. Stem cuttings from a number of houseplants such as *Impatiens*, *Fuchsia* and *Oleander* root very easily. Of the herbs

tarragon and mint cuttings root readily in water and can be put in pots for use in the kitchen.

Finally there are those most amenable of plants, the ones that are always spontaneously self-propagating, so that all you need to do is watch and wait until the babies are large enough to be plucked from the parent plant and potted. Spider plants and *Saxifraga stolonifera* produce long tendrils which spray out in all directions with their little ones fully formed at the end of each tip. *Ceropegia woodii* is some-

times called the hearts-on-a-string, because of the heart-like shape of the little leaves which pop up in the axis of the parent leaves. Perhaps the most fascinating of all of these simple self-propagators is the *Bryophyllum* which sprouts miniature plants all round the outer edge of its leaves and these are easily separated from the parent plant.

All these baby plants are a delight to children, and they appear in such large numbers and are so straightforward to pot that there are few disappointments.

A nursery of young cacti (top left) grouped together in their traditional position on a sunny window sill. These are easy for children to care for, providing you remember to keep them cool in winter.

Plants growing in glass are always attractive. An additional bonus can be gained by growing them in water, like this trailing ivy (*Hedera*), so that root and stem can be easily observed.

Make your own desert (left) with baby cacti and cuttings imaginatively arranged in a bowl of sandy soil. Model cowboys and Indians in action set a convincingly wild western scene.

Special containers are not necessary for childrens' gardening projects. A lush water garden can thrive perfectly, and be closely observed in an ordinary glass-stoppered storage jar.

Herbs

Basil (left) is a powerful herb that grows quickly and easily, but remember that both the leaves and the roots need daily watering, otherwise the plant will collapse. Bush basil has small leaves and is better for indoor growing, but garden basil will do just as well. If you pinch out the centre stem, the side stems will flourish to make a small handsome, bush.

Basil growing with two other culinary standbys, fennel and parsley, in a kitchen herbery (right). Fennel needs care, as it can reach heights of up to 1.22 m (4 ft), and will not grow in the same pot with certain other herbs such as dill. Ever-useful parsley needs lots of nitrogen-rich compost and germinates very slowly, so don't despair if it does not seem to be growing.

Herbs are currently enjoying a great revival. Their fresh flavour provides an alternative to the tasteless monotony of sterilized, frozen and dried foods. If you are lucky enough to have a large garden plot you can cultivate your own crops. And even if you are a city dweller limited to a couple of window boxes and a few pots you can improve the flavour of everything you eat by growing some of the many varieties of delicious herbs. Not only will they lend their individual flavours to your cooking, they will also permeate your rooms with their sweet fragrance.

A herb is a plant whose stem, leaves and flowers contain certain mineral salts and aromatic oils that help maintain good health, add savour to food and spread fragrance. Once you have cooked with herbs, you will not willingly do without them.

Some herb and food combinations have a long tradition. Mint and lamb are an age-old partnership as are sage and fatty foods, such as pork and goose. Savory has always been cooked with beans for its flavour and also because it acts as an antiflatulent. Dill and fennel have been added to indigestible foods such as cabbage and cucumber.

Today there is such a wide range of influence and inspiration in the use of herbs that it is no longer possible to refer simply to the traditional use of one particular variety. It depends entirely on whose tradition you are referring to whether you say, for example, that basil belongs in a pasta, a digestive tonic or a curry. The present revival of interest in herbs and their cultivation is the rediscovery of a host of lost flavours and perfumes, remedies and preparations.

As a rule herbs are untemperamental and amenable plants. They need a well ventilated spot, preferably out on a window ledge, and regular sunshine. The exception is chervil which actually seems to grow better inside and needs shade when outside. They like an even temperature and not too much water. Grown indoors they may turn out to be rather dwarfed specimens, but their flavour is in no way affected, and they easily taste as good as garden grown herbs.

Among the many varieties the deep rooted ones such as comfrey and horseradish are impossible to grow indoors. Nor should you attempt anything really tall like lovage, chicory or tansy. Apart from these the range of possibilities is very wide. They can be grown together in mixed groups or they can be added to a display of flowering plants. They are lovely to look at in themselves; there is feathery leafed fennel, and borage with its greyish foliage and its pale blue flowers, while the small prostrate form of rosemary trails itself decorously over any window box rim. Some have the special attribute of releasing their delicate scents when touched; pots of basil are often placed around a house just for the gentle burst of fragrance which suddenly permeates a whole room. Some antisocial varieties of herbs such as the notorious mint must be grown alone: its smell blends well, but its root system develops so rapidly that it soon takes over a whole pot.

Herb plants may be bought and potted at any time. 10–12 cm (4–5 in) pots are large enough for most of them. If you have room on a balcony or roof, a wooden planting box is useful. This should be 45 by 90 cm (18 by 36 in) and 30 cm (12 in) deep and can be planted with chives, rosemary, tarragon and parsley.

Seeds of chervil, basil and parsley can also be sown in the box. Mint can be grown in a 1 kg (2 lb) bucket or tub. A good compost is necessary: a mixture of fibrous loam, peat, leaf mould, well rotted manure and some coarse sand will suit most plants. The compost in permanent boxes and large pots needs to be changed once a year. Food for herbs should be organic if possible such as bonemeal or dried blood.

Fresh picked herbs are best in cooking, but remember that three times the quantity should be used to give the same amount of flavour as freshly dried herbs. Pickings that aren't used at once can be dried for future use. The best time to cut herbs for drying is just before flowering when the essential oils are at their strongest. The simplest way to dry them is to spread them out on screens of netted material which will give them maximum ventilation. Put them in a place where the air circulates all around as they dry: a laundry shelf, a cupboard, anywhere dry and well ventilated is suitable. Or you can hang them upside down from a shelf in the kitchen. Do not leave them in the sun as this will drain them of their natural oils. It will probably take a few days for the leaves to become brittle and crisp. Rub them from their stalks and store them in airtight jars. Remember to write the names on each jar: they become very anonymous in their dried-out state. Dried herbs are not immortal. When a year has passed your stock should be thrown away, even if you haven't used it all up, and new supplies should be prepared and safely stored.

Thyme is the foolproof herb. It actually thrives in poor soil and needs very little watering. A positively luxuriant growth can be achieved by standing the plant on a warm stone sill with plenty of sunshine (above).

Herbs need not always be grouped with each other. Make up a 'health' garden growing herbs like chervil and purslane (square dishes, bottom right) with soya, wheat-germ and all kinds of cress.

Basil (*Ocimum basilicum*)
The name of this sweet and pungent herb is derived from Basileus, the Greek word for king. Originally it came from India, where it was and still is much used in curries. Basil has had a place in the folklore of many countries. The Hindus regarded it as a plant sacred to Vishnu and Krishna, and pots of basil were grown in the temple courtyards. For the Romans it came to symbolize hatred. In Italy it stood for love and a lover wore a sprig of basil when he visited his sweetheart.

Appearance and Cultivation:
There are two common varieties of basil, sweet basil and bush basil, and the latter is best suited for indoor growing. It is an annual plant. Sow it in spring and it dies down in winter. It can easily be raised from seed in a small pot with a heated propagator if you have one. Germination takes one to two weeks. Six seedlings in a 20 cm (8 in) pot are all you will need. Pinch out the tops of the young plants to make them bush. Their sweet fragrance is delightful indoors.

Harvesting and Use:
The fresh green leaves can be picked as soon as they unfurl. Basil has many practical uses. It is an essential ingredient in all tomato dishes, and egg, cheese and fish dishes are enhanced by its savour. It gives off a beautiful fragrance, and also repels flies.

Bay (*Laurus nobilis*)
The bay was considered sacred to the sun god Apollo and was used as a protection against evil. Bay leaves were a symbol of glory forming the crowns awarded to poets and heroes. The Romans placed a leaf of bay behind one ear to avoid overdrinking at banquets. In medieval times bay was used as a protection against witches and devils, thunder and lightning.

Appearance and Cultivation:
Sweet bay is an evergreen, aromatic shrub often clipped into formal shapes. It thrives in a large pot or tub on a window sill with a lot of sunshine. In winter it can be brought indoors or placed in a conservatory. Bay can be easily propagated from cuttings of half-ripened shoots.

Harvesting and Use:
The leaves can be picked all year round. They should be allowed to dry out for at least 12 hours before use. They should be stored in air-sealed containers, as the strong aromatic oils are exuded very quickly. Bay leaves stimulate the appetite and they play an essential part in a bouquet garni; the other two ingredients are parsley and thyme or marjoram. Bay leaves add flavour to marinades, stews and casseroles, fish, poultry and game dishes, and can be boiled with vegetables, such as potatoes and carrots. They can be added to meat while it's roasting, and boiled with ham, tongue and fish.

Borage (*Borago officinalis*)
The 'herb of gladness' has a long standing reputation for making people merry and courageous. Traditionally the leaves and sometimes the little blue flowers as well were steeped in wine and used as a tonic. They were also made into a tea.

Appearance and Cultivation:
Borage grows to a height of 45–90 cm (18 in–3 ft). Its grey-green furry leaves and bright blue flowers make it an attractive addition to a window box display. It is an annual plant which can easily be propagated from seeds planted directly into a window box or a pot.

Harvesting and Use:
Once the plant has flowered cut the young leaves. Ideally they should be used fresh; drying is inadvisable. The fresh leaves are delicious in a salad or chopped up on bread and butter. They improve the flavour of soups and stews. A sprig of flowers together with the leafy tips is a marvellous addition to any alcoholic drink.

Chervil (*Anthriscus cerefolium*)
Chervil originally came from the Mediterranean and spread through Europe with the Romans. It later developed diverse uses as a preventative against the plague, a cure for hiccoughs, and a reliever of rheumatic pains, and bruises.

Appearance and Cultivation:
An aromatic annual, chervil has delicate feathery foliage. It can be sown at intervals through the spring and summer, and needs to grow in a cool, moist place, not in full sunlight. Many people still believe that the best results come if chervil is sown two days before the full moon. It does well in pots and troughs. Ideally a whole box should be allotted to chervil alone, so that more can be sown from time to time to keep up the supply.

Harvesting and Use:
Chervil should be cut six to eight weeks after sowing. Don't wait for the plant to flower since only the leaves are used. Use it fresh in generous amounts. Its mild, delicate flavour goes well with any dish and also makes a good garnish.

Chives (*Allium schoenoprasum*)
Chives are among the most ancient of herbs: there is a record of their use by the Chinese in 3000 BC. In the Middle Ages in Europe, as well as having their place in cooking, they were used as a remedy for bleeding and an antidote to pain.

Appearance and Cultivation:
Chives are the smallest member of the onion family with the most subtle flavour. They grow in pots and window boxes like little clumps of fat grass. They need a rich soil and moderate light, not too much direct sun. And they need a lot of water. Sow the seeds in spring; a small clump of chives will spread well in a year and may be divided and replanted.

Harvesting and Use:
Once the plants are well established they can be cut regularly to within 5 cm (2 in) above the soil, and used for cooking. This also keeps them in a healthy condition. Today, many cheese and egg dishes, particularly scrambled eggs and omelet, soups and stews, benefit very much from a sprinkling of finely cut chives. They are delicious on new vegetables, such as new potatoes, and on bread and butter. Also essential in cream soups, such as vichysoisse.

Dill (*Peucedanum graveolens*)
The word dill comes from the Norse word dilla meaning 'to lull', and the herb does have a mild soporific effect. Dill water is soothing for babies and dill tea is used to encourage sleep. Dill comes from Asia Minor and is mentioned as a medicinal herb in an Egyptian papyrus written 5000 years ago. The Greeks used it in perfumes and the Romans wore it entwined round their heads at festivals. It has always been considered lucky; at one time it was the custom for brides to carry a sprig of dill at their wedding.

Appearance and Cultivation:
Dill is a feathery herb with bluish-green leaves. It's an annual that can be sown in a sunny window box in a well-drained compost. Its asparagus-like foliage make it an attractive pot plant.

Harvesting and Use:
Dill seeds and leaves are used for flavouring. The leaves can be used six weeks after planting. It's a good idea to allow the plant to flower and go to seed. When both flower and seeds are on the plant it can be cut for pickling. If the seeds are wanted for flavouring or sowing, they should be harvested when the plant is fully mature. Use the chopped leaves in fish dishes and salads, and with bland vegetables such as cabbage. The seeds and flowers have a stronger flavour good for pickles, and vegetable dishes.

Fennel (*Foeniculum vulgare*)
Fennel has been a cultivated herb for many years. It is mentioned in papyri from ancient Egypt. The Romans ate its leaves, roots and seeds in salads, and baked the seeds in bread. In medieval times it was used as a strewing herb for its insect-repellent qualities. Like dill, it was thought to be highly efficacious against witches, particularly when it was hung over the doorway on Midsummer's Day, and it was often stuffed into keyholes to ensure that nothing harmful found its way in during the night.

Appearance and Cultivation:
Fennel is a hardy perennial. It needs a large container, but this feathery and attractive plant will happily limit its growth when kept in a window box or pot on a sill. It is especially suited for cities, since it is tolerant of a smokey atmosphere. It can be easily grown from seed, and is not fussy about soil; but it does need regular sunlight.

Harvesting and Use:
The leafy part can be cut and used fresh just before it flowers and until it dies down in winter. The leaves and pieces of stem can be used in all fish dishes, with chicken and eggs, and in salads.

Lemon Balm (*Melissa officinalis*)
Melissa is Greek for honey and this herb has always been known as the bee plant. There is a belief that the bees will never leave a garden where lemon balm is growing, and it was an invaluable herb in the days when honey was the only sweetener. It is believed to be good for soothing pain and relieving tension and was worn as an amulet by people who wanted to be loved.

Appearance and Cultivation:
Lemon balm is a perennial shrubby plant, whose leaves give off a strong lemony scent. Its appearance is similar to mint and, like mint, it is a dominating plant that needs to be grown alone, in a pot of at least 12 cm (5 in) in diameter. It can be grown from seeds in spring, or propagated from cuttings taken in spring or autumn, and is a resilient plant that adapts readily to window sill growing.

Harvesting and Use:
Lemon balm is a delicate flavoured herb. The leaves can be picked regularly at any time, which also improves the growth of the plant. Chopped up finely it gives a pleasant lemon flavour to salads, stuffings and puddings. It can be added to all fish dishes and is also delicious with lamb and chicken. The leaves make perhaps the best of all tisanes, and it is said that you will live to over a hundred if you drink lemon balm tea every day.

Sweet Marjoram (*Origanum marjorana*)
There are three different kinds of marjoram of which the sweet is the most popular for flavouring. It is one of the oldest herbs, which came originally from the eastern Mediterranean and was brought over to northern Europe by the Romans. Unlike most herbs the pungency of its flavour increases when it is dried and kept in a sealed container.

Appearance and Cultivation:
Sweet marjoram is a half hardy annual, which grows into a tough little bush about 20 cm (8 in) high. The shape of its flower buds has given it the name 'knotted' marjoram. It is easily affected by the cold and should be grown indoors from seed, and then transplanted into window boxes when the seedlings have developed.

Harvesting and Use:
Cut the leaves and flowers in summer. They can be used fresh but the flavour is better if they are dried first. Sweet marjoram is essentially a meat herb, especially good with sausages, but use it cautiously since it tends to overpower all other flavours.

Mint (*Mentha spicata*)
The Greeks regarded mint as a magical herb. The name is derived from Menthe, the nymph who was loved by Pluto and was changed into a herb by his wife Prosperpine. Mint is an important herb in many cultures. It is believed to have magical powers as well as being used medicinally and as a food flavouring.

Appearance and Cultivation:
There are several varieties of mint. Spearmint is the most common and also the best suited for window box cultivation. All mints need to be grown alone, since their rambling roots soon dominate any patch of ground. Mint is easily propagated by laying a rooted runner 5 cm (2 in) deep in compost in late spring. It will grow well in a 10 cm (4 in) pot on a window sill, as long as it has good moist compost and some sunshine.

Harvesting and Use:
Mint leaves can be cut any time before the plant begins to flower, and frequent cutting is good for growth. Mint leaves can be dried, as long as they are not damp. Mint is most commonly used for making mint sauce, but it is also delicious sprinkled on new potatoes, and in salads.

Parsley (*Petroselinum crispum*)
Parsley is an essential in any herb garden. The Greeks believed parsley to be a favourite herb of Hercules and wove it into victors' crowns at athletic festivals. It was also worn to absorb the fumes of wine and delay drunkenness. Gardeners believed that it should be planted on Good Friday. And to be sure of a good crop it should be planted by a pregnant woman. Parsley seed in the hair was said to keep away baldness.

Appearance and Cultivation:
Parsley is a hardy biennial herb, ideal for window boxes. The curled variety is the best. It likes rich, well-drained soil and should be sown in spring. Seeds take 8–10 weeks to germinate, so seedlings are slow to appear. They may be sown in succession from early spring to late summer. Seedlings should be thinned out when they are 2.5 cm (1 in) high. During the winter parsley can be grown in pots inside.

Harvesting and Use:
Only a few leaves should be picked at a time, and it is best to use them fresh. Parsley goes well with many dishes: soups, stews, sauces, salads, vegetables, fish; it also forms part of a bouquet garni.

Rosemary (*Rosmarinus officinalis*)
Rosemary was named the 'dew of the sea' because it grew near to the Mediterranean coast. It is beneficial to the body and is now much used in skin and hair cosmetic preparations. It has become a symbol of constancy, trust and memory.

Appearance and Cultivation:
Rosemary is a perennial with pine-like leaves, woody trunk and delicate blue flowers. The best varieties for indoor cultivation are dwarf rosemary which grows no higher than 45 cm (18 in) and prostrate rosemary which looks very pretty in a window box with its trailing stems. They can be propagated from seeds or from root divisions taken from a mature plant. Rosemary grows well in a sandy soil, and should be regularly clipped to keep it healthy.

Harvesting and Use:
It takes about two years for a plant to be sufficiently established for use. Then it can be regularly picked in small quantities. Late summer is the best time for picking leaves for drying. The pine-like, pungent flavour of rosemary gives a unique taste to many dishes, and it is especially suited to Mediterranean cooking. It is delicious with lamb and with many meat, egg and vegetable dishes.

Sage (*Salvia officinalis*)
In ancient Greece all ailments were relieved with sage. It was thought to preserve the memory, remove depression, retard the effects of old age, cure consumption, snake bites and grief. These beliefs are borne out by the old saying, 'how can a man die who has sage in his garden?' Sage tea was a popular drink long before conventional tea became known in Europe, and it is still an excellent tonic.

Appearance and Cultivation:
Sage can easily be grown from seed or stem cuttings in a window box. Pineapple sage and dwarf garden sage are especially suited. Plants will need to be renewed quite regularly. Keep them bushy by clipping back the young shoots.

Harvesting and Use:
Sage can be used fresh or dried. Its strong flavour demands that it be carefully used. It is ideal with fatty meat and cheese, since it aids the digestion. It is also an essential flavouring in many highly spiced dishes.

Savory (*Satureia*)
In ancient Egypt savory was considered to be an aphrodisiac. It was also thought to cheer people up, enliven tired eyes, cure ringing in the ears, and soothe wasp and bee stings. Both the Romans and the Saxons made much use of this spicy herb.

Appearance and Cultivation:
Summer savory is ideal for window boxes; it is a small bushy plant 30 cm (12 in) high, purplish green in colour. It is sown in spring in a sunny position and the seedlings are thinned to at least 15 cm (6 in) apart. It can also be bought as an established plant. Winter savory is a perennial, greyish bush similar in appearance to thyme. Raised from seed it is usually sown at the end of summer. Both savories do well in pots.

Harvesting and Use:
The young shoots of both summer and winter savory can be collected as required. They strengthen the flavour of other foods, giving them a slight 'bite' without superimposing their own flavour. They are traditionally known as bean herbs, since they are always added to bean dishes. They are also good in stuffings, salads and casseroles.

Tarragon (*Artemisia dracunculus*)
The word 'tarragon' is derived from 'estragon', meaning 'little dragon'. Tarragon was a late arrival in most European gardens. It did not appear in Britain until the fifteenth century. A mixture of the juices of tarragon and fennel was once the favourite drink of the kings of India.

Appearance and Cultivation:
There are two varieties of tarragon, French and Russian. The French one is small and has a finer flavour, while the Russian one grows to 1 m (3 ft) and is less pungent. Tarragon can be grown in pots and window boxes but it needs a lot of room. Like mint, it can be bought as a small plant or a rooted runner of the parent plant. It roots well and does best in compost which is not too rich. When first planted in a box or pot, it should be cut down to 5 cm (2 in) above the compost, and kept bushy.

Harvesting and Use:
Fresh leaves can be used throughout the summer, and leaves for drying should be cut before the plant flowers. Tarragon is a much-used herb, especially in France. It is added to sauces, marinades, salads and stuffings, fish dishes and poultry, particularly chicken. It is excellent chopped finely and sprinkled over new potatoes.

Thyme (*Thymus vulgaris*)
Thyme is one of the most strongly flavoured herbs, and has deservedly been much prized for its medicinal and seasoning properties. For the Greeks it was a symbol of courage, and apparently in the Middle Ages in Europe thyme soup was considered to be a cure for shyness. The Romans used it to flavour cheese and various drinks.

Appearance and Cultivation:
The most common varieties are garden and lemon thyme. Both are perennial, reaching a maximum height of 30 cm (1 ft). Plants should be planted or seeds sown in spring. A mixture of compost and sand suits thyme in pots. Plants in pots and boxes must be well watered.

Harvesting and Use:
Thyme is usually used in its dried form. Shoots of about 15 cm (6 in) should be cut just before or during the flowering period, and dried out in a dark warm place. It is best preserved in sealed containers. Thyme, like so many other herbs, aids the digestion of fats, and so is used with pork, mutton, eels and shell fish. It is also good with cheese and in sausages. Mixed with boiling water and honey it makes a pleasant remedy for a hangover.

Food plants

It used to be presumed that only people with big gardens could indulge in the luxury of growing food plants, while those limited to pots, boxes and tubs had to be satisfied with decorative plants to look at, but definitely not to eat. This presumption has been thoroughly shaken, and many people nowadays know the satisfaction of picking their own crops of vegetables from boxes which used to be thought fit only for window displays of flowers.

It is possible to grow some vegetables under artificial light conditions and manufacturers are at this time developing fluorescent tubes specially adapted for vegetable growing. Movements of air can also be supplied by a slow moving electric fan. Hydroponics can be used and many enterprising indoor farmers are able to grow good crops in this way.

But vegetables are not house plants as such, and with one or two exceptions they need to be out in the fresh air with regular exposure to sunshine. They are therefore best grown in window boxes.

When setting up a container for vegetable growing, good drainage is especially important. Before you put in the compost or soil mixture it is a good idea to add a layer of gravel or small pebbles. If you have a balcony then all kinds of odd and unlikely containers can be commandeered into service. Since most vegetables are annuals you can change the groupings and arrangements and try new experiments each year. Seeds that germinate quickly such as radish, lettuce and spring onions, can be sown in succession every three weeks to give you a small fresh crop all through the summer, while lettuces and climbing cucumbers do well in a mixed window box display along with herbs and flowers. Although they have not been bred for appearance, vegetables are very attractive to look at especially when they are laden with ripe fruits. The tomato, which looks and smells particularly delicious, was in fact first cultivated as a decorative plant and even considered dangerous to eat.

Not surprisingly, vegetables grown in small containers are going to be smaller in size than those grown outside and growers have even been experimenting in producing special miniature varieties that are ideal for container growing. We include here all the possible varieties although a lot does, of course, depend on what sort of climate faces the plants as they sit on your window ledge or balcony.

As with every sort of gardening the soil mixture must be right for the plant, and the plant must be given enough room, light, water and feeding. It would be foolish to attempt to grow a giant cabbage or cauliflower in a window box, but nor do you need to feel limited to the traditional crop of tomatoes, peppers and climbing beans. Little carrots, climbing cucumbers, eggplants and onions can be grown in pots, containers or window boxes, and one encouraging gardener declares that he sees nothing against growing your own potatoes in a large, deep pot. Most of these vegetables can be easily propagated from seed or bought as seedlings in a garden nursery. They are usually very inexpensive so it's worth while experimenting.

With vegetables it's a question of fast non-stop growing, so you do need to water them every day, and give them a weekly dose of plant food to keep them going. They grow much more energetically and vigorously than your stately potted palm, which moves slowly into maturity producing maybe one new leaf every three months. Some vegetables, such as lettuces, are ready for harvesting in 55 days. Others take 60 to 70 days, but once underway vegetable growing is nearly always a speedy process.

Train a runner bean plant to grow vine-like around a town house window. It makes elegant foliage.

Conservatory conditions are ideal for certain food plants such as tomatoes, peppers and aubergine or egg plants. These not only provide a useful crop but also look attractive contributing their own charm to the mass of elegant greenery.

The flower-like beauty of lettuce is highlighted when grown in individual containers rather than rows or trays. Lettuces cultivated in this way will not grow very large but will flourish with a gratifying rapidity as long as they stand in a sunny place.

Lack of land need not prevent you from raising a satisfactory indoor vegetable crop. Gro-bags, as their name implies, are convenient, tidy and portable 'beds' of ready fertilized soil. This is prepared especially for the growth of various vegetables, in this case tomatoes.

Aubergine (Egg plant)

The aubergine like the tomato is a warm weather vegetable, ideal for growing on a sheltered window ledge receiving much sunlight. Plants can be raised from seed sown in late spring and then transplanted into large containers in a sheltered spot. With regular watering and a lot of sunshine they should bear fruit in 70 to 90 days. The large purple coloured fruit should be picked as soon as it is ready, or else it will turn bitter. There are several good varieties that can be used for container growing.

Capsicum (Sweet Peppers)

Miniature sweet peppers are hardy plants and can be grown quite easily in containers, as long as they stand in a warm sheltered spot. Seeds are sown in spring and germinate at a temperature of 15–18°C (60–65°F). When the seedlings develop three little leaves, they can be planted in 7·5 cm (3 in) pots, and potted on to 15 or 18 cm (6 or 7 in) pots when they are about 12 cm (5 in) high. They grow to a full height of about 75 cm (2½ ft) and become attractive bushy plants with dark green leaves. Keep them moist and feed them regularly with tomato fertilizer once the fruit has formed.

Beans

Climbing beans are attractive plants. They used to be grown for their decorative appearance alone. They grow quickly and easily and are one of the 'musts' for indoor food plant growing. Planted in a window box they make excellent leafy screens, diffusing the sunlight and giving a cottage effect to a kitchen window. The many varieties of bean range from the scarlet runner, which reaches a height of up to 2–5 m (8 ft), to the dwarf varieties which rarely get taller than a few inches. The most popular for window boxes are the climbing French beans, which grow to a height of about 1·5 m (5 ft). They can be sown directly into a box at a depth of 4 cm (1½ in) with 15–25 cm (6–10 in) between them. The 'mange tout' varieties bear fruit from early spring to summer and never get stringy. They need canes as climbing frames. A large pot with three or four canes in it will make the plants grow into a leafy obelisk. The dwarf varieties of French beans are sown directly into pots in late spring or early summer. They make bushy plants that need no support. You can eat them young and small, or harvest them when they have dried out on the plant and use them as haricot beans in autumn.

Mung Beans

The Mung beans produce the bean shoots used in Chinese cooking. They are easy to grow in a warm place on a wet flannel, or on a layer of cotton wool in a bowl or flat tray. Soak the beans overnight and wash them again before sprinkling them on to the damp lining. Put them in a plastic bag in a dark place for a week, by which time the beans will have sprouted into plump shoots 2.5–4 cm (1–1½ in) long. Remove the sprouts from the bean case and plunge them into boiling water for 2 minutes before cooking.

Carrots

Some people say that it is unwise to try and grow carrots in containers. But they can be easily raised, as long as they have sufficient room. They are especially delicious when harvested young. The seeds can be sown directly into your container, and germination takes up to four weeks. Thin out the seedlings when they are 7·5 cm (3 in) high. They take about 70 days to mature, but can be harvested earlier.

Chilli

These are the hot, spicy little capsicums that are dried to make chilli powder or pickled to make a delicious, fiery relish. You may find them a little hot to use very often in cooking but they make exceptionally pretty window box plants. The seeds are cultivated in the same way as capsicum. To make chilli powder the fruit is dried in a wire basket in a low oven for twelve hours, and then pounded down with a quarter of their own weight of heated salt. However, if you wish to make the powder, you must protect your face with cream and your eyes with glasses; ideally the pounding should be done in the open air, as the fierceness of this fruit is not to be trifled with.

Courgettes (Zucchini)

Courgettes, also known as zucchini, are small, young and very tender marrows. They can be eaten whole even with the stalks. Specific courgette types have now been developed that grow numerous small fruits instead of the solitary giants that the marrow usually produces. The plants are very pretty with large butter-yellow flowers. Seeds should be sown in trays in early summer and then planted out in a large pot or box with a distance of about 45 cm (30 in) between each plant. The fruit is ready when it is approximately 10–12 cm (4–5 in) long. The more you pick the more they grow. The plants need regular watering and feeding and a good light soil mixture.

Cucumbers

The only type of cucumber for container growing is the ridge cucumber. For a long time these plants were unjustly maligned because they did not look like 'real' cucumbers, but they have a good flavour and are sturdy growers. They can be grown in boxes and tubs and they appreciate a very rich soil mixture. Seeds of the midget plants should be sown in spring directly into their container, as long as the temperature is not below 15°C (60°F). Cucumbers are trailing plants, and need stakes or trellises up which to climb. They bear fruit after approximately 42 days. The cucumbers that aren't used fresh in salads can be made into sweet pickles.

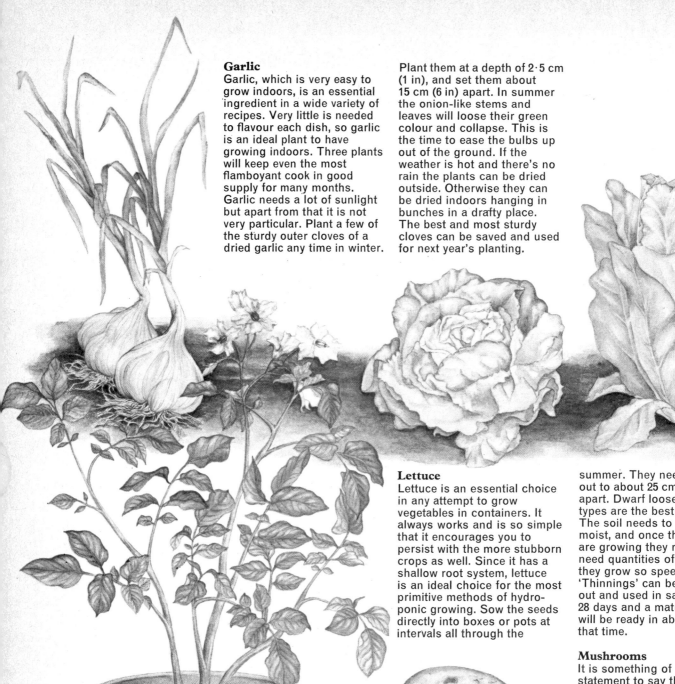

Garlic

Garlic, which is very easy to grow indoors, is an essential ingredient in a wide variety of recipes. Very little is needed to flavour each dish, so garlic is an ideal plant to have growing indoors. Three plants will keep even the most flamboyant cook in good supply for many months. Garlic needs a lot of sunlight but apart from that it is not very particular. Plant a few of the sturdy outer cloves of a dried garlic any time in winter.

Plant them at a depth of 2·5 cm (1 in), and set them about 15 cm (6 in) apart. In summer the onion-like stems and leaves will loose their green colour and collapse. This is the time to ease the bulbs up out of the ground. If the weather is hot and there's no rain the plants can be dried outside. Otherwise they can be dried indoors hanging in bunches in a drafty place. The best and most sturdy cloves can be saved and used for next year's planting.

Lettuce

Lettuce is an essential choice in any attempt to grow vegetables in containers. It always works and is so simple that it encourages you to persist with the more stubborn crops as well. Since it has a shallow root system, lettuce is an ideal choice for the most primitive methods of hydroponic growing. Sow the seeds directly into boxes or pots at intervals all through the summer. They need thinning out to about 25 cm (10 in) apart. Dwarf loose-head leafy types are the best choice. The soil needs to be rich and moist, and once the plants are growing they really do need quantities of water, since they grow so speedily. 'Thinnings' can be plucked out and used in salads within 28 days and a mature plant will be ready in about twice that time.

Mushrooms

It is something of an understatement to say that mushrooms are suitable for indoor growing, since they can be grown in total darkness at any time of the year. An otherwise useless cellar or empty cupboard can be converted into a growing bed for this mysterious vegetable as long as the temperature is never above 10–16°C (50–60°F). Mushrooms need ventilation but not draughts, and apart from this they are very amenable plants. You can buy mushroom spawn already sown in a specially prepared compost from most garden centres. This comes complete with its own container, and your only task is to keep the compost moist. If you follow the instructions you will have a crop of button mushrooms ready in 40 days and bigger ones in 60 days.

Potatoes

There is nothing to stop you from growing a good crop of potatoes indoors, except perhaps a natural unwillingness to give up valuable and limited space to this most common of all vegetables. This unwillingness is worth mastering, since potatoes grow very easily and quickly indoors and they do taste that much better than anything bought in the shops. Tubers (seed potatoes) begin to sprout eyes quite unaided when they are kept indoors in the winter, and you may unintentionally have enough for a spring planting already waiting in the vegetable rack. Pinch out some of the eyes, so that only two or three are left. Plant the tubers in 25 cm (10 in) pots, placing them on a shallow bed of compost and initially covering them with just 2·5 cm (1 in) of compost. As the growth progresses more compost should be added, until it reaches about 2·5 cm (1 in) below the rim of the pot. The potatoes need to be watered regularly with a weak liquid fertilizer. 12–14 weeks after planting knock the root ball out of the pot and there will be your potato crop.

Radishes

Radishes are like lettuces both in the way that you grow them and in the near certainty that nothing can possibly go wrong as long as you give them water and sunlight. Seeds can be sown directly into their container through late spring to summer. The plants will be ready for harvesting in the record time of about 30 days after sowing, so several crops can be grown in succession.

Tomatoes

Tomatoes are one of the most popular and successful food plants to grow in pots. Very often the types which are sold commercially have been reared for their ability to travel and are not the most tasty. Nothing beats the flavour of a freshly picked home grown tomato, especially the little thin-skinned ones which have a delicious sweetness. Tomatoes are tender plants and must not be exposed to frost. They need a lot of water and regular feeding with tomato fertilizer. Apart from this, they are not particularly temperamental. You can buy young plants in early summer from garden centres, or raise them yourself from seeds germinated in a heated propagator in the early spring. When the leaves of the seedlings are fully opened the plants are ready to be potted into 7–10 cm (3–4 in) pots in potting compost. At this stage they need to be in a temperature of 18°C (64°F). In early summer the plants can be potted on into 25–30 cm (10–12 in) pots and put out of doors on balconies and window sills. An ideal position is against a wall, where they will get maximum exposure to the sun and be protected from draughts. The smaller plants are best for window boxes and containers. Full sized plants tend to need the support of stakes. The small yellow blossoms appear in early summer and may need pollinating. This can be done by tickling them with a feather or gently shaking the whole plant. New blossoms open daily over a long period, and the fruits go on appearing and ripening well into late summer. Side shoots should be removed when they are about 7·5 cm (3 in) long. These appear between the main stem and the foliage and distract the plant from its fruit producing activity. The very top of the plant should be pinched out in late summer to encourage the last fruits to ripen. Apart from being delicious, the miniature types of tomato are very attractive to look at, especially when they are studded with their bright red fruits.

Strawberries

The traditional way of growing strawberries is either in a big wooden barrel or a special little earthenware pot with holes. The little plantlets are inserted into the holes and when the plants mature they appear to be crawling all down the sides of the pot. You can easily convert an old barrel by drilling 5 cm (2 in) holes in it and removing one end, or you can buy a special pot from a garden shop. Hanging baskets are also good for growing and displaying these pretty plants, especially the smaller types of strawberries. They need a good quality soil, plenty of humus, regular watering and a good drainage system. You can either buy young plants, or propagate them by pegging down runners from parent plants.

Indoor plant calendar

Spring

Check all house plants to see if they need repotting and repot before spring growth really starts. Place plants which need very humid conditions, such as ferns, inside a larger container and fill the space between the containers with moist peat or moss. Remove any dead leaves and keep all plants sprayed and free of dust.

Plants will now begin to need more water, so water them more frequently as the weather gets warmer. Start watering cacti again.

Move delicate or flowering plants away from direct sun to west facing windows. If the weather gets really hot remove all plants except cacti and succulents from the hottest windows.

Plants in bud and those you have had for six months or longer can have a little liquid fertilizer at the beginning of spring. Increase amounts of fertilizer and start feeding all plants as conditions become hotter and dryer, but do not feed unless plants are showing signs of strong growth.

Prepare pots and seed trays for continuous spring planting. Stem and leaf cuttings should be taken now. Root cuttings of such plants as *Tradescantia* and *Impatiens* in water and take leaf cuttings of *Begonia rex* and African violets. Other plants which may be rooted in water are *Chlorophytum*, *Peperomia Rhoicissus* and *Philodendron*. Pot up young offshoots of bromeliads and spider plants. Sow seeds according to instructions on packet.

Put in parsley, tarragon, rosemary and other herb plants. Miniature shrubs and trees can be planted in boxes, and seeds of hardy annuals sown where they are to flower, or planted out if you have got them off to an early start in indoor seeds trays. Remove spring bulbs from window boxes as soon as they have ceased to look attractive, and replace them with bedding plants such as geraniums, heliotrope and *Calendula*, which will happily last the summer in the window box.

Summer

All plants must be watered and fed liberally throughout the summer until the weather starts to cool. If possible, put them outside during gentle rain showers; this not only waters them in the best possible way but also washes off dust which may have built up on the leaves while the windows are open. Another way to increase the humidity as the days get warmer is to spray the plants with tepid water. You will find that ferns particularly are grateful for extra humidity as they cannot survive hot, dry conditions. On the other hand, cacti can be placed in direct sunlight in the hope that they might flower.

If you are going away on holiday and have to leave plants with nobody to look after them, there are several ways to ensure their wellbeing during your absence. Put them in the coolest room of the house. Plunge the pots in moist peat or, if they are not too big, water each plant thoroughly and slip a plastic bag over it; blow into the bag to prevent it touching the plant and seal with a rubber band. Several proprietary systems of automatic watering are available and, if you are going away for any length of time or if you are keeping very delicate plants, it is well worth investing in them.

Pots outside and window boxes will need watering at least once a day. Hanging baskets need constant checking during the hot weather and may need watering twice a day.

It is still not too late to take leaf cuttings of begonias and you can take advantage of the need to trim geraniums and fuchsias by getting cuttings from old, straggly plants. All flowering plants will benefit from having their dead heads taken off frequently so that they flower more profusely and do not go to seed. Cut and dry herbs.

Keep a look out for aphids and white fly and spray plants or wash with soapy water to remove them.

Put in lily bulbs at the height of summer and, as autumn approaches, choose bulbs for early winter flowering.

Autumn

Gradually reduce the watering and feeding of house plants as winter approaches. Cacti and succulents will need much less water now.

Bring indoors pot plants that have been outside for the summer and remove any dead leaves and stems. Give the plants a thorough soaking in lukewarm water to settle them in the new atmosphere. Move delicate plants away from windows, particularly on cold nights, and check that no plants are in a draught. Plants which like a lot of light can be moved from a west-to a south-facing window. This is a good moment to try plants in different rooms, as the move will not impede their growth. Bearing in mind the requirements of individual plants, experiment with moving them around.

Check plants carefully for red spider mite and, if you find them, use a derris or malathion spray or any other acaricide, or sponge the leaves with insecticide. Change your pesticide regularly as spider mite soon build up a resistance. Humidity in the atmosphere also helps control them.

As you turn up the central heating, watch out for the detrimental effect it may have on plants. They will almost certainly need more humidity; do not increase the water directly, but place pots on trays of gravel that is kept damp all the time. Keep a small bowl full of water in the room and put plants that like a lot of humidity in a large container packed with moist peat round the edges.

Bulbs for winter flowering may be put in bowls of bulb fibre in a cool dark place. Plant window box bulbs before the weather gets too cold. Put wallflowers and other biennials in window boxes for spring. For winter interest outside plant dwarf conifers, ivies and heather.

In the kitchen you can grow mustard and cress and keep useful herbs going all through the winter by bringing them indoors. Any dark corner can be used for growing mushrooms.

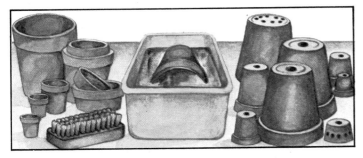

Winter

Watch that plants are not being overwatered; yellowing and falling leaves will soon let you know if they are. Put cyclamen in a cool place and water only from the bottom. Water begonias very sparingly and soak new plants such as azaleas in a bucket of water. Plants should be kept warm enough, but not exposed to direct heat. Keep up the humidity as in autumn and check that plant positions are draught-free. Remember that it is particularly important in winter to see that plants have enough light indoors, but ensure that they are not placed too near to cold windows. Do not feed them at all unless they are growing particularly strongly or flowering.

Bulbs should be watered slightly and removed from cool, dark place into the light when blades show well above the surface.

Winter is the time to take stock of all your plants and plan for the coming year. Consult seed catalogues for seeds and bulbs. Look for flowering annuals such as *Ipomoea* and *Cobaea scandens* which are suitable for window boxes or pots. Prepare pots and other containers for new plants. Put new soil into window boxes and top dress soil that has been in pots for a long time. Window boxes may need treating with preservative; make sure they are secure on window sills and that they have sufficient drainage space underneath.

Keep an eye on plants to see if they need any treatment. It may be necessary to throw some away and replace them, which is best done before the growing season begins. Some may need repotting, but it is best to wait till early spring to do this. When you do repot the plants break up the soil around them slightly, and top dress the soil in the new pot.

Leaves of all plants should be kept clean by wiping gently with tepid water. Waxy leaves can be given an extra shine with proprietary leaf polish solutions. Plants can be trimmed and tidied up by having any yellowing leaves or spindly growth removed.

241

Bibliography

Hydroponics and artificial lighting
DICKERMAN, Alexander and John
  Discovering Hydroponic Gardening
  Woodbridge Press, California, 1975
DOUGLAS, James Shalto
  Hydroponics, The Bengal System
  Oxford University Press, 1959
DOUGLAS, James Shalto
  Guide to Hydroponics
  Pelham Books, 1972
ELBERT, George A
  The Indoor Light Gardening Book
  Crown Publishers Inc, New York, 1973
KRANZ, Frederick H & Jacqueline L
  Gardening Indoors Under Lights
  Viking Press, New York, 1976
MCDONALD, Elvin
  The Complete Book of Gardening Under Lights
  Popular Library, New York, 1965
MOSSMAN, Keith
  Indoor Light Gardening
  William Luscombe, 1976

Bonsai and miniature gardens
SUNSET Editorial Staff
  Bonsai Culture and Care of Miniature Trees
  Lane Books, California, 1965
KRAMER, Jack
  Miniature Plants Indoors and Out
  J M Dent, London/Charles Scribner, New York, 1971

Herbs and food
HALL, Dorothy
  The Book of Herbs
  Pan, London, 1976
LOWENFELD, Clare
  Herb Gardening
  Faber & Faber, London, 1964
VILMORIN-ANDRIEUX, M M
  The Vegetable Garden
  John Murray, London, 1905

General
BLUNT, Wilfred
  The Art of Botanical Illustration
  Collins, London, 1950
FAUST, Joan Lee
  New York Times Book of Houseplants, 1973
HAY, Roger/MCQUOWN, F R/BECKETT, G & K
  The Dictionary of Indoor Plants in Colour
  Ebury Press/Michael Joseph, London, 1974
HERWIG, Robert/SCHUBERT, Margot
  The Treasury of Houseplants
  Macmillan, New York, 1974
KROMDIJK, G
  200 Houseplants in Colour
  Lutterworth Press, London, 1967
ROYAL Horticultural Society
  The Dictionary of Gardening
  Clarendon Press, Oxford
SHEWELL-COOPER, W E/ROCHFORD, T C
  Cacti as Houseplants
  Blandford, 1973
SWINDDELLS, Phillip
  Ferns for Garden and Greenhouse
  Dent, 1971
TOMPKINS, Peter/BORD, Christopher
  The Secret Life of Plants
  Penguin, 1975
WHITTLE, Tyler
  The Plant Hunters
  Pan, 1975

Glossary of terms

Annual
A plant that completes its life cycle—seed to seed—growing, flowering, seeding, and dying in one season.

Anther
The part of a stamen which contains the pollen grains.

Areole
A hairy or woolly tuft on some cacti.

Aroid
A plant belonging to the *Aracae* or arum family such as *Philodendron*, *Caladium* and *Monstera*.

Axil
The angle between a stem and a leaf petiole from which grow further (axillary) buds.

Bedding plant
A hardy, half-hardy or tender annual or perennial used for temporary display in summer.

Biennial
A plant that completes its life cycle in two seasons, growing from seed one year and forming leaves, over-wintering, and flowering, seeding and dying the second year.

Bract
A modified leaf often taken for a petal; in some cases conspicuous and highly coloured as in poinsettia.

Bromeliad
A member of the *Bromeliacae* family eg pineapple, *Aechmea*, *Billbergia* and *Guzmania*.

Bulb
A swollen underground bud which acts as a storage organ made up of fleshy leaves or leaf bases, closely wrapped eg onion, *Narcissus*, *Vallota*. Unlike a corm, a bulb always contains the young plants.

Cactus
Succulent plant of the *Cactacae* family, usually desert dwellers having to conserve water, also forest-growing epiphytes.

Callus
Protective tissue formed by a plant to cover wounds. Many cuttings need to callus before rooting.

Compost
Two meanings. The mixture of loam, peat, sand, leaf mould, etc in which plants are grown in pots and other containers, sometimes called potting mixture or soil. Also manure made of decomposed plant remains, rotted down to make a rich, crumbly humus.

Corm
A swollen underground stem base, usually covered with a papery skin, and, like a bulb, a storage organ. A corm always has a bud at the top.

Crocks
Pieces of broken clay flower pot put in a pot to aid drainage.

Cultivar
A cultivated variety of plant.

Cutting
A piece of plant, leaf, stem or root, which forms roots and makes a new plant.

Deciduous
A plant which loses its leaves at the end of the growing season.

Dormant
The resting period of a plant when it temporarily stops growing, usually autumn and winter.

Epiphyte
An air plant, growing above the soil, often on tree branches or rocks, usually in rain forests eg most bromeliads and orchids. Not to be confused with parasites which derive nourishment from the host tree.

Family
Major groupings of plants made up of genera whose members are similar.

Forcing
The method of bringing plants into flower or fruit abnormally early, usually in the dark eg daffodils and other spring bulbs, rhubarb and chicory.

Genus
A botanical term identifying plants of allied species.

Gesneriad
A member of the *Gesneria* family eg African violets, *Sinningia*.

Glochid
A hooked hair found on some cacti eg *Opuntia*.

Habit
The natural shape or growth of a plant.

Half-hardy
Plants which will be killed by frost or which will need sheltering in very cold weather.

Harden off
Getting plants gradually used to outside conditions when they have been grown under glass or in heat.

Hardy
Plants which can survive frost in the open air.

Humus
Sweet-smelling, rotted and decayed vegetable matter.

Hybrid
A plant derived from crossing two plants of different varieties, species or genera eg *Fatshedera*.

Inflorescence
The arrangement of one or more flowers in a group eg umbel, raceme, whorl, spike.

Leafmould
Partly decayed dead leaves, such as oak or beech; an important soil conditioner, like peat, to maintain fertility.

Loam
Good fertile soil, rich in minerals. Not wet and sticky or dry and sandy.

Offset
A young plant growing from its parent, which can be detached and grown separately.

Osmunda fibre
Rotted roots of *Osmunda regalis* (royal fern) used in orchid compost.

Peat
Partially decayed organic matter, particularly dead mosses and sedges from boggy areas. It supplies humus to poor soils.

Petiole
A leaf stem.

Perennial
A plant which lives for a number of years or indefinitely, as distinct from annuals and biennials.

Phyllodes
Flattened leaf-like petioles without blades, sometimes performing the functions of leaves.

Raceme
Individual flowers in an unbranched arrangement, stalked and arranged spirally as in hyacinths.

Rhizome
A horizontal swollen underground stem, acting like a bulb or corm as a storage organ eg some iris.

Root ball
The mass of matted roots and soil filling the pot of a house plant.

Sharp sand
Coarse, lime-free generally river sand used in composts to improve porosity, especially for growing cacti and succulents.

Shrub
A woody stemmed plant usually with no trunk or with a short trunk.

Spathe
A modified leaf-like organ sometimes coloured, surrounding the flower spike (spadix) of arum lilies (*Zantedeschia*).

Spadix
A fleshy flower spike found in the arum family whose small flowers are surrounded by a white or coloured bract or spathe eg *Anthurium*, *Spathyphyllum* and *Zantedeschia*.

Sphagnum moss
Bog mosses which hold water well, used in orchid culture. Partly rotted sphagnum moss is moss peat.

Species
A distinct plant or group of plants, with unique characteristics and which always breed true. A sub-division of a genus.

Spore
A dust-like single cell, the equivalent of a seed in lower plants like ferns, fungi and mosses by which they reproduce.

Stamen
The male reproductive organ of a flower made up of the filament and two anther lobes which hold the pollen grain.

Stigma
The tip of the female reproductive organ of a flower.

Stipe
The leaf stalk in ferns, and the erect, cylindrical stem of a palm or a tree fern.

Strike
The rooting of a cutting.

Succulent
A plant with thick, fleshy stems and leaves that store water in arid regions eg cacti, *Crassula*, *Lithops*.

Tender
A plant liable to frost damage and having to be grown indoors or under glass in cold climates.

Tuber
A thickened underground root or stem acting as a storage organ like a corm or bulb eg *Begonia* × *tuberhybrida*.

Umbel
An inflorescence made up of individual flower stalks coming from a central point like an umbrella.

Variegated
Leaves that are spotted or blotched with contrasting colours.

Variety
A naturally occurring sub-division of a species. It is also used incorrectly to describe a cultivar.

Whorl
The arrangement of leaves and flowers round a stem, all emerging from one point like spokes in a wheel.

Acknowledgements

Our thanks to the following people for their contribution:

Valerie Allam
Allenby Joseph Associates
Judy Bardrick
Barralets of Ealing
Kenneth A. Beckett
Berkeley Nurseries
Jackum Brown
Fons Bruys
Casa Pupo
Tchaik Chassay
Chelsea Nurseries
Jamie Chewton/Tiona Dorrien-Smith
David Chipperfield/Paul Florian/
    Jackie Lynfield
Chivers Flowers
Clifton Nurseries
Ronnie Cohen
The Craftsman Potter
Sara Ellis
Mr and Mrs Elton
Esso
Florocasion
Fonthill Pottery
Fraser's Giftware
Richard Gliddon
Germaine Greer
Habitat
Bill Hackett
Hampstead Garden Centre
Heals
T. M. Hewitt, Hollygate Nurseries Ltd.
Ajud Horst
House and Bargain
Bernard and Florence Hunt
Ali Jabri
John Jefferies and Son Ltd., Cirencester
Charles Jencks/Maggie Keswick
Pamela Jencks
Jungle Jim at Habitat
Sebastian and Jackie Keep
C. D. Kenrick
Kew Gardens

Klong, Camden Town
Lynn Kramer
Mrs L. Lenthal
Malcolm Lewis
Longmans Ltd., Fenchurch Street
Lady Parker of Waddington
Rick Mather
The Neal Street Shop
Pat's Club (Pat Gibb/Gary Cockrell)
PEN Centre
Rassells of Kensington
Richard and Jennifer Raworth
Phil Rhodes
Katie and Adam Ridley
Rochford's Nurseries
Rocket Records
Dennis Rolfe
Mr Adnant Samman
Sandersons Wallpapers
Mrs Audrey Sant
Jim Sayer/John Carter
Selwyn Davidson, Berwick Street,
    London W.1.
Shell Centre
William Siddens Associates
Southwoods Village Nurseries
Springfield House, Gloucestershire
Syon Park Nurseries
Tanqueray Gordon
Lillian Temple
The Terrarium Company, Campden,
    Gloucestershire
Dorothy Thickett
Tokonoma Bonsai
Matt Townsend (Tiles)
Treasure Island
Jane Tressider
The Warehouse, Neal Street
Georgie Wolton
Christopher Wray Pot Shop
Sylvia and Andrew Wright
Mr Yoo

Illustrators

Key: t=top, b=bottom, r=right

Dave Ashby: 72–73
Jim Bamber: 99
Lynn Cawley: 86: 110–111: 240–241
Harry Clow: 62–63
Helen Coucher: 68–69: 75
Bill Easter: 87
Chris Forsey: 70–71: 85 br: 104–105
Richard Gliddon: 10–11
Juliet Glynn-Smith: 26–27
Vana Haggerty: 232–233
Clive Hayball: 214–215: 220–221
Ingrid Jacob: 208: 236–239
Paul Kern: 82 b: 83 b: 106–107
Sally Launder: 76–77
Kevin Maddison: 97
Peter Morter: 16–23
Gill Platt: 96: 108–109
Prue Theobald: 82 t: 83 t
Dave Watson: 74: 84–85

Photographers

Key: des=Designer, arch=Architect, coll=Collection
t=top, b=bottom, l=left, r=right, c=centre

Glossary of common names

A

African evergreen *Syngonium podophyllum*
African hemp *Sparmannia africana*
African violet *Saintpaulia*
Albany bottlebrush *Callistemon speciosus*
Aluminium plant *Pilea cadieri*
Amaryllis *Hippeastrum*
Angel's tears *Billbergia nutans*
Arabian coffee *Coffea arabica*
Areca palm *Chrysalidocarpus lutescens*
Arum lily *Zantedeschia*
Avocado *Persea gratissima*

B

Baby's tears *Helxine soleirolii*
Ball fern *Davallia mariesii*
Balsam *Impatiens balsamina*
Banana, dwarf *Musa cavendishii*
Barbados gooseberry *Pereskia aculeata*
Basil *Ocimum basilicum*
Bay *Laurus nobilis*
Beefsteak plant *Iresine herbstii*
Bellflower *Campanula*
Bird of paradise flower *Strelitzia reginae*
Bird's nest fern *Asplenium nidus*
Bishop's cap cactus *Astrophytum*
Black-eyed Susan *Thunbergia alata*
Bleeding heart vine *Clerodendrum thomsonae*
Blood flower *Haemanthus katharinae*
Blood lily *Haemanthus*
Bloodleaf *Iresine indenii*
Blue cape plumbago *Plumbago capensis*
Blue glory bower *Clerodendrum ugandense*
Blushing philodendron *Philodendron erubescens*
Boat lily *Rhoeo spathacea*
Borage *Borago officinalis*
Boston fern *Nephrolepis exaltata* 'Bostoniensis'
Bottlebrush *Callistemon*
Bowstring hemp *Sansevieria*
Brake *Pteris*
Bunny ears *Opuntia microdasys*
Burro's tail *Sedum morganianum*
Bush coleus *Coleus thyrsoideus*
Busy lizzie *Impatiens wallerana holstii*
Butterfly palm *Chrysalidocarpus lutescens*
Button fern *Pellaea rotundifolia*

C

Cabbage palm *Cordyline*
Calamondin orange *Citrus mitis*
Calla lily *Zantedeschia*
Canary Islands palm *Phoenix canariensis*
Candle plant *Plectranthus coleoides*
Cape grape *Rhoicissus capensis*
Cape jasmine *Gardenia jasminoides*
Cape primrose *Streptocarpus*
Cardinal flower *Rechsteineria cardinalis*
Cast-iron plant *Aspidistra elatior*
Castor oil plant, false *Fatsia japonica*
Cat's jaws *Faucaria tigrina*
Chenille plant *Acalypha hispida*

Chervil *Anthriscus cerefolium*
Chestnut vine *Tetrastigma*
Chilean bell flower *Lapageria rosea*
Chincherinchee *Ornithogalum thyrsoides*
Chinese evergreen *Aglaonema*
Chives *Allium schoenoprasum*
Christmas pepper *Capsicum*
Climbing fig *Ficus pumila*
Clock vine *Thunbergia*
Cobweb houseleek *Sempervivum arachnoideum*
Coffee, Arabian *Coffea arabica*
Common Ivy *Hedera helix*
Common maidenhair fern *Adiantum capillis-veneris*
Cone plant *Conophytum*
Coral berry *Ardisia crispa*
Coral vine *Antigonon leptopus*
Cornflower *Centaurea*
Cotton rose *Hibiscus mutabilis*
Crab cactus *Schlumberga truncata*
Creeping moss *Selaginella*
Croton *Codiaeum*
Crown of thorns *Euphorbia milii splendens*
Cup and saucer plant *Cobaea scandens*
Curly sentry palm *Howeia belmoreana*

D

Daffodil *Narcissus*
Date palm *Phoenix dactylifera*
Delta Maidenhair fern *Adiantum raddianum*
Desert privet *Peperomia magnoliifolia*
Devil's ivy *Rhaphidophora*
Devil's tongue cactus *Ferocactus latispinus*
Dill *Peucedanum graveolens*
Dragon tree *Dracaena*
Dumb cane *Dieffenbachia*
Dwarf banana *Musa cavendishii*
Dwarf mountain palm *Chamaedorea elegans*
Dwarf painted feather *Vriesia psittacina*

E

Easter cactus *Rhipsalidopsis*
Ebra rush *Scirpus*
Egyptian papyrus *Xanthosoma*
Egyptian star cluster *Pentas lanceolata*
Elephant's ear *Philodendron hastatum*
English ivy *Hedera helix*
European fan palm *Chamaerops*

F

Fairy moss *Azolla caroliniana*
Fairy primrose *Primula malacoides*
False Aralia *Dizygotheca*
False castor oil plant *Fatsia japonica*
Fennel *Foeniculum vulgare*
Fiddleleaf fig *Ficus lyrata*
Fig *Ficus*
Fingernail plant *Neoregelia spectabilis*
Fish-tail fern *Cyrtomium falcatum*
Five fingers *Syngonium auritum*
Flame of the woods *Ixora coccinea*
Flame pea *Chorizema*
Flame plant *Anthurium scherzeranum*
Flaming sword *Vriesia splendens*

Flamingo flower *Anthurium scherzeranum*
Flowering inch plant *Tradescantia blossfeldiana*
Flowering maple *Abutilon*
Flowering rush *Butomus umbellatus*
Forget-me-not *Myosotis*
Freckle-face *Hypoestes sanguinolenta*
Friendship plant *Pilea involucrata*
Frogbit *Hydrocharis morsus-ranae*
Fuchsia begonia *Begonia fuchsioides*

G

Galingale *Cyperus*
Geranium *Pelargonium*
Glory bower *Clerodendrum*
Glory lily *Gloriosa*
Glory of the snow *Chionodoxa luciliae*
Gloxinia *Sinningia*
Gold dust Dracaena *Dracaena godseffiana*
Golden barrel *Echinocactus grusonii*
Golden plume *Rhaphidophora*
Golden trumpet *Allamanda cathartica*
Goldfish plant *Columnea microphylla*
Grape hyacinth *Muscari*
Grape ivy *Cissus antarctica*
Grape ivy *Rhoicissus rhomboidea*
Grass palm *Cordyline australis*
Green pepper *Capsicum*
Guernsey lily *Nerine sarniensis*

H

Hare's foot fern *Davallia canariensis*
Hart's tongue fern *Phyllitis*
Heath *Erica*
Hen and chicken fern *Asplenium bulbiferum*
Holly fern *Cyrtomium falcatum* 'Rochfordianum'
Houseleek *Sempervivum*
Hurricane plant *Monstera deliciosa*

I

Inch plant *Tradescantia albiflora*
Indian azalea *Rhododendron simsii*
Iron cross begonia *Begonia masoniana*
Ivy *Hedera*
Ivy-leaved geranium *Pelargonium peltatum*
Ivy-leafed Peperomia *Peperomia hederifolia*
Ivy tree *Fatshedera lizei*

J

Japanese Aralia *Fatsia japonica*
Japanese Pittosporum *Pittosporum tobira*
Java glorybean *Clerodendrum speciosissimum*
Jerusalem cherry *Solanum*

K

Kafir lily *Clivia miniata*
Kangaroo thorn *Acacia armata*
Kangaroo vine *Cissus antarctica*
Kentia *Howeia fosterana*
Kohuhu *Pittosporum tenuifolium*

L

Lace orchid *Odontoglossum crispum*
Lady's supper *Paphiopedilum*
Leadwort *Plumbago*
Lemon balm *Melissa officinalis*
Lily-of-the-valley *Convallaria*
Living stones *Lithops*
Lollipop plant *Pachystachys lutea*
Lucky clover *Oxalis deppei*

M

Madagascar dragon tree *Dracaena marginata*
Madagascar jasmine *Stephanotis floribunda*
Madagascar periwinkle *Catharanthus roseus*
Maidenhair fern *Adiantum*
Marigold *Calendula*
Marjoram *Origanum*
Marsh marigold *Calthas*
Mexican breadfruit *Monstera deliciosa*
Mimosa *Acacia*
Mind-your-own-business *Helxine soleirolii*
Mint *Mentha spicata*
Mistletoe cactus *Rhipsalis cassutha*
Mistletoe fig *Ficus deltoidea*
Morning glory *Ipomoea*
Moses in the cradle *Rhoeo spathacea*
Mother-in-law's tongue *Sansevieria trifasciata*
Mother of thousands *Saxifraga stolonifera*
Myrtle *Myrtus*

N

Nasturtium *Tropaeolum*
New Zealand cabbage tree *Cordyline australis*
Nightshade *Solanum*
Norfolk Island pine *Araucaria*

O

Oil cloth flower *Anthurium andreanum*
Old lady *Mammillaria hahniana*
Old man cactus *Cephalocereus senilis*

P

Painted net leaf *Fittonia verschaffeltii*
Painter's pallette *Anthurium andreanum*
Panamiga *Pilea involucrata*
Pansy *Viola*
Paper flower *Bougainvillea glabra*
Paradise palm *Howeia forsterana*
Parlor palm *Chamaedorea elegans*
Parsley *Petroselinum crispum*
Partridge-breasted Aloë *Aloë variegata*
Passion flower *Passiflora*
Peace lily *Spathiphyllum wallisii*
Peacock plant *Calathea makoyana*
Peanut cactus *Chamaecereus*
Pebble plants *Lithops*
Persian violet *Exacum affine*
Piggy-back plants *Tolmeia*
Pineapple *Ananus comosus*
Pink quill *Tillandsia cyanea*
Pocket book plant *Calceolaria*

Poinsettia *Euphorbia pulcherrima*
Pomegranate *Punica granatum*
Powder puff *Mammillaria bocasana*
Prayer plant *Maranta leuconeura*
Prickly pear *Opuntia*

Q

Queen of the night *Selenicereus grandiflorus*
Queen's fears *Billbergia nutans*
Queensland umbrella tree *Schefflera actinophylla*

R

Rabbit's tracks *Maranta leuconeura*
Rattlesnake plant *Calathea lancifolia*
Red-hot cat's tail *Acalypha hispida*
Regal elk horn fern *Platycerium grande*
Rex Begonia vine *Cissus discolor*
Ribbon fern *Pteris cretica*
Ribbon plant *Dracaena sanderiana*
Rice *Oryza sativa*
Rooting fig *Ficus radicans*
Rose geranium *Pelargonium graveolens*
Rose heath *Erica gracilis*
Rose mallow *Hibiscus*
Rose-of-China *Hibiscus rosa sinensis*
Royal red bugler *Aeschynanthus pulcher*
Rubber plant *Ficus elastica*
Rugby football plant *Peperomia argyreia*

S

Sage *Salvia officinalis*
Savory *Satureia*
Scarborough lily *Vallotta speciosa*
Scarlet paintbrush *Crassula falcata*
Scarlet plume *Euphorbia fulgens*
Screw pine *Pandanus*
Sea urchin cactus *Echinopsis*
Sedge *Carex*
Sensitive plant *Mimosa pudica*
Shrimp plant *Drejerella*
Silk oak *Grevillea robusta*
Silk net leaf *Fittonia argyroneura*
Slipper flower *Calceolaria*
Slipper orchid *Paphiopedilum*
Snowdrop *Galanthus*
Song of India *Dracaena reflexa*
Spear flower *Ardisia crispa*
Speedy Jenny *Tradescantia fluminensis*
Spider Aralia *Dizygotheca*
Spider fern *Pteris multifida*
Spider plant *Chlorophytum*
Spiderwort *Tradescantia*
Spleenwort *Asplenium*
Spotted flowering maple *Abutilon striatum*
Spurge *Euphorbia pseudocactus*
Squill *Scilla*
Stag's horn fern *Platycerium*
Star of Bethlehem *Ornithogalum umbellatum*
Stonecrop *Sedum*
String of hearts *Ceropegia woodii*
Striped inch plant *Callisia elegans*
Striped squill *Puschkinia scilloides*
Summer torch *Billbergia pyramidalis*
Swedish ivy *Plectranthus oertendahlii*
Sweet marjoram *Origanum majorana*

Sweet William *Dianthus barbatus*
Sweetheart vine *Philodendron scandens*
Swiss cheese plant *Monstera deliciosa*
Sword fern *Nephrolepis exaltata*

T

Tail flower *Anthurium andreanum*
Thread Agave *Agave filifera*
Thyme *Thymus vulgaris*
Tiger's jaws *Faucaria tigrina*
Torch thistle *Cereus*
Touch-me-not *Impatiens*
Tree ivy *Fatshedera lizei*
Tree philodendron *Philodendron bipinnatifidum*
Trumpet lily *Zantedeschia*
Tulip *Tulipa*

U

Umbrella grass *Cyperus alternifolius*
Umbrella plant *Cyperus*

V

Velvet flower *Sparaxis tricolor*
Velvet plant *Gynura aurantiaca*
Venus slipper *Paphiopedilum*
Veronica *Hebe*

W

Wallflower *Cheiranthus*
Wandering Jew *Tradescantia albiflora*
Wandering Jew *Zebrina pendula*
Wand flower *Sparaxis*
Water crowfoot *Ranunculus aquatilis*
Water hyacinth *Eichhornia crassipes*
Water melon *Peperomia argyreia*
Wax plant *Hoya carnosa*
Wax privet *Peperomia glabella*
Weeping fig *Ficus benjamina*
White flag *Spathiphyllum*
White paintbrush *Haemanthus albiflos*
White sails *Spathiphyllum wallisii*
White velvet *Tradescantia sillamontana*
Window linden *Sparmannia africana*
Winter cherry *Solanum capsicastrum*
Wood sorrel *Oxalis*

Y

Yesterday, today and tomorrow *Brunfelsia calycina*

Z

Zebra plant *Aphelandra squarrosa*
Zebra plant *Cryptanthus zonatus*

Index

Numbers in italics refer to illustrations and photographs

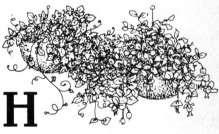

I

J

K

L

P

R

S